What People Say about Prem Rawat

"Prem Rawat provides enlightened guidance and leadership on the path to self-knowledge. He helps people gain most valuable insights into life and has helped me gain such insights into my own life."

> —Neil Evans, former chief information officer of Microsoft Corporation

"Prem Rawat's message is simple and straight to the heart. He speaks in a unique and most valuable manner about real life, about how much there is to enjoy in life, and about how to appreciate what an incredible gift it is."

> —Prof. Giulio Cossu, MD, president of the Italian Society for Cell and Development Biology, and director of the Stem Cell Research Institute, Milan

"I'm convinced that the people of India and from other countries need to embrace in their hearts Prem Rawat's call to peace. For the last forty years, as a messenger of peace, he has been making a constant effort to teach a lesson of peace. I would like to express my heartfelt feeling towards him as a most trusted and respected person who takes a message of joy to society and society puts it into practice. Doing so is the greatest success there can be in life. I want his message to reach the people around the world."

> —Shri Bhairon Singh Shekhawat, vice president of the Republic of India

"I have great admiration for Prem Rawat as a leading voice for peace because of his absolute refusal to allow anything to contaminate the integrity of his teachings. He has a unique understanding about the self and about life. He gives a fresh perspective that has little to do with the scales of success and failures. That is freedom."

> —Dr. Sandy Hewitt, former director of Business Excellence, Rolls-Royce, plc

"Many people in this world speak of peace from different angles. Some speak of peace as a result of good socioeconomic policies or of a sound distribution of wealth. Prem Rawat speaks of peace from a perspective that is both original and intriguing. Rather than looking only to institutions or policies for creating peace, he speaks of a peace that, he says, each person is personally responsible for finding. His message is directed at each individual who comes to hear him, and the people who enjoy his message come from all walks of life."

> —Dr. Jaime Pages, former rector of the Polytechnic University of Catalonia, chief executive officer of the Universal Forum of Cultures, Barcelona, Spain

"Prem Rawat's message addresses in an original manner the areas of education for a culture of peace and the fundamental human right to happiness, understanding, tolerance, and solidarity—all essential elements for a thriving culture of peace. His view is that, while institutions can do a lot to promote peace, the primary responsibility for peace lies in the hands of each individual."

—Helen Disney, president of the United Nations Association of Australia, Australian Capital Territory

"While many television programs are special, some are essential. *Words of Peace*, which presents Prem Rawat's message, is one of these unique programs. It makes an important contribution towards building a culture of peace in Brazil. The feeling within that Prem Rawat introduces people to is very important; it is very important to spread this feeling of peace to everyone in all Brazil. This program is a great contribution to the triumph of inner peace. Prem Rawat's message has the potential to unite all Brazilians in inner contentment."

—Fernando Mauro Trezza, president of the Brazilian Association of Community TV Channels

"Prem Rawat's message is one of hope and peace, and he has inspired millions throughout the world. Prem Rawat reminds us that magic begins with people, and it's within each person. That the possibility of peace and the possibility of living a life to the fullest begins with recognizing the value of life itself. That is, in my opinion, the deepest learning and is certainly a curriculum for everyone."

—Dr. Eduardo Padrón, president of Miami Dade College, Florida

"Peace, says Prem Rawat, is possible. His message is valuable, original, and profound."

—Dame Laurie Salas, former vice president of the World Federation of United Nations Associations

"Over the years, I have come to admire Prem Rawat's passion for existence, and I remain enthused by the content of his message in my own personal growth as a human being. It has had a significant impact—sometimes a source of strength when required, sometimes a force for stability when everything else shifted. And I must confess that, even in my career, it has helped me develop a worldview that underpins my thinking and writing."

—Professor Ron Geaves, Chester University, introducing Prem Rawat at Oxford University

"Prem Rawat, the International University of Peace grants you the title of Ambassador of Peace. You do not need any title because, from your heart, you labor to pursue your mission, to awaken and to spread peace in the hearts of all people, to help them find where peace is. But many people need to know who the Ambassadors of Peace are, and that's the reason we give you this title."

—Pierre Weil, rector of the International University of Peace, recipient of the UNESCO Prize for Peace Education

"The charter of UNESCO says, 'Since wars begin in the minds of men, it is in the minds of men that the defense of peace must be constructed.' Little progress has been achieved towards making this vision a reality. Prem Rawat brings a message of peace. He speaks of a peace that is more than the absence of war. A peace that institutions cannot bring. To establish peace on the outside, he says, peace needs to be established first on the inside. He brings a remarkable message of hope."

—Richard Patten, member of the Parliament of Ontario, Canada

"Prem Rawat's message is extremely simple, extremely easy to learn, and one wonders why we don't learn it when we're small and keep it going that way. The secret of civil society seems to be no secret."

—Clive Hildebrand, president of the Australian Institute of International Affairs

"Prem Rawat travels the world bringing people a unique message of hope and peace, which deserves to be heard with great attention."

—Manu Leopairote, permanent secretary of the Thai Ministry of Industry, and chairman of the Petroleum Authority of Thailand

"It's not possible in a few words to convey the breadth of Prem Rawat's achievements. Or, indeed, what he has to offer in the context of peace. While we tend to first look to institutions to bring peace, Prem Rawat says we need first and foremost to look within. His message is original and profound."

—Paul McDonald, executive director of the Committee for the Economic Development of Australia

"We all lead busy lives and all seek worldly success. While such pursuits are important and help us have a better life, peace within is vital for leading a life fulfilled. Prem Rawat brings a message of hope and peace. Such a message is very much needed in this world today. Each of us as individuals can benefit from it. Prem Rawat's message can help us lead more fulfilled lives, whatever our circumstances might be."

—Mahendra Swarup, chief executive officer of the Times Foundation

PEACE IS POSSIBLE

Peace Is Possible

The Life and Message of Prem Rawat

ANDREA CAGAN

MIGHTY RIVER
P R E S S

2006

Book design and composition by Scribe Typography
Set in Aldus, designed by Hermann Zapf
Cover photo by Greg Gorman

ISBN-10 0-9788694-9-4 (soft cover)
ISBN-13 978-0-9788694-9-6

If not available at your local bookstore, this book may be ordered directly from
the publisher at www.mightyriverpress.com

Contents

Part Two
1966–1971

Part Three
1970s and 1980s

Part Four
1990–2006

Part Five

Foreword

In our own ways, we all seek to improve the world we live in. We do this both as individuals and by participating in many different institutions. Unfortunately, this has proved to be easier said than done.

We try to use our best capabilities to facilitate the best courses of action in order to provide a standard of living for every human being and for society that allows us to thrive in peace and lead a fulfilled existence. Prem Rawat would probably say "a happy life."

However, we are often both enticed and limited by our own selfishness and vulnerability. Who is exempt from these traits? We feel helpless, and this is the worst thing that could happen to us. As we try to pursue this vision, we mainly focus our attention on society—the world around us and its traditions, governments, international organizations—and all the various means we believe can help bring about peace.

There is, however, a perspective that is not often put forward. This perspective focuses on the human being as the source of peace—every single human being living on earth.

We are reminded of this in the preamble to the UNESCO constitution, which says, "Since wars begin in the minds of human beings, it is in the minds of human beings that the defenses for peace should be built." There are two definitions for peace that are part of our culture: peace as harmony and peace as justice.

The question becomes, can peace exist and permeate our nations and institutions if it is not first present in the hearts of human beings and guides their actions? How effective would it be to have "peace as justice" if such peace were not already rooted deeply in the heart of each human being? And so, as we move along a path of an inner quest, a path in search of peace and fulfillment, we come across the message and inner practice of Prem Rawat.

In our culture, we tend to hold a rather pessimistic definition of *peace*. We tend to say that peace is the interval between wars. Prem Rawat sees peace as much more than a mere absence of war. He looks at peace as a profound feeling within oneself, a seed that has to germinate, grow, and bear fruit within the heart of each human being. His words urge us to reflect deeply, and they deserve to be heard because what they are inviting us to know is essential.

The word *know* is predominant in Prem Rawat's message. He offers an invitation to ponder, to *know,* and to express the values that are present within us but that too often are buried like a lost treasure, or even worse, entirely neglected.

Prem Rawat invites us to learn the basics of life, to discover what is within us, and then to project it outside and around us.

—Emilio Colombo
Former President of the European Parliament
Former Prime Minister of Italy

Author's Note

In 1971, I was living in a rustic cabin in Laurel Canyon, surrounded by poets and musicians. All of us were steeped in the "hippie" lifestyle of the period, and the arrival of the thirteen-year-old "boy guru" in Los Angeles was the talk of the canyon. However, it would be more than thirty years later, in 2006, that I would hear him speak. I was writing for a living, the boy had become a forty-eight-year-old man, and I was impressed with his message of inner peace that had spread internationally throughout his entire life.

At this point, the idea of a biography emerged to tell the story of the message and life of Prem Rawat, known also by the honorary title, Maharaji. It felt like the right time, but when I discovered that Maharaji rarely stayed in one place for more than a few days at a stretch, the concept of personal interviews with him to gather information seemed impractical and next to impossible.

So, in preparation for this book, I decided to interview those who knew him well, and I met with everyone from his cook to his photographer, from his friends to his lifelong students. I taped conversations, I watched DVDs, and I read his talks that have been meticulously saved for posterity. Finally, after reviewing thousands of pages of interviews and media clippings, watching many of his taped addresses, and speaking to a multitude of people who knew him during different phases of his life, a picture began to emerge.

Doing justice to such a huge life was a daunting task for me. I realized early on that there was no way I could tell his story in its entirety, so I fashioned this book to paint a picture of an extraordinary man in love with life, whose one-pointed dedication to spreading the message of peace—a message his father entrusted to him when Maharaji was eight years old—remains unadulterated and filled with promise. I feel enriched from having written about Maharaji, and, in the spirit of his teachings, I feel honored to have helped in a small way to articulate his timeless message of peace.

—Andrea Cagan

Because man wants peace, if it is not found in one place, he will search in another and another and another. But where is this peace?
This peace lies in your own heart.
But people don't know.

MAHARAJI, AGE THIRTEEN,
DELHI, INDIA,
NOVEMBER 8, 1971

Prologue: June 1971

On June 17, 1971, at 8:15 a.m., a thirteen-year-old Indian boy named Prem arrived at Heathrow Airport in London. During this explosive era in world history, the Vietnam War was full blown and peace demonstrations were taking place all over the world. Since the late '60s, "hippies" in the West had been dropping out of society, looking for something or someone to show them a better way. Drug experimentation to reach altered states of consciousness was common among these rebellious youngsters who were willing to travel to the Far East to find the truth and simplicity they felt were missing in their societies. But now, with the arrival of Prem and his simple, practical message, those who were meeting his plane felt that, at last, it was coming to them.

Prem's father, Shri Maharaji, known to many Indians as a "perfect master," had passed away when Prem was eight, and the boy had taken up his work of spreading the age-old message of peace and hope. Prem had talked his reluctant mother into letting him leave his hometown of Dehradun, in northern India, during his summer vacation from St. Joseph's Academy. He had never been outside of India, but a number of young English men and women who had met him in India had offered to finance and arrange things when he got to London. They had done what they promised and were responsible for the large and enthusiastic welcoming committee gathered at the airport.

To them, Prem was not just a thirteen-year-old boy. He had given them hope at a time when nothing else did—not rock music, acid trips, or a peaceful "love revolution," which Beatle John Lennon and many others sang about. They had spent many nights before they met him talking about natural living, the healing power of herbs, Eastern mysticism, and the secrets of the medieval Christian monks and nuns. But when morning came, they were still frustrated, wondering if they would ever find the peace of mind and the joy they dreamt about.

Then they heard a simple message from a child, which seemed almost too simple to be credible. Many had overlooked it, but some had become interested. Now they were gathered at Heathrow Airport.

It could be argued that Prem's arrival in the West was perfectly timed. However, the child's mother—known simply as Mataji—was a devout Hindu, a strict disciplinarian, and always a force to be reckoned with, and she did not condone her teenage son leaving the nest so early. Fearing Western influence on him, she wanted Prem to focus on his high school education; to enter a university when he was old enough; and to eventually marry a Hindu woman of her choosing, as tradition dictated. Then he could travel all he wanted, she had assured him. These were not unusual desires for a traditional Indian mother, but as much as Prem respected her, he refused to take no for an answer. He was on a mission, and he believed that going to the West at this particular time was an important step in achieving it.

His mother finally relented. After several teary outbursts and loud demonstrations of disappointment from her son, she had allowed him to make the trip, on the condition that he would return after the allotted two weeks. Bihari Singh, formerly Shri Maharaji's valet, cook, and driver, was chosen to travel with Prem. Bihari had witnessed this extraordinary boy grow up and quickly assume more and more control of his own life. While he understood Mataji's concerns, Bihari had learned that with Prem, there was no way to predict the future. All he knew for sure was that the boy had his own will and the courage to do whatever he set out to do.

Thinking they were in England, Bihari and Prem had exited the plane during a short refueling stopover in Rome and had nearly missed the second leg of the trip. But now they were in London as Qantas Flight 755 touched down on the tarmac and taxied to the gate at Terminal Three. They waited in line as the first-class passengers exited the plane. Prem's British friends had purchased a pair of first-class tickets for the two Indians, but since neither Prem nor Bihari had ever heard of first class, they had taken empty seats in the economy section and had remained there for the entire flight.

Prem, who was dressed all in white, looked out from his window seat at a world brand-new to him. He had boarded the plane in India wearing a cream-colored Indian business suit with fitted pants and a Nehru collar, with his traditional Indian pajama and *kurta* (cotton pants and loose white shirt) underneath. He'd removed the outer clothing in the lavatory, and Bihari Singh had put the suit in his carry-on bag.

Prem welcomed the mild summer weather in London after having endured the scorching heat in several Indian cities when he had toured the country—at first with his father and then with his mother after his father's death. No stranger to being the center of attention amid large crowds of people, Prem had spoken in front of hundreds of thousands during the last five years in India. He could not imagine the crowds that would gather for him here. As much as he had wanted to leave school, he was suddenly grateful that his father had put him in a school that taught English.

As Prem disembarked, he wondered what it would be like here and what kind of reception he would receive. Two years before, he had asked one of his close associates, Charan Anand, to go to London to prepare the way. He had told Charan Anand, "Young people will come to listen to you. They will have long hair and a peculiar lifestyle. They will be taking drugs like LSD, but don't criticize them or they will hate you and will not listen to what you have to say. Don't support them in their interests, either, because if you join them in what they're doing, the police will arrest you."

He had learned this from the people who had visited him in India, whom he had questioned in great detail about contemporary life among young Westerners. "But," Prem had continued, "these young people are the ones who will be looking for something more in their lives. Just convey my message to all who are interested." His message, which offered the same hope as his father's, said that there was infinite peace and joy within each human being and that finding this peace was possible during their lifetime.

As Prem and Bihari were ushered into the public arrival area, Prem scanned the crowd, quietly taking in the familiar faces of people with whom he had talked and played in India. He glanced with little curiosity at a reporter who was busily taking pictures. He was far more interested in the close to 200 people of all ages who had come to meet him—many of them in tie-dyed clothing, threadbare jeans, and sandals—the very ones he had described to Charan Anand.

When Prem and Bihari emerged from immigration and customs, a cry of excitement rose up. People called out Prem's name, sat with their eyes closed, or hugged each other and laughed. Tchekof Minosa, a French film director, was there with his Arriflex 16 mm camera, capturing the moment in black and white. If Prem harbored any misgivings or fears, he kept them to himself as he humbly acknowledged the people. He had no idea what to expect when he arrived, and this was beyond anything he had imagined.

To all who saw him, he appeared enthusiastic and excited. He didn't seem to care that he had less than thirty English pounds in his pocket due to Indian currency export regulations, a few simple changes of clothing, and a limited knowledge of English, spoken in a voice that was still changing. Or that he had been traveling for close to twelve hours and had eaten little food that he was comfortable consuming. This young man who had just touched down in a foreign land, seemingly empty-handed, had in his possession what his students considered to be an extraordinary gift—not only a riveting message of peace, but also something called *Knowledge*, a practical means for attaining an inner peace and contentment that he declared he could show to anyone who truly desired it.

Many of those present had already received this Knowledge and were enjoying inner peace in an outer world filled with war, anxiety, and turmoil. That was what it was all about—Prem's desire to take his gift worldwide and to reach as many people as possible, in whatever manner was most effective, while retaining the purity and simplicity of his message.

He smiled at Airport Press Officer Smellie, who watched over the welcoming committee. The crowd beamed at the short, slightly plump, black-haired boy, whom they swore was illuminated with a golden light from within. While he may have looked like a regular young boy to passersby, those who came to meet him saw him as neither regular nor particularly young. To them, he was extraordinary and ageless, someone who could help them transcend the limitations of worldly pursuits and offer them a profound message and inner experience that would make their hearts blossom like never before.

A few people stepped forward and, in Indian tradition, draped Prem's neck with so many flower garlands that they began to rise above his chin, obscuring his face. With a good-natured smile, he adjusted the garlands and strolled through an underground tunnel, along a petal-strewn path to a waiting vintage Rolls-Royce Phantom limousine. The bonnet of the car had been decorated with fresh flowers purchased at Covent Garden at 5:30 that morning, formed into the shape of a heart, with additional floral arrangements covering most of the limo.

Several greeters bowed and reached out to touch Prem's feet (an Indian practice of respect called *pranam*) as he passed them. Someone stuck wilted flowers into his hands, and another person emptied a bucketful of rose petals over his head, and he broke into a wide smile. Then he waved and climbed into the waiting limo, taking the passenger seat beside the chauffeur. Bihari Singh got into the backseat and closed the door. The hired driver, a stout, sweaty man dressed formally in green livery, started up the engine. Several cars filled with students fell in behind them, forming a caravan toward a borrowed town house on Lincoln Street, just off King's Road in fashionable Chelsea.

Long after Prem and his greeters left Heathrow, the airport buzzed with news of his arrival. The press reporter headed back to his office to report on the arrival of the "boy guru." As a child, Prem had been called Sant Ji, then Balyogeshwar (child master of yogis), and later Guru Maharaji. Today he is known around the world either as Maharaji or Prem Rawat.

Prem rode along the streets of London, in awe of the sights and sounds of the cosmopolitan city. Although he had frequently visited Delhi, where the sheer number of people was overwhelming, he was stunned when he saw the amazing shops with luxury goods and flashing lights in the middle of the day. As he gazed out the limo's window, he saw young people with revealing clothing kissing openly in the London streets, unheard of in his native land. He was clearly in foreign territory now, and even though he had friends, he was as alone as a thirteen-year-old could be.

For the first time in his life, there was no one to advise or console him. His father was deceased; he was the messenger now. There was no one to help him figure out how to best reach the people. And yet, his determination was unswerving, as was his absolute confidence in the power of his message. He had seen firsthand how people's lives were changed by what he offered. It had been obvious to those around him that Prem had a special gift from an early age—when he spoke from his heart, people were touched, and many lives were transformed.

I can truly and sincerely tell you this Knowledge is over-brimming with love. There is so much love that if you take the water of all the oceans on one side and you take this love on the other side, the ocean will shorten up, but the love will still be more.

MAHARAJI
London, England, November 2, 1971

Part One
1957–1966

You praise many things, but do you ever remember the One who made them?

MAHARAJI, AGE SIX,
DEHRADUN, INDIA,
MARCH 1964

Sant Ji

Prem Pal Singh Rawat, the future Maharaji, was born on December 10, 1957, in Kankhal, India. This small village is located on the outskirts of Haridwar along the river Ganges, several hours' drive north from Delhi.

When Prem was born, the family consisted of his father, Shri Hans Ji Maharaj (Shri Maharaji); his mother; his stepmother; and his three older brothers: Sat Pal (Bal Bhagwan Ji), born in 1951; Mahi Pal (Bhole Ji), born in 1953; and Dharam Pal (Raja Ji), born in 1955. Shri Maharaji's daughter from his first marriage, Savitri (Didiji), was married and lived several hours north, in the hillside area where Shri Maharaji and both of his wives were born and spent their childhoods.

Shri Maharaji, considered a "perfect master" by tens of thousands, was away from home on one of his numerous speaking tours across northern India when Prem was born. When he got the message about Prem's birth, he promptly cancelled all engagements and hurried home to greet his fourth son.

Shri Maharaji was a popular public figure, speaking about peace and inner contentment, but people sought him out for much more than his eloquent and inspiring words. He offered them something practical—a way to go inside themselves and experience the peace and contentment he talked about. The method he offered was called *Knowledge*, consisting of four techniques to help a person focus their attention within and discover a world of profound peace. But Knowledge was hardly Shri Maharaji's creation. He had been initiated into it by his master, who had

3

been initiated by *his* master, who had learned from his master, and so on.

It is important to note that sometimes the word *Knowledge* refers to the four techniques designed to turn one's attention inward. But at other times, the word is used to denote the realm of peace itself. Many people who practice these techniques say that the experience cannot be gained, understood, or appreciated through imagination, the intellect, or the outer senses, or even fully described in words. It cannot be seen with the eyes, heard with the ears, or felt through touch. Rather, it is an experience in the heart, something to be felt, and the practice of the techniques opens the door to having this inner experience.

Shri Maharaji, like many before him, sang the praises of Knowledge. He said, "Knowledge gives man an understanding of the source of life itself. By knowing that, happiness is found. The dumb suddenly become eloquent, the deaf receive ears, and the lame find legs." He had dedicated his life to spreading the message that peace was within, that it could be experienced in this lifetime, and that this Knowledge made it possible.

Those who received this gift from him were known as "premies." As *prem* means *love,* the word denoted a lover of life, of truth and peace within.

ى

Prem's days in Kankhal, his birthplace, were short-lived because Shri Maharaji and his second wife, Mataji, wanted to provide their children with first-rate educations that were unavailable in Haridwar. Within three weeks of Prem's birth, the family moved twenty-five miles north to Dehradun, a modernized Indian city with several first-class educational institutions. This idyllic city, nestled in the lower foothills of the Himalayan Mountains, boasted an unusually temperate climate. Years earlier, when India was under colonial rule, British army personnel purchased summer residences in Dehradun to provide relief for themselves and their white-skinned families, who were unaccustomed to the intense heat and humidity of a typical Indian summer. For these reasons, this relatively small town had become India's most modern in terms of facilities such as electricity and sewage.

During World War II, Dehradun had housed the British intern camp for foreign nationals from Germany, Austria, and other countries at war with Great Britain. Toward the beginning of the movie *Seven Years in Tibet*, imprisoned Heinrich Harrer, an Austrian mountain climber played by actor Brad Pitt, looks up from the camp in Dehradun at the majestic snow-clad Himalayas. Harrer escaped across the treacherous mountain range to become the English teacher of the Dalai Lama, who was then eight years old. It so happened that less than two years after Prem was born, the Dalai Lama and his Austrian teacher escaped the Chinese regime by descending that same mountain range on horseback and mules, leaving Tibet forever.

The uncommonly splendid view of the Himalayas was to become a familiar sight during Prem's thirteen years in Dehradun, where the family lived in rented homes until 1960. Finally, they moved into a large house on 13 Municipal Road, a sprawling estate they purchased from a queen whose husband, Patiala Maharaj, had been the king of a small state, now a part of the new India. The large old mansion, sitting on abundant acreage, was run-down, which made it affordable. Mataji had secretly saved money over the years, and, combined with loans from generous friends, there was just enough to buy the house, restore it, and redecorate it. The property eventually became a haven for multitudes of guests and students to visit from all over the world.

"A master's students," Shri Maharaji often said, "should be able to see him daily or as often as possible." His belief in the necessity of the master-student relationship to achieve self-realization was clearly expressed in his public addresses. But it was a contentious issue for some local Hindu religious groups, which advocated worship of mythical gods over a relationship with a living master.

Still, the family was content in Dehradun, where the lack of industry caused the skies to appear unusually dark blue, nearly black in the middle. The modest-sized town was relatively wealthy, and the local shops and food markets extended credit to anyone living there whose faces they recognized. "Pay at the end of the month," they told the local residents, and that was how business was conducted.

～

A white one-story structure, the main house had five bedrooms and a large living room. The dining room opened onto a long veranda with two study rooms attached. The property's entrance was guarded by two heavy wooden gates, one of which swung open onto a lush garden with a swept gravel walkway between well-tended lawns. Some of Shri Maharaji's students would arrive to help in the household every day, and more showed up in the garden to hear him speak on Sundays when he was home from his tours. Since he was often gone three weeks out of four each month, his talks in the garden were all the more attractive.

Shri Maharaji responded spontaneously to people's invitations and therefore would often leave unexpectedly for a speaking tour. Even during a tour in progress, he would sometimes grant a student's wish for him to visit their village, causing sudden changes of plans and leaving no way for anyone to know when he would return home. Consequently, in the early days of his work, before Prem was born, people often camped out in front of his hillside house for a week, a month, or even several months, waiting for him to return.

Whoever wished to spend time with the master would leave their villages and walk along dirt roads, sometimes for weeks, to reach his house. There they camped under makeshift tents in the fields around Shri Maharaji's house, sleeping on the ground on blankets or on beds made of planks, and they cooked simple meals on wood fires. Parents, children, and grandparents alike waited to see Shri Maharaji or ask him for Knowledge. When he got home, the place would buzz with activities and with people connected to his work.

The family had always understood his mission, but they felt his absence—except for rare occasions when they went along on his tours. In one of the cities they visited, a trusted student of Shri Maharaji's named Gyan Bairaganand often took Prem in his baby carriage to a nearby park. There, among the roses and other aromatic flowers and greenery that covered several blocks, a *sardar* (a Sikh) in a turban showed up every day with flowers and sweets for the little boy.

"Why are you doing that?" Gyan Bairaganand asked the sardar one day.

"I recognize him as the reincarnation of Sant Tukaram," the Sikh said.

Gyan Bairaganand understood. Sant Tukaram was a poet from the Mumbai (then Bombay) area in the 1600s, one of the *sants* from the state of Maharastra. Like many other Indian sants, he did not express himself in Sanskrit, the language of the religious elite, known as *pundits*. Rather, he brought his message in the local language to the common people, including the poorest of the poor, better known as the *untouchables*. He used metaphors from daily life and work to describe the experience within. Like other sants before him, he often delivered his message through songs, called *bhajans*, disregarding the barriers between literates and nonliterates and between castes.

When Gyan Bairaganand returned with Prem to where the

family was staying, he told them about the sardar's offerings to the baby and his claim about Prem's previous incarnation. Shri Maharaji turned to his small son who couldn't talk yet and asked with a smile, "Are you a sant?" Prem nodded his head, and from that moment on, he was called "Sant Ji."

It must be explained here that the word *sant*, derived from the Sanskrit word *sat*, meaning *truth* or *reality*, is often mistakenly translated as *saint*, even by Indians. But a sant in an Indian context is different from a saint in the Christian tradition. The Christian context of the word *saint* is characterized by goodness, sacrifice, and miracles, while the Indian word *sant* means someone who communes with the divine and tells others about his experiences.

Indian tradition is rich with stories of these mystics and masters. The timeless, inspiring bhajans from poet sants like Kabir, Mira, Tulsidas, Surdas, Tukaram, Nanak, Namdev, and Brahmanand, all known to most Indians, have been performed for hundreds of years.

The sants, who typically were neither yogis nor renunciates and wore no special attire, have been described as "seekers of the absolute" or "lovers of God." They did not share a body of doctrine or a rigid set of beliefs. Rather, they claimed that the path to liberation was open to all and could be achieved in this lifetime, independently of religion and creed. They spoke of the possibility of merging into an ultimate reality within and becoming one with it, regardless of circumstances.

There had been many sants from the Hindu, Muslim, Sikh, and Jain religions, but there were also sants who distanced themselves from religion altogether, as did Kabir—whom Maharaji would later often quote and who wrote the famous lines, "I searched in the temple and didn't find it. I searched in the mosque and didn't find it. Then I looked in myself and found it there."

Shri Maharaji was particularly fond of the following bhajan

of Brahmanand, a sant from the mid-nineteenth century. With its rich metaphors, this poem was Brahmanand's attempt to convey his inner experience, which defied description:

> O Sants,
> I have seen a great wonder.
> There is a well in the sky
> from which nectar is falling,
> and a lame man climbs up to it
> and drinks his fill.
>
> There are gongs ringing,
> drums beating, cymbals clashing,
> and trumpets sounding,
> yet no one is playing them;
> a deaf man listens to them
> and dances, beside himself with joy.
>
> There is a palace
> built where no world exists,
> and it shines with a brilliant light
> day and night.
>
> A blind man is overcome with joy
> simply to behold it.
> There are living people who die
> and are brought back to life again.
> They are full of vitality,
> yet they take no food.
>
> Brahmanand has this to say:
> Rare and fortunate among holy men
> are those who understand my riddle.

᠑

Shri Maharaji, an imposing figure who stood six feet tall and who had a smile that spread across his wide-open face, was the center of the family and the extended household, the pivotal point of all that happened. For more than thirty years, he worked tirelessly to spread the word that anyone who really wanted to could rise above their circumstances and discover peace within. "Come to me," he claimed boldly, "and I'll show you the way to liberate yourself from all suffering and attain the state of consciousness where you experience true bliss and joy and know who you are."

He made it abundantly clear that the prevailing *mantras* (short religious syllables or poems that people would repeat), rituals, yoga exercises, prayers, and chanting of verses from holy books would *not* help anyone attain inner transformation.

But this claim did not sit well with the traditional Hindu establishment in his part of India, the very heartland of Hinduism. In ancient times, King Rama had established a glorious kingdom there, magnificently described in the *Ramayana*, the great epic by Tulsidas, a book Shri Maharaji often quoted. The original *Ramayana* was much older, but Tulsidas, a 1600s sant, rewrote the story. And that's why Shri Maharaji loved to explain the underlying meaning of the words in Tulsidas's *Ramayana*, while he maintained that Hindu priests got lost in literal beliefs.

Despite years of criticism and, at times, even organized opposition, Shri Maharaji remained true to his belief that each human being could realize truth and inner contentment, no matter their caste, religion, gender, or life circumstance. He took this message from the hillside regions in Punjab to Delhi and northern India all the way to Mumbai in the south and Patna in the east. Slowly, over three decades, his following grew, and at the time of Prem's birth, his students were starting to organize themselves with several centers, a small office in Delhi, and a monthly magazine containing excerpts from his addresses.

Shri Maharaji had a daughter with his first wife, Sinduri Devi, but the legend goes that before his master, Swami Swarupanand, died, he'd spoken about Shri Maharaji having as many as four sons. Perhaps that was why he felt the need to marry again after Sinduri Devi was no longer able to bear children.

In fact, his daughter, Didiji, who passed away in 2005, claimed that her mother herself had suggested that her husband take a second wife to produce a son. And so, in 1948, Shri Maharaji married a young woman named Rajeshwari Devi from the Garwhal district, which today forms the western segment of the newly established state of Uttaranchal. This ancient ancestry shows up in the physical appearances of various family members. While Shri Maharaji was tall and lanky, his new wife and her son Prem had shorter, broader builds with faces reminiscent of Tibetans to the north. The genetic explanation for this could be that Garwhal had been a part of the Nepalese kingdom as late as the 1800s, and the Nepalese are a mix between Indians and Tibetans.

In the traditional Indian fashion of that time, Shri Maharaji remained married to his first wife after he married the second, and both wives lived with him in the house. As custom dictated, the first wife was called *Badhi Mataji* (Older Mother), while the younger one was called *Chottee Mataji* (Younger Mother). Eventually, the younger one was known simply as Mataji. Didiji remarked, "Both the mothers lived together, and there was great affection between them." A longtime member of Shri Maharaji's traveling staff commented, "It was not unusual in India at that time for a man to have two wives at the same time and for them to live under the same roof. But it was rarely suggested by the first wife."

In this atmosphere of peaceful acceptance, surrounded by the natural beauty of the Himalayan foothills, young Sant Ji developed a great affinity with nature. "I remember when I was just small, lying between my parents, wide awake," he says. "I was waiting for them to open their eyes. I could hardly resist it anymore—

waiting for the light to come, watching the windows. We had two windows, one on one side of the room and one little window way up above." The small child would lie quietly in the dark, knowing his parents would not allow him to go outside until he could see the light. "It would come so slowly," he said. "I wanted that day to come so bad, I would close my eyes a little, so when I opened them, I could tell if the light was really there."

When he knew for sure that day was breaking, he would cry out, "Yes, it's here!" and then jump up and rush outside to stand beside the bright yellow sunflowers in the garden. When he looked into the fuzzy brown faces of these magnificent flowers, which were as tall as he was, he recalls, "I wanted to see if their faces really followed the sunlight. They did, but you had to be very still to see the movement."

Everywhere he looked, Sant Ji saw magic. He would touch the shimmering leaves early in the morning to watch droplets of dew fall to earth, and to him they looked like "liquid chrome." While the sun gained potency and climbed higher in the clear sky, he listened to birds calling out their joy in trilling notes. "I had no apprehensions," he recalls. "I didn't go to school yet, and I knew the day would bring nothing but beauty. I had no memory of what had happened yesterday. I had no reason to call anyone a friend or an enemy. I had no jealousies, angers, or fears."

In fact, the natural beauty of Dehradun during his youth was so primal and resilient that when Maharaji returned there thirty years later, he would find it basically intact. "The town was as magical as when I left it," Maharaji said in 2003 after flying over the area in a helicopter. "There were the same waterfalls, the forests, the crystal-clear skies, the valleys, and the river so clear, you could see right through to the bottom."

Cherry plums covered the garden walls of the family residence, surrounding a birdhouse where a group of doves nested and cooed. Fruit trees grew in abundance, including litchi, papaya, banana, peach, and mango (Sant Ji's favorite). "I loved eating bananas with salt, but I was a complete mango fanatic," he recalls. "It fascinated me to think about where the mango tree came from. The seeds were fairly large, and I thought the tree must be all curled up inside the seed. I figured when they got planted and watered, they would fill up with liquid and expand like a balloon. I took a hammer once and opened up a seed to see the fruit tree in there, but there was no trace of a mango.

"When spring came, the trees bloomed with tiny green mangos, but they were up too high. In summer, they would turn a golden color and get bigger and bigger. We were too short to reach the mangos at first, but if we waited for them to get large and heavy, the branches would dip down, down, down under the weight of the ripening fruit. We draped a sheet across the branches to catch the mangos before they fell to the ground and smashed open. Then we ate so many, we got sick. There were five different varieties, and they were all delicious! When I finished a mango, I sometimes planted the seeds in the ground, and soon enough, small mango trees popped up all over the garden."

The house itself was always teeming with people and activities, with every space put to good use. The area above the two-car garage beside the wooden gate had been converted into a guest quarters with two bedrooms and two baths. In front of the main house was another building for guests, with four rooms on the ground floor and six on the second floor. The kitchen, a two-story structure separate from the main house, was always bustling with two cooks preparing meals on a wood-burning stove.

Just above the kitchen structure, a hallway led into a small room where Sant Ji set up a makeshift dispensary. He nailed up a board with the words "Dr. Prem Pal Singh Rawat" and played one of his favorite games—doctor. When someone asked for a "diagnosis," he would sometimes suggest they change their diet and stop eating sweets.

Beside the kitchen was a storehouse for rice, wheat, and other supplies, and a large grinding stone for grinding wheat into flour. After the meals were prepared, a server would first bring Shri Maharaji his food in his room, where he preferred to eat alone. Then the rest of his family would eat. This was only one of the ways in which Shri Maharaji appeared as a somewhat distant figure in the family, eating alone, meditating alone, and traveling for long periods of time.

Shri Maharaji was always seen as both the master and a family man, and everyone, including his family members, paid him the utmost respect. Whether he was speaking or not, moving or standing still, his mood prevailed. If he was quiet and thoughtful, nobody dared invade his silence. If he was joking and playful, everybody followed his lead.

When he was home, he and his family and whoever else was there that day would take a walk for an hour or so, and there was no way to tell how those afternoon walks would turn out. Shri Maharaji might start a conversation with some of his students, or he might have them all running around playing hide-and-seek. He loved telling everybody to stay and count, and then he would run off to hide. When they couldn't find him (which happened more often than not), he would appear behind their backs, smiling coyly.

Back at the house, the parents shared their bedroom with the youngest child, Prem, as is often the case in India. The first wife had two rooms of her own, and the three elder brothers shared a room until two of them went off to boarding school. In typical Indian tradition, the dining room had two altars on large cornerstones, around which the family would gather and sing. Above one altar was a picture of Shri Maharaji's teacher, Swami Swarupanand. There were separate study rooms and storage rooms, as well as an enclosed, rounded glass terrace.

About twenty miles from the house was the family farm where they grew their own sugarcane and basmati rice. On the farm, cows grazed and fruit trees flourished, and two miles beyond the farm was a well-known meeting place called Sahastradhara (Thousand Streams), where the children went on picnics in summer and played in the water.

Sant Ji was rarely alone during his childhood. In addition to his three brothers and two mothers, several of his father's students and the household staff either lived on the premises or came by to help during the day. In India in the '50s, when people were satisfied to work for room, board, and a modest stipend, the residence staff consisted of two drivers, one night guard, two cooks, an elderly woman who cut vegetables and ground flour, a food server, someone who sewed, and someone who hand-washed and ironed clothing. To complete the staff, there was a staff supervisor; an attendant to Mataji; a handyman; and a live-in friend of Shri Maharaji's named Amir Singh, who was called Uncle and helped the children with their homework.

Sant Ji thrived on being around people, especially his father's students. A fun-filled child always eager to laugh and play, he recalls warm thunderstorms when he and his brothers would rush outside to celebrate the rain as each little drop did its dance. The lawn, a foot lower than the road, would be transformed into a veritable lake, and Sant Ji would jump up and down in the water, feel the rain hit his body, and open his mouth to catch the droplets.

He found inspiration in the clouds, wondering, "Are they air or solid? Can a person walk on them?" His favorite color was blue, and Sant Ji would lie on the ground, imagining himself flying through the clouds across the blue sky. As he got older, he dreamt of being a pilot, but back then, it was enough to inhale the delicate scent of the sweet peas climbing the garden walls, which he found irresistible. Neither could he resist squeezing the dog flowers to make them open their little green mouths.

At night, the stars appeared to him as pinholes in the heavens that leaked light from a big black sheet of sky. A child who appreciated the beauty of life and nature, Sant Ji could often be found sitting quietly under a magnolia tree, apparently in deep contentment without a care in the world.

The religion of every human being is to access supreme joy. Creation is the same for all. Just as the sun is the same for all, the moon is the same, fire is the same, the way everyone eats is the same—to access that joy is also the same for all.

MAHARAJI
Dehradun, India, April 1965

God is in the stone; He is in the water also, in mountains also, and in everyone's heart also. But the people of the world keep searching for God outside. God is within, and until man finds Him within himself, he will not find Him in the world outside either.

MAHARAJI, AGE SEVEN,
DEHRADUN, INDIA,
APRIL 1965

Emergence

When winter warmed into spring, the heavens in Dehradun turned a clear bright blue. The sun rose, the dew evaporated, and giant clouds appeared like blankets of wonder across the sky, giving off a silvery hue. Truly his father's son, Sant Ji's cheerful and playful attitude reminded people how to be happy in one's self, and he often repeated what he heard his father say.

But he was as mischievous as any child his age. When the family got their first refrigerator—the old white kind with a rounded top and a metal handle—Sant Ji would open the door, stare at the empty shelves, and ponder the blue light inside. The fridge had cost a lot of rupees, but the family had nothing to put in it since the cooks bought fresh vegetables each day. And the family had its own cows, so they drank as much milk as they wanted and turned the rest into yogurt and butter. No need for a refrigerator. So it was put in a bedroom.

Sant Ji was plagued, however, with a burning question: Did the light stay on after the door was closed? As hard as he tried, he could not devise an effective way to determine whether or not the blue light went off. Finally, he took out the shelves, climbed inside the refrigerator, and closed the door. He got his answer: The light did go out when the door closed. But now he was facing a much more pressing problem—how to avoid becoming refrigerated, since the door could not be opened from the inside. And it was pitch black.

Fortunately, someone came along and opened the door right away, stunned to find the small boy inside. He was scolded, and the shelves were put back in place, but it remained empty. Eventually, the cooks put pots of water inside. "We drank water when we weren't even thirsty," Maharaji says, laughing. "Imagine having cold water all the time, even when it was boiling hot outside. That was new for us."

◇◠

Shri Maharaji, captivating his audiences, would speak for hours, and during breaks, everyone would celebrate by making music, singing, and dancing. The events usually took place in the late night to take advantage of the cooler air. Maharaji has talked about his father's sweet voice and how, as a young boy, the talks lulled him into calmness and eventually sleep.

In the 1920s, Shri Maharaji had started inspiring people to find peace, and he began teaching the techniques of Knowledge to those whom he recognized as sincere seekers. Over the years, as his audiences grew, he allowed a small number of his disciples to teach the techniques on his behalf. Such a handpicked disciple was called a *mahatma* (great soul), a title that Shri Maharaji had held when his teacher was still alive, although he had a family and was not a renunciate. Most of Shri Maharaji's instructors were renunciates and lived in ashrams. The men were called *mahatmas* and the women were called *bais*.

In India, traditionally, mahatmas were renunciates. People joined the ashram for life. At least that was the intention, as they renounced material pursuits, lived a life of service, took vows of celibacy, and dedicated their time and efforts to the practice of Knowledge and spreading the message of peace. In this way, a large part of their lives was spent engaging in *seva*—service in support of the guru's efforts.

However, Shri Maharaji had never been a renunciate. So when people approached him to establish ashrams in his name, at first he was hesitant. Contrary to the majority of so-called spiritual teachers in India, he did not preach renunciation as a prerequisite. In fact, he consistently maintained that renunciation had nothing to do with his message. If something were to be renounced, he said, it was the ignorance, the darkness, within a person, not things on the outside.

In the end, however, he allowed his students to set up ashrams as centers for spreading the message. Because the residents had no family obligations, they were free to focus on assisting Shri Maharaji in his efforts. So even though Shri Maharaji was not living in the ashram and didn't require renunciation from his students, the ashrams became a backbone of his work.

By the time Prem was born, Shri Maharaji had assembled a core group of Knowledge instructors (mahatmas), some of whom were in their twenties, including Sampurnanand and Charan Anand. They and others would often stay at the guesthouse in Dehradun, and little Sant Ji enjoyed their company. He remembers how these gentle, sweet-natured men carried with them a clarity and certainty that he found compelling, even at a very young age. There was a purity to them, a loyalty to his father and to Knowledge, and a sense of comfort that exudes from people who dedicate their lives to what they feel in their heart is right.

A slim man with a gentle, loving personality and intelligent eyes, Charan Anand, now in his seventies, has been a student of Shri Maharaji's since he was about twenty. No one knows his exact age because in the province of Rajasthan where he was born, they did not keep track of dates or times of birth. A carpenter by trade, he had been sent to Delhi to apprentice with an uncle when he heard Shri Maharaji speak. He was immediately taken by him and his message.

About his lifetime of practicing Knowledge, Charan Anand says, "In the beginning, my curious mind really wanted to know the beginning and the end of that feeling. But slowly and gradually, I began getting more and more deeply absorbed into it. It was like a story I read somewhere: Once, a grain of salt wanted to know how deep the ocean was. As the grain of salt entered into the water, it slowly dissolved and never came back with any information.

"The same thing happened to my curious mind. I became convinced that there was something fathomless and timeless. Something that was never ending. From my own experience, I started putting more and more effort into it. Now, I *know* that there is something timeless. Something infinite. These are not mere words for me. I have my direct experience. There is nothing more real and reliable and exciting in this world than this feeling that I enjoy all the time, and I am always the same inside. For fifty years now, it has been constant, real, and reliable."

Charan Anand wanted to help Shri Maharaji however he could while he apprenticed with his uncle. But soon he felt compelled to move into the ashram and became a mahatma. Charan Anand's open personality and his loving acceptance of all people endeared him to everyone, and today he is one of the few remaining people who remember hearing Prem's cries soon after he was born.

Charan Anand witnessed firsthand the amazing affinity Sant Ji had for his father's mission right from the start. He recalls, "I would sometimes wake up early in the morning, look out on the veranda, and there was Sant Ji, sitting with his eyes closed, deeply absorbed within, while everyone else was still sleeping. I was impressed and inspired. He was barely more than three years old.

"Sometimes Sant Ji would knock at our doors early in the morning and tell us to wake up. 'Don't stay sleeping,' he would say with a smile. 'Be ready. Practice Knowledge or I'll beat you with a stick.' He was imitating his father, who could be at times a stern master wielding a long stick, occasionally tapping people with it to make a point, (never hurting them). But Sant Ji was so charming and gentle despite his tough words, we would open our doors and invite him to sit down with us."

Sant Ji would sit down with his father's students, close his eyes, and remain very still. What a vision it must have been to see the small boy dressed in white, sitting in the midst of a circle of mahatmas in saffron robes and shaved heads, all deep in meditation.

Even though the fascinating guests in his house and the infinite gifts from nature awed Sant Ji, no one would ever inspire him as much as his father did. "He was touching the hearts of people everywhere, so he didn't spend too much time with us," says Maharaji now. But he recalls a time when his father took him for a drive into the center of the city. There, gathered in front of a huge Hindu temple, were thousands of people, some of them bowing down. At first Sant Ji thought they were there to greet his father because he was used to that sight. But he soon discovered that was not the case. His father explained to him that they all had their desires. Someone wanted a son; someone else wanted a job, a piece of land, or a husband. They stood in front of the temple, asking for something and praising the gods when their wishes were fulfilled.

Sant Ji had his own desires and wishes, and his father rarely deprived him of anything he wanted. "I once sent my father a note while he was away," Maharaji recalls, "telling him I wanted an airplane with a propeller that turned and made noise. He found one and brought it home to me." In response to another request, Shri Maharaji once arrived home with two fish tanks in the back of the car, filled with goldfish. But with four boys and a housekeeper eager to care for the new family pets, the fish got overfed and quickly died.

"In my household," Maharaji says, "there were very few rules and a lot of understanding. My father told us to take the dead fish and bury them at the roots of a jackfruit tree. He said the fish would be nutritious fertilizer and would help the tree grow tall and strong. I was shocked. My little mind could not grasp how the dead fish could swim through the roots and end up in the jackfruit. I went into the kitchen and watched our cooks open the jackfruit, but I never found a fish inside."

When Shri Maharaji was at home, he often sat in his rattan chair in his study while people lined up outside waiting to see him. A greeter stood outside the door and brought them in, one person or one delegation at a time, as Shri Maharaji listened to their woes and needs, giving them advice and accepting invitations to travel to distant cities. When he was finally alone at the end of a long day, sitting by himself in his chair, nobody tried talking to him. In fact, Mr. Goel, a stenographer who traveled with Shri Maharaji to notate his speeches, never saw father and son engaging in a casual conversation. Whatever went on between them was very deep.

When the young boy once asked if he and his siblings could watch a movie, his father replied, "Why do you want to see a movie? Just look around you. It's all moving, isn't it? I can show you a movie that never ends."

This extraordinary man was the primary motivating force in his youngest son's world. "He had a huge personality," Maharaji recalls, "and when he talked, everyone listened. Even the house listened. I don't think there was a gentler and kinder person on the face of this earth than my father. Maybe he was stern; maybe he had his way of doing things that only he knew. It is not my position or anybody's position to judge. I have met a lot of people in my life, but none as kind and gentle as he was."

*I used to have the opportunity to go to Shri Maharaji's
events when I was a young child. Even though at the events
there would be bhajans and singing and dancing, to me,
the event began when Shri Maharaji started speaking and
ended when he stopped. Sometimes it was too long for me,
so I would go to sleep. But I didn't want to leave.*

MAHARAJI
Lisbon, Portugal, July 30, 2005

This life is invaluable. If one wishes to get a breath at the time of death by offering all the riches of the world for it, nobody can give it to you. We are wasting such precious breaths!

SHRI MAHARAJI,
DELHI, INDIA,
JUNE 4, 1952

Shri Hans Ji Maharaj

In the 1920s, colonial India was alive with a fervor of nationalism. A decade earlier, Mahatma Gandhi had revitalized the decaying Congress party with his nationwide *satyagraha,* a campaign of civil disobedience. The Indians were clamoring for independence from the British. For many, nationalism was equated with the rigid, mandatory rites and rituals of fundamental Hinduism, while for others it meant becoming modernized. This atmosphere of upheaval in the large cities was juxtaposed with traditional life in the countryside, where Maharaji's father, Shri Hans Ji Maharaj, was born on a chilly morning on November 8, 1900, high in the hillside country beneath the towering Himalayan mountain range.

As Hans grew up in a stone house in the village of Gadh-ki-Sedhia, his light-filled face, broad forehead, shining eyes, and ready smile made him a family favorite. While his father, Ranjit Singh, was busy working in the fields every day, his mother, Kalindi Devi, would take Hans to visit the Hindu temple. As he matured, his mother's prayers and devotion to Hinduism left a deep and lasting impression on him. Although he would seek a more practical approach toward life and worship, he admired his mother's unwavering dedication to her beliefs.

Sadly, she died when Hans was eight (the same age Maharaji was when his father died), and he was brought up by "Aunt Tai," his elder brother's wife. Despite the loss, however, Hans's happy spirit continued to shine. Aunt Tai heard him laugh so often she called him Hans Ram, which means "Swan of the Soul," alluding to the majesty of ancient King Ram.

27

Even though Hans was happy and playful, he also enjoyed being alone in the hills, where he sometimes had so-called mystical experiences. But he didn't know what to think of them. It was only later in life that he would understand the true nature of what had moved him so deeply in his childhood.

Like many other young men, when Hans turned twenty, he went to look for work in nearby Lahore, the second largest city in present-day Pakistan, then the capital of Punjab. Looking for the truth about life, Hans visited many teachers in Lahore, but he always left unsatisfied and with more questions than before.

Disenchanted with the separatist and elitist traditions he felt were stuck in the Hinduism of the past, he turned to *Arya Samaj*, a movement formed to purify Hinduism of its caste prejudices and idolatry. Initially it attracted many forward-thinking Indians. In the end, though, Hans did not derive satisfaction from Arya Samaj or from reading scriptures or from following intellectual pursuits. He needed something practical to help him understand the mystical experiences of his youth. However, the wider he searched, the more dissatisfied be became—until he met Swami Swarupanand Ji in Lahore. This swami's caring words and luminous presence struck a chord in Hans's yearning heart.

There is a famous story about the time Hans received Knowledge from Swarupanand in 1923. Hans had to cross a fast-flowing river to reach a city where he either had work or perhaps was on his way to see his master. There had been a storm the day before, and a powerful current caught him up and swept him away. He knew how to swim, but the pull was too strong. Just when he thought he would drown, he saw the face of Swarupanand and heard his words: "Without a living master, no one can find true freedom." Hans thought to himself, "I'm about to die, and I still don't have freedom."

In the next moment, he felt someone pulling him out of the river. Hans had no doubt that it was Swarupanand. He could see him, hear him, and feel his hands on his body. But when he sat breathlessly on the riverbank and looked around for his rescuer, no one was there. Today, more than eighty years later, it remains unknown whether this event really occurred or whether Hans was simply using it as a metaphor—a common theme found in Indian bhajans where the poet sants describe the feeling of drowning in unconsciousness until the master comes and saves them. Fact or metaphor, Hans wept with gratefulness each time he said, "I was being swept away in a river of darkness. My master pulled me out, and he showed me this beautiful place inside. Then I was content. Without my asking anything, my master answered all my questions."

While he worked to support himself, his wife, and his daughter, his dedication to the message and to Swarupanand became his top priority. In 1926, Swarupanand invited Hans to be a mahatma and to take the message outside of the ashram environment to people in cities and villages. Hans asked if he should leave his wife and daughter to become a renunciate like most of Swarupanand's mahatmas.

"No," said Swarupanand, "stay with them."

During the next decade, Hans introduced the message to everyday people who worked in the factories, the fields, or in offices. He enthusiastically embraced his mission, touring isolated and largely inaccessible areas in India, traveling extensively through what is now Pakistan and northern India. Hans even started his own centers, unusual for a disciple of a master. But there was nothing usual about Hans and his relationship with Swarupanand, who actually had done the same thing when his own master, Advaitanand, was still alive. Hans often toured with Trilok Singh, a loving, amiable, and entertaining person, also a disciple of Swarupanand's. Trilok Singh helped Hans write a wonderful book called *Hans Yog Prakash*, published in 1934, two years before Swarupanand's death. For the next three decades, Trilok would be Hans's beloved companion, spending time in Dehradun where he was known for making everybody laugh.

Hans was touring on April 9, 1936, when a telegram arrived with the disturbing news that his teacher had died in the village of Nangli Sahib near Haridwar. Upon his return to the ashram, Hans was told that, on Swarupanand's deathbed, he had instructed the small group of disciples present to follow Hans. Hans was fully prepared to take up the master's mantle, but it caused a great deal of unrest among the majority of Swarupanand's followers.

Those who had not received a direct communication from Swarupanand before he died maintained that Hans, a married man and—in their terms, a "householder"—was not an appropriate person to carry on the work. They, on the other hand, were renunciates, just as Swarupanand had been and Advaitanand before him. They saw themselves as the holy ones, the true disciples who wore saffron and shaved their heads. With their vows of chastity and poverty, they felt they had earned the right to decide who should be in charge, and they were not about to commit all their work and property to a householder! In the end, Hans did not skip a beat as he left behind the wealthy center to begin his own mission with a few loyal followers. "Let's start from scratch," he told those who supported him. Unfazed, he never demonstrated discouragement.

Hans continued his tireless effort to bring the message to people who were thirsty for truth, but his life was far from smooth sailing. Not being influenced by anyone's marital status, caste, religion, or social standing, the new master, now called Shri Maharaji, was not afraid to be a bold critic of social injustice and never felt he had to compromise in the name of political correctness. In a conference attended by religious leaders who differentiated between castes, Shri Maharaji once said that the similarity between the rich and the poor was that they both produced excrement—and the difference between them was that the excrement of the rich person had cost a lot more money to produce.

Even though Shri Maharaji had been raised in a Hindu family, he maintained that religion alone did not hold the answer to man's eternal quest for truth—a point that he would make wherever he went in the devout Hindu India of that time and that his son would later make as well. Both of them worked to assure people that the message was compatible with any religion and remained free of religious associations. Shri Maharaji warned people against getting locked into a rigid mindset, especially around religion. "If you want to have your rites and rituals, fine," he said, "but don't forget the real ritual that we all share—the ritual of one breath in and one breath out." He felt that what he offered was an immaculate, pure inner experience, and he was determined to keep people from mixing it up with their religious beliefs or cultural habits.

Shri Maharaji often reminded people that religions were created after a master or saint passed away and that nothing could replace a living teacher. Not during his life. "What was the Buddha's grandfather's religion?" he would ask anyone who challenged his views about the irrelevance of religion in his work. "Obviously, he wasn't Buddhist. Who did Krishna's father pray to? Krishna wasn't around yet. Just like you need a living doctor, so you also need a living teacher."

Shri Maharaji traveled almost continuously across northern India, using any mode of transportation he could find, such as bullock carts, bicycles, and horses. He crowded into second-class train compartments, slept on station platforms, and wore holes in the soles of his shoes trudging over bumpy dirt stretches to reach remote villages with no paved roads.

He ate what he could find and afford, often surviving on dried lentils and sugar or roasted chickpeas with salt and chilies. Sometimes he had a mango and a glass of milk for dinner, and he was satisfied. Other times he went hungry, taking his sustenance from the joy of the people who came to see him—all for the sole purpose of sharing the experience that Swarupanand had gifted him with.

Shri Maharaji forgot all else when he was communing with people. He would travel at night to reach his next destination by morning, avoiding the heat of the day. Once there among his followers, he would talk, sing, and dance late into the evening, often without much sleep, as if there were not enough time to give people everything they wanted.

In Shri Maharaji's later years, people who were jealous of his growing following or detractors who held a grudge against him would sometimes try to disturb his meetings. One such man was Ram Mahir, who was from the state of Haryana and who showed up in the audience one night. He was waiting for the perfect moment to disturb the talk, but when he didn't find it and began to listen more deeply, he suddenly liked what he heard. From then on, he became a trusted student of Shri Maharaji, who would sometimes start his events by calling Ram Mahir to the stage to tell his inspiring story of transformation.

Shri Maharaji held events in people's backyards and living rooms, where he was open to giving Knowledge to most everyone—unless he detected a lack of true desire and respect or an ulterior motive. Then his words could cut to the quick. Everyone agreed that when he smiled, he could charm the world, but when he was upset, people around him would be stunned into silence.

In the summertime, Shri Maharaji stayed in the hillsides of his birthplace. But in the winter, he traveled to the Delhi and Haridwar areas, eventually taking up residence in Haridwar. There, in 1944, a group of his followers raised enough money to buy a large piece of property with a small house at the banks of the Ganges River. Shri Maharaji called the place Prem Nagar (Town of Love), and over the years, during the holidays, people from all over India arrived to develop the land, help build facilities, and listen to Shri Maharaji's discourses.

Charan Anand, who first began attending Shri Maharaji's meetings in Delhi in the mid-1950s, recalls that, in the early years, there were usually small groups present when Shri Maharaji spoke. It was only toward the end of his life that the size of his audiences started growing by the thousands.

Because Prem Nagar could not accommodate large indoor audiences, the need was felt for a medium-size hall that could accommodate meetings for a few thousand in any weather. In 1961, the first stone of the indoor meeting hall in Prem Nagar was laid. The president of India had agreed to attend the ceremony, but on his way there from Delhi, he was diverted by riots and didn't make it. The ceremony happened anyway, and eventually the hall catered to thousands of guests for meetings and three-day events at which Shri Maharaji would go with little sleep for days on end, inspiring his students late into the night.

Shri Maharaji could be totally overcome by joy, but he could also be very stern. One day, Dhirendra Brahmchari, the yoga teacher of Indira Gandhi (the first female prime minister of India and daughter of Nehru), came to see Shri Maharaji. A controversial figure, Dhirendra Brahmchari had come into prominence at the time of Indira Gandhi's father. Something of a spiritual adventurer, he had studied hatha yoga (physical postures) with different teachers, had created his own school, and had published books that sold extensively. Perhaps at the time they met, Shri Maharaji sensed his duplicitous character. It seemed that Dhirendra Brahmchari was interested, and Shri Maharaji told him about an event he was doing in Delhi. "Why don't you come hear me speak tomorrow night?" he suggested. "Then you can see for yourself what I have to say."

The man balked. "I can't do that," he said. "I can't leave the ashram where I live, in case I am needed."

Shri Maharaji saw that understanding his message was not the most important thing to Dhirendra, and he became angry. "You cannot have Knowledge," Shri Maharaji stated clearly. "You cannot have Knowledge in this lifetime. I will make sure you don't have it."

In a similar episode, a politician from Rajasthan approached Shri Maharaji and asked for the gift of Knowledge. "I know why you want it," he told the man. "If I give you what you want, you will go to others who have received this gift and ask them for their votes. I am never going to give it to you."

The man argued and debated, but Shri Maharaji held strong to his decision. "You can argue as much as you like," he told the frustrated politician, "but it's my Knowledge to give, and you cannot have it."

In 1958, Shri Maharaji purchased his first car, a green Austin Somerset, an Indian-built copy of the British Austin motorcar. Now, with a personal driver at his disposal, he was free to travel at a moment's notice as he went from Mumbai to Kashmir to Patna and from Assam back to Rajasthan, putting more than 100,000 miles on the car. And still, after an engine overhaul, it looked brand-new and ran perfectly. The truth was that, as happy as he was to have the car, little mattered to him besides his passion to distribute his message. And just as nothing could dissuade him from offering his gift to the people, nothing could stop the people from clamoring to receive it.

Peace cannot be attained by an agitated and unsteady mind, and no society can be peaceful and loving unless its individual members are peaceful and loving. Knowledge gives man a complete understanding of the source of life itself. The entire universe emanates from this source of life. By knowing that, happiness is found, and the deathless state of self-realization is attained.

SHRI MAHARAJI
New Delhi, India, November 18, 1963

I had a funny relationship with my father. Of course he was my father. That's a wonderful thing. But he was also the one who gave me this precious gift. He is not here anymore, but the gift that he gave me has created a bond between us, a relationship that transcends everything. In the light of this relationship, nothing else matters. Not even the fact that he is— or was—my father.

MAHARAJI,
BRIGHTON, ENGLAND,
JUNE 7, 1992

Sant Ji Speaks

In January 1961, while a young and charismatic John F. Kennedy was inaugurated as president of the United States, Shri Maharaji went on his winter tour around the Mumbai area, accompanied by his wife Mataji and their three-year-old son, Sant Ji. This was an era of an epic battle between the two superpowers—the United States and the Soviet Union—with nuclear threats looming. Tensions between Cuba and the United States were reaching a boiling point, and the Berlin Wall was being constructed. At the same time, India (under the leadership of Jawaharlal Nehru), along with many other countries in Africa and Asia, were declaring themselves neutral. Rather than aligning themselves with the West or the Soviet Bloc, they were forming a new bloc that French demographer Alfred Sauvy called the "Third World."

Shri Maharaji was quite aware of the world situation. He actively promoted his point of view that peace and harmony in the world could only come about as a result of individuals finding peace within. He believed that no institution, government, or politician could bring peace. After all, they had tried for centuries, and so far, it had not worked.

In 1960, Shri Maharaji had a well-publicized meeting with the Soviet ambassador. He also attended a large all-caste conference where he made these points. At the end of November in Patna and later in a discourse at Laurence Square, New Delhi, he addressed an important issue facing the world. Mankind, in his view, was obsessed with material progress. This obsession, together with a disregard for true peace, was bound to destroy it. True progress, he said, could only come from within. The Patna newspaper *Dainik Aryavart* featured a story under the headline SANT HANS JI MAHARAJ'S THOUGHTS.

In January 1961, Shri Maharaji made a 2,000-mile round-trip journey across India, talking at events set up by his students. His seven-day event in Mumbai was presided over by the president of the Mumbai Legislative Assembly; the mayor of the city; and the ex-governor of the state of Uttar Pradesh, Shri Maharaji's home state.

For this event, Shri Maharaji, his family, and his staff were invited to be houseguests in luxurious mansions. Charan Anand recalls that some of these wealthy people invited Sant Ji to speak to them. One evening, the small boy stood at the front of a large room, and his riveted audience listened in deep silence, impressed with the child's clarity and wisdom as he talked about the gift of life and the possibility of being happy and fulfilled—until some ladies on the residence staff bustled into the room, walked to the front row, and sat, causing a disturbance.

Sant Ji frowned. "I am not going to talk to you people any more today," he said suddenly. "You have no respect for *satsang*" (a Hindi word meaning "company of truth"). He looked directly at the women and was about to walk out when they apologized and moved to the back of the room. He resumed speaking, leaving his listeners amazed at his command of the situation. Later, when someone asked Sant Ji's father how such a small child could take control like that, Shri Maharaji said, "The self is neither small nor big, neither old nor new."

On the way back to Dehradun, they stopped in Nasik, 200 kilometers northeast of Mumbai, where neighbors gazed out their apartment windows to watch a stage being erected between their building and the one adjacent. A large empty space had been cleared in front for people to sit and listen, but so far, it was unoccupied. The amateur band had not attracted people (maybe it was even keeping them away), and no one came down from their apartments until three-year-old Sant Ji made his presence known.

Shri Maharaji was taking a nap at the back of the stage before his talk when he was awakened by the sweet, confident voice of a young boy booming over the public-address system. It was Sant Ji. Shri Maharaji sat just inside the entry to the stage, listening to his son, who was sitting in his chair, speaking in a gentle childish voice.

In the meantime, people slowly meandered downstairs from their apartments, flowing into the seating area for a closer look at the phenomenal child. Sant Ji spoke calmly and clearly about this body being a gift from the Creator and about the need to fully appreciate this life. The first time he opened his mouth in public, he was urging people to appreciate the gift they already possessed—a theme that remains the foundation of his message nearly fifty years later.

When Sant Ji walked off the stage, the area was teeming with people who were amazed at what they had just seen and heard. Shri Maharaji met Sant Ji at the side of the stage and said, "I want to ask you a question." Sant Ji lifted his eyes to meet those of his father, who was dressed completely in white with a *tilak* (traditional red mark often worn on special occasions) on his forehead. "You were speaking about Knowledge," said Shri Maharaji, "and about peace and the gift of the human body. What if somebody in the audience asked you a question? How would you answer?"

Bihari, who was standing close by, remembers Sant Ji answering his father matter-of-factly: "I already know what there is to know," the child said. "I can give them the answers they want." From that day forth, whenever he could accompany his father, he did. Little Sant Ji was often Shri Maharaji's opening act. At other times, he was the closing act, coming onto the stage and sitting in the chair after his father had spoken. When he felt inspired, he danced onstage to the beautiful and uplifting Indian devotional music.

"When I sat and listened to my father," says Maharaji, "I couldn't think at all. There was nothing to think about. All I had to do was let go and enjoy. What he said was nurturing some deep, deep place inside me."

No one was more aware of the child's rare nature than Sampurnanand (also known as Sampu), one of Shri Maharaji's young instructors. Sampu had the rare distinction, along with a very few others, of watching Maharaji grow up. "See how young my son is," Shri Maharaji told Sampu, "and how well he presents himself. Imagine when he is grown up, how he will present this beautiful message to people around the world."

Sampu, a powerful man with a past military career, recalls that one afternoon when he was talking with Shri Maharaji, he sensed a light out of the corner of his eye. He felt compelled to turn his attention away from Shri Maharaji to look, and there stood Sant Ji, smiling, dressed all in white, from his shoes to his shirt. When Shri Maharaji saw his son, he waved him over and asked him to sit on a small chair beside them. "Do you know him?" he asked Sant Ji, gesturing toward Sampurnanand.

"Yes," the boy declared.

"What is his name?" the master asked.

"Sampu Nanand," Sant Ji said, slightly mispronouncing Sampu's name.

"Talk to him," he instructed the boy.

Sampu listened to Sant Ji speak spontaneously for a few minutes. The essence of his speech was that the body and this life were precious gifts given for one purpose only. Even though his language was that of a young child, it was obvious that Sant Ji spoke from a place in his heart where he truly felt everything he was saying.

After this occurrence, Sampu was fascinated by the young boy. However, he became concerned when he would sometimes choose to play with Sant Ji instead of listening to Shri Maharaji's talks.

But Shri Maharaji put him at ease. "It's okay," he assured Sampu. "Being with Sant Ji is like helping me. Don't ever feel badly about being with him."

∾

There was a time in his early childhood when Sant Ji cried bitterly over a toy car that his mother did not want him to have. It was a little car he had seen in the shop across the street. But when he eventually talked her into getting it for him, the attraction disappeared quickly. His own swift change of emotion made a stark impression on the little boy, and he still talks about this life lesson that helped him realize the elusive quality of desires.

But Sant Ji did not just *play* with his toys. He tinkered with them, using a screwdriver to open them up and take them apart, piece by piece. He wondered what made them tick, and his Swiss Army knife made it easier to cut to the insides of things. Sant Ji did this with great gusto and without considering how he would fit it all back together, often ending up with a handful of screws and nowhere to put them.

One time, frustrated at trying to reassemble a toy, he turned it upside down and jammed the screws inside. Soon enough, though, after some thinking and reasoning, he was able to put it back together.

It was not only the inner workings of objects that fascinated the boy. He was also interested in the inner workings of people. One afternoon, he was in the car with his parents when he saw several people on the road who would walk a few steps, bow to nobody, and then crawl along the road on their hands and knees. "What are they doing?" Sant Ji asked his father. "Why are they bowing and crawling?"

Shri Maharaji said with a smile, "They think they need to do this. Maybe they made a promise to God that if He would do something for them, they would do this for Him. And now they are honoring their promise."

Another time, Shri Maharaji took Sant Ji to see a man in a tattered jacket who gave shows in the center of town, hoping to get a few rupees from people who gathered to watch. He waited until a crowd formed and then fed a piece of plain paper into a small machine he carried around. When rupees flew out the other side instead of the paper, people applauded and gave him a few coins.

Sant Ji assessed the practical value of such a thing. "We can really use this machine," he thought. "It will be the end of our money problems." For a few consecutive days, he got someone to bring him back to watch the man perform his trick, until one day he realized that something was not right. "If this man can turn paper into money," the boy reasoned, "why is he still so poor? Why doesn't he buy himself a new jacket?"

He approached the magician after the crowd had dispersed and said, "I know this is a trick. Show me how it works." The tattered man revealed the illusion, explaining that the money was already in the machine before people arrived. Sant Ji lost interest in the machine, but he continued to be fascinated by how things worked. When a puppet show came to town and he discovered the puppeteers working the dolls from underneath the stage, he was less interested in the puppets and more interested in the people who were making them dance, sing, and tell stories.

On another occasion, Shri Maharaji showed Sant Ji a man who had been standing on only one foot for several months. People from adjoining villages came to observe him in the middle of the city in his saffron robes, one leg held off the ground in a white cotton sling. Shri Maharaji told Sant Ji that the man considered this strange mode of worship as his sacrifice to God.

"We stood there quietly," Maharaji recalls, "and it was very weird to watch this man standing on one foot. Then I noticed my father was smiling from ear to ear. Suddenly, he said out loud, 'God has made a terrible mistake.'

"The man looked at my father, frowned, and said, 'What do you mean, God has made a terrible mistake?'

"My father, still smiling wide, said, 'He gave you two legs. He should have given you only one.'"

There is one childhood story that Maharaji often used as a metaphor in his talks when he toured the world in the '70s. When he was very young, he attended a fair in Dehradun that attracted close to 50,000 people. The sidewalks were crowded with people, and Sant Ji was holding tight to his nanny's fingers when something caught his eye—a bunch of brightly colored balloons. He let go of his nanny to try to reach for a balloon, but when he turned, she was gone. He panicked, suddenly caring nothing about the balloons. Afraid and alone, all he wanted was to find his nanny's hand so he would no longer feel lost. Sant Ji and his nanny were soon reunited, but he never forgot the fearful experience.

When he grew up and spoke around the world, Maharaji would often refer back to this frightening but symbolic moment in his life. "There's that little child," he would say, "and everything looks so attractive. You walk into the fair and you're holding on to your mother's finger, and the mother looks at the child and says, 'You stay close to me, okay?'

"'Oh, yes, yes, yes.'

"Holding on to the finger, he doesn't want to get lost, and off they go. Then he says, 'Oh, look at the balloons. Look at the candy, the rides, the colors. Oh, look at all this and look at that!' And all the time, why didn't he know he'd lost his connection to his parent? Because his attention wasn't there. It was on everything else."

Throughout his life, Maharaji's experiences would provide him with stories and anecdotes, as he turned many seemingly insignificant occurrences into metaphors that would help enrich his public addresses and inspire people.

I remember the day I was left at school. I cried
and I cried. I did not want to go to school.
I remember I just hated it the first day.
And then I understood that this was my
responsibility. I had to go to school, and I did
very well. The best I could do, I did.

MAHARAJI,
ESCOBAR, ARGENTINA,
JANUARY 27, 1991

School Days

Ihen Shri Maharaji dropped Sant Ji off at the convent of St. Mary's for his first day of kindergarten, the four-year-old wept. As he stood on a balcony watching his father walk away, he thought, "This isn't worth it. If I can't be at home, what is it all about anyway?"

All he wanted was to go home where he was free to wander the gardens, help out with the work, and play games. But when his father said he *had* to stay in school, he understood that this was now his primary responsibility. He did not like it, but he found some comfort sitting beside a large stone statue of Mother Mary just outside the convent entrance. There was a shallow cave there with a little fountain running into a pond. Sant Ji would listen to the calming sounds of the cascading water until the school bell rang and he had to return to class.

The next year, 1963, he was more accepting of his fate, when he started first grade at prestigious St. Joseph's Academy, a strict Catholic school that Indira Gandhi's children had attended. But he didn't like it there, either. Actually, his father had enrolled him there for one purpose only—to learn English. Religion had nothing to do with it. But in order to get a good education, the five-year-old had to comply with many rules and regulations he did not like, such as having to wear a uniform of gray pants and a dark blazer with a collar and tie. He was far more comfortable in his Indian pajama and kurta, which were perfect for the climate and lifestyle in his village. And he didn't like carrying his books in a leather satchel. But he had no choice.

And then the teachers—a group of pale-faced Irish monks who wore long white robes fastened around their bodies with thick green cloth belts—were far too anxious to whip their students into submission. "Yes, Brother Duncan," or "Right away, Brother Duffy," the children had to say. Maharaji later realized that these sad, frustrated monks were probably resentful they'd been ordered to leave their native Ireland to teach a group of kids in the sweltering heat of India. Maybe this was where they sent disobedient monks who needed some hard service far from home. Why else were they so bad-tempered?

Accustomed to his father's kindness and lack of household rules, Sant Ji was disheartened by an average day in school. "First we recited the Lord's Prayer," he recalls. "The teachers would place their canes in plain sight on a table, wiggling and shaking them around to get our attention. 'Have you done your homework today?' a sour-faced monk would ask, considering it his right to smack us around as much as he wanted. We could not take our eyes from the cane that hurt so much. The teachers were overly attached to hitting."

Whack, whack, whack, was a familiar sound in that schoolroom, and beating was a practice Sant Ji dreaded and for which he had no respect. To this day, he does not believe in the use of force to make a point. But in India when he was growing up, hitting was a familiar cultural practice. He recalls people saying hello and giving each other a hearty slap on the back or even across the face. In the same way, parents and teachers alike considered it their privilege to hit their children, ending the beating with something like, "It's only because we love you."

To Sant Ji, such violence had nothing to do with love. The teachers did not seem to realize the negative impact of their actions, and the kids bore the brunt of their frustration. On the other hand, when someone behaved himself or got a good grade, that child was rewarded with a miniature pocket Bible.

Early on, he felt the hypocrisy of the monks and the so-called love they touted under the guise of religion. "Love thy neighbor," they proselytized, but the school did not love its neighbors, as the monks talked behind the neighbors' backs. And neither did the neighbors love the school, as they were always upset by the racket the children made. Only later did Sant Ji discover that conflicts among neighbors were not isolated incidents occurring only around his school. He would find the same kinds of conflicts occurring everywhere else in the world, as neighbors, friends, and even countries rose up against one another.

As Sant Ji reluctantly eased into the routine at St. Joseph's, one can only imagine the opposing forces that were at play in his life. As little importance as religion played in his father's world, his mother was rigidly attached to Hindu caste distinctions as well as to the various mandatory thousand-year-old rites and rituals. She expected her children to follow her lead in Hinduism as she arranged each distinctly different ritual—one for buying a house, one for building a house, one for blessing the foundation, and others for taking long journeys, weddings, births, and anything else concerning the comings and goings of family life.

At a very young age, Sant Ji became aware that his father merely tolerated his mother's dedication to Hinduism. He recalls being in the car one day with his parents when they came upon a Hindu temple located immediately after a tunnel on the way out of Dehradun. In order to pay homage to attract the favors of the gods, people would aim carefully and toss a coin into the temple's front door without stopping the car. When Shri Maharaji saw his wife reaching into her purse that day, he asked her what she was doing.

"I'm going to throw a coin into the temple," she said.

"Why?" he asked.

"Maybe by throwing this coin, I will have salvation or liberation," she said.

"Do you *know* this will happen?" he asked.

"No, but everybody does it."

Shri Maharaji broke into a wide smile. "Give me the coin," he said, "and I will make sure you have liberation."

"No!" she said. When he held on to her wrist and urged her to give him the coin, Mataji became angry and tried to shake off his grip. "Let go of me. Let go!" she cried.

From the backseat, little Sant Ji witnessed his parents fighting, his father laughing and his mother becoming angry. Finally, he let go of her wrist and Mataji tossed the coin, whereupon Shri Maharaji turned his head to Sant Ji and said, "Well, there went liberation right out the window!"

Religion was often a topic of contention for Sant Ji. When he was older and the school became aware of his public talks, his teacher once asked him to what religion he belonged.

"I am from the ancient religion," he answered.

"Surely, then, you believe in caste distinctions," the teacher said.

Sant Ji said that he did not.

"Then you cannot be Hindu," the teacher said.

Sant Ji explained to her that the word *Hinduism* actually meant "ancient religion." To him, it meant nothing more and nothing less, but the arguments never ceased.

Once he had begun school, gone was Sant Ji's early morning anticipation for the light to appear so he could rush outside to revel in nature. Now, his arduous six-day weeks began at 4:00 a.m., whereupon he got up, put on his school uniform, and went directly to the little classroom in the house. There, he and his brothers studied with Uncle before breakfast. After eating, Sant Ji headed off to St. Joseph's for the rest of the day, which began with reciting the Lord's Prayer and then catechism. They studied Hindi for the next forty-five minutes and went on with the rest of their schoolwork.

When the school day ended in the afternoon, Sant Ji happily rushed home and changed into his Indian pajama and kurta. He alternated his free time between watching the carpenter and the people in the kitchen making *chapatis* (Indian bread) and playing with the mahatmas. After dinner when his schoolwork was done, he fell into bed, exhausted. "I used to think how great it would be," Maharaji remembers, "when I didn't have to go to school anymore. I imagined it would be sleep, sleep, sleep until I felt like waking up."

For his Hindi study in school, Sant Ji was assigned to read and interpret a poem by Kabir, the beloved Indian poet from the 1400s:

> Wherever I looked,
> I saw this incredible redness.
> So one day, I became curious
> And I went over to that redness.
> And when I went over to that redness,
> I also became red.

Sant Ji knew that his teacher had no sense of what the poem meant. But *he* did. His father had explained that the "incredible redness" did not represent only a color—it was the color of the passion Kabir experienced inside of himself. When he embraced this passion, the redness overwhelmed him and catapulted him into endless joy.

Sant Ji learned the hard way to keep his understandings to himself because no one put any stock in his ideas. During his lunch break, he often sat alone in a corner of the schoolyard, gazing up at a number of tall, fragrant pine trees that graced the area.

He would laugh out loud as he watched hawks and eagles swoop down from the tallest branches and grab sandwiches from the hands of unsuspecting children. But one wonders how isolated the boy must have felt when keeping his distance was a welcome alternative to having his deepest convictions and his father's efforts questioned by his peers and his teachers.

He turned his attention to nature, marveling at the miniature pinecones adorning the massive trees, and wondered, "Who does it? Who puts the pinecones there?" He imagined a gardener arriving at the schoolyard each night, pinning pinecones on trees, opening flowers, and pulling out withered petals—until he had a higher realization: No mortal gardener could pull off such a magical act. "Wait a minute," he told himself, "it's not the gardener who does this. There is Somebody beyond the gardener."

During school holidays, Sant Ji accompanied his father on tours where he would get on the stage and dance to the same traditional devotional songs that were played when he was still in his mother's womb. "I was taken to any event I had time for," recalls Maharaji. "I'd sit off to the side of the stage, and it was so peaceful, I would start to doze off. My father's voice was melodic, and I didn't want to sleep because I liked his stories so much, but I couldn't help it. I stayed in that twilight zone for a long time. Sometimes the people sang and danced, and it was so beautiful, I joined in."

*As a child, I heard there was a force greater than me,
greater than my teacher, greater than the principal and
every human being on the face of this earth. I wanted to
know what that force was. I wanted to know what that
energy was.*

MAHARAJI
Baltimore, Maryland, June 23, 1981

I have always seen Shri Maharaji as my teacher
more than as my father. Essentially I am filled
with two kinds of gratitude—one for his being
my father. But really, the day he gave me this
Knowledge far outweighs the fact that
he was my father.

MAHARAJI,
BRIGHTON, ENGLAND,
JUNE 7, 1992

Completing the Puzzle

How does a child decide that, above all else, he wants to dedicate his life to peace? It is difficult to imagine such a decision being put before a young boy, but Sant Ji was accustomed to musing over things that few children would contemplate. For example, he often praised his Creator, emphasizing to people many times his age that this life was not to be wasted in vain pursuits, but rather to be used for a meaningful purpose.

He spoke beautifully, expressing a simple and original understanding of the creation. When he was four and a half, he said at one of his father's events, "Look how good God is. He made us. Then He made the days and the nights. Then He made good things to eat. Then He sent us into the world. How beautiful the human body is. A nose to breathe. Can we live without a nose? Just think, God made all parts of our body properly, but if we don't use them properly, then it is our fault, not God's. So do something with your life before it's too late." This talk was published a few months later in *Hansadesh* magazine in India.

Sant Ji's directness and simplicity often shocked people. Charan Anand remembers when an elderly man, an expert scholar of Sanskrit literature, once visited the residence at Dehradun. Charan Anand, a simple man with very little schooling, was talking with this highly educated pundit when in the midst of their conversation, Sant Ji entered the room. When he heard the two men speaking, he sat on Charan Anand's lap and quickly saw that the elderly man was not listening to Charan Anand. Rather, the conversation had become a debate that was deteriorating into an argument, as the older man kept speaking aggressively to the mahatma, trying to make his point.

Sant Ji interrupted the conversation. "How old are you?" he boldly asked the visitor.

"Seventy-five," said the scholar.

"Have you seen God?" asked Sant Ji.

"Not yet."

Sant Ji pressed on. "Have you realized your own Self, since this is what you are arguing about?"

"Not yet," the elderly man admitted.

Sant Ji looked directly into his eyes and told him that he had no right to argue with the mahatma, who was talking about something real, something that Guru Maharaji had revealed to him within himself. "You are only talking about what you study in books," Sant Ji said. "This book learning has not given you any direct experience of God."

The scholar remained silent.

"Don't waste your time anymore," Sant Ji said. "You are already old. Very little time is left, and this book learning has not brought you the experience you want. You should go to Guru Maharaji and ask him for the gift of Knowledge. That will bring you the experience your heart is longing for."

When the child left the room, the scholar asked, "Who is this boy?"

"The youngest son of our Guru Maharaji," said Charan Anand.

"In my life," the visitor said, "I have met many learned people, great pundits and gurus. But no one made me speechless like he did. He asked such a direct question, I could not escape. Now I really want to learn about Knowledge."

❧

Once, at an event, Shri Maharaji remarked to his wife, "Look at the stage. Your youngest son always comes and sits in my chair.

No one else does that." It had become a regular routine for Sant Ji to sit in his father's chair and speak while people gathered.

"I'm dying," a woman asked the six-year-old at one event. "What should I do?"

He looked at her with an unwavering gaze and said, "Until you do, extract everything from this life that you can. If you do that, it will be fine." Perhaps some thought this was arrogant. What did a child know about death and life? But Sant Ji, following his father's example, said what he felt in the moment and was actually proud to be of help. Back at the residence, he often asked the grown-ups, "How can I help my father? What can I do for him?"

They always answered in the same disappointing way: "Do your homework" or "Do well in school."

Like most children, he didn't like homework, but he applied himself and got excellent grades. "I was the only one in my family who did not fail a class," he recalls. "I just kept at it, and I got all As." But he still saw little practical use in it.

Maharaji recalls Muslim students in his class who were his friends. "We never thought of each other as different," he says. "They had different names from us, but we all ate together, played together, passed and failed tests together, and everybody got caned—Muslims, Christians, and Hindus alike. The monks didn't care what your religion was."

Once again, Sant Ji's father was his role model as he interacted with a Muslim neighbor, even though he was a member of an organization that was against gurus. And still, Shri Maharaji listened, demonstrating that it was better to be friends than enemies. Sant Ji shared his father's views, pursuits, and values, but not everyone in his household did. Maharaji recalls that two of his elder brothers, obsessed with buying lottery tickets, used to go on and on about the Cadillacs, houses, and airplanes they would buy with the prize money. They frantically rifled through the newspaper in the mornings to find the winning numbers to make their dreams come true. They always lost, but each day, they would optimistically go out, buy another lottery ticket, and start the process all over again. Sant Ji, however, had a different idea altogether about what would make his dreams come true.

His home environment was conducive to contemplation, and as a six-year-old in the first grade, he wondered at times if peace was something he really needed. What was the necessity? Was his childish happiness not enough? Did he need something more? He was not sure, but he felt a longing for something that was missing. He now describes it as the need for a "coloring," a filling in of something in his life.

While he contemplated the meaning of Knowledge and how it might affect his life, he also had a strong feeling in his heart about it. But since he didn't have it yet, it was hard for him to put a finger on exactly what it would be like. And yet, deep within himself, he knew that it had to be the greatest, the most superb thing in the world.

In January 1964, six-year-old Sant Ji was playing with his brothers in the dining room when his father called the four boys into his sitting room. "Uh-oh, something's up," they thought, wondering if they had done something wrong.

"Do you want Knowledge?" Shri Maharaji asked his sons, one after the other, from his seat on the sofa.

They all said yes. Two of the brothers were about to leave for boarding school, and perhaps Shri Maharaji wanted to give them something essential to take with them on their journey. "Do you know how to meditate?" he asked his sons.

Sant Ji sat on the carpet, crossed his legs, and closed his eyes. "Like this," he said.

"Okay," said Shri Maharaji, "that's right, but there is more to it. There's your inner experience. Now, are you sure you want Knowledge?"

"Yes," said Sant Ji and his three brothers.

Shri Maharaji proceeded to introduce the four techniques to his sons. He made sure they understood, gave them some time to practice, and explained how to find privacy in a crowded dormitory in a bunk bed—by pulling sheets over their heads.

Today, Maharaji distinctly recalls how the experience moved him in its simplicity and beauty. "I could recognize myself in it," he says. "It was as simple as that. That was me and I liked what I saw. I saw my Creator in His most perfect form, most elegant form, most complete form, in a form that to this day, I cannot say if it even had a form. It was so alive, so vibrant, that when I experienced that Ultimate Life itself, I started to understand what I was a part of, and that life had just begun for me."

Upon receiving Knowledge, Maharaji says that his questions and doubts disappeared, never to return: "It was like having someone place a mirror in front of my face. I didn't see my face, and I didn't see my body either. I only saw the kindness, the beauty that had been placed inside of me. That was the sign I wanted, the proof I was looking for.

"Before, everything was like a scattered puzzle—what Knowledge was, how to meditate, all of it. All this had no real significance. But afterwards, I found it easy to speak from my heart, trusting that the words would flow from the kind and beautiful part of myself that I'd glimpsed. It was as if everything *had* to go wherever it belonged. The puzzle had to be completed and it was completed. But I was surprised to see that the biggest hunk of that puzzle was not Knowledge. It was my father and my master, Shri Maharaji."

Sant Ji, who was fond of writing poems, expressed what Knowledge meant to him:

> Without Knowledge
> I am food without salt.
> I am a glass without water.
>
> I am the ocean without fish.
> There is no beauty in me.

I am the plant that doesn't have any greenery.
I am the mountain which is barren.
I am the sky that's pale.
I am a man who is not a human being.

"Because of that gift," says Maharaji, "I am prospering within today. I'm still growing. I am ageless, and I have found my immortality in the truest sense of the word. It will never end and neither will my gratitude to my master."

When I was very little, my happiness was my toys. My smile, my laughter, was playing and running around the house. But I saw in myself that I needed something; I was missing something. When Shri Maharaji revealed this Knowledge to me, it was beautiful. Then everything was so clear.

MAHARAJI
Orlando, Florida, November 9, 1975

There is a great lamp within you, and the rays of that lamp are your life. In these little lamps [pointing to lamps on the wall], the wick burns oil and then burns out. The lamp within does not burn anything, but gives bliss.

MARAHAJI,
DEHRADUN, INDIA,
DECEMBER 1965

Speaking in English

By 1964, Shri Maharaji had carried his message to many large Indian cities and to a multitude of smaller towns and villages in the states of Uttar Pradesh, Bihar, Haryana, Punjab, and Rajasthan. The number of his students was increasing rapidly. He had created a center in Haridwar called Prem Nagar, and there was a smaller ashram between Delhi and Haridwar called Satlok (Place of Truth).

Earlier, some of his students had encouraged him to establish an organization. They assured him it was the best way to get maximum support for spreading the word. Although Shri Maharaji agreed to receive the help, albeit a bit reluctantly, he didn't trust the concept of organizations. He felt that his work was made possible by an individual connection between himself and each of his students. This was how it had worked for him until now and how it had worked for his master. If his master's work had been in the hands of an organization, he, as a married man, might never have been given the chance to go out and spread Knowledge. Furthermore, he feared that the inevitable bureaucracy and politics of any organization would stand in opposition to what he was trying to do. But since his master had asked him to avoid disputes with his students, Shri Maharaji decided to remain open and give it a try.

The first organization founded to support his work was short-lived, as its managers quickly tried to sue Shri Maharaji for control. "When the organization turned on him," says Maharaji, "I heard tell that my father made a gesture and said, 'I wish somebody would take some honey and ash, stir it all together, mix in the organization, and eat it.'"

In 1960, however, Shri Maharaji decided to give it one more chance, and a new entity was registered in Patna, Bihar. He hoped that joining forces with others under one umbrella would help him achieve his ultimate purpose, but his initial misgivings soon returned.

Shri Maharaji had misgivings partly because he was used to setting up his own events. When he saw people at his residence, he might agree to attend events or discuss projects they suggested. When he was on tour, people would line up to greet him and request his presence in their locality. If he felt the people were coming from their hearts and had the ability to set up an event, he would agree to show up in their cities.

However, although such spontaneous and unpredictable behavior delighted his students, it was a headache for any organization with established policies and set procedures. But Shri Maharaji was not interested in giving up the joy and beauty of individuals interacting spontaneously with him.

There is a widely told story that exemplifies his attitudes about who he considered was truly responsible for the work. One day he had a discussion with some organizers who believed that he couldn't function without them. "You need us to arrange your events and invite the people to come and listen to you," they told him.

Shri Maharaji was not buying it. "Oh yes?" he said. "That is what you think? All of you stay here, and I will go out alone."

Shri Maharaji put on his *dhoti* (cloth draped around the waist and legs), his kurta, and tilak. Then, looking elegant and beautiful and brimming with serenity, he walked quietly through the streets of Jwalapur. When people spotted him, they were so touched by his presence that they began following him down the street, creating a parade behind him. When Shri Maharaji returned to the ashram, a crowd of several hundred people followed him there. He had made his point.

Ironically, a little more than ten years after Shri Maharaji's first organizers sued him, the Indian branch of the organization turned against his son. As with his father, the son would be taken to court, but this time, the organizers weren't the only ones trying to sue him—his own family members wanted total control over organizational decisions and assets as they attempted to assert their authority over his work.

After dealing with such disappointing situations, Maharaji adopted his father's ambivalence about organizations supporting his work. And like his father, he struggled to find a balance between the need for logistical help with his work and the need for unencumbered, spontaneous interaction with people.

In 1966, Sant Ji spoke at three of his father's large events—one in Dehradun, one in Meerut, and one in Haridwar—astonishing people with insights that seemed beyond the understanding of a child. Even Shri Maharaji did not know what his son would say on any given day, because the young boy had his own views and could extract lessons from stories that at first seemed devoutly Catholic or Hindu.

But this talent was not received so well in school, when his teacher gave the class a written assignment to answer the question, "Where is God?" Sant Ji knew that the Catholic religion said that God was omnipresent, so he wrote, "God is omnipresent. He is everywhere, but it is in yourself that you can find Him." The answer they wanted was that God was in heaven, and Sant Ji failed the assignment.

However, his sense of purpose was clear, and he continued to speak his mind. After faithfully practicing Knowledge daily for two years, the young boy had come to believe that without realizing the real self, a life was useless. When Indian prime minister Jawaharlal Nehru died, Sant Ji boldly referred to his death in a manner that risked angering his listeners. He pointed out that while Nehru had led an apparently successful life, he had wasted time if he had not come to know his own inner secrets.

Jawaharlal Nehru had been India's prime minister since they had won their independence in 1947. Worn out after seventeen years of being the "father" of the country, he came to rest in Dehradun on May 24, 1964, an idyllic "hill station" to which his family had always been connected. Ramachandra Guha, an Indian writer who had been a student at St. Joseph's Academy at the same time as Maharaji, describes how he and the other students at St. Joseph's were hustled out of their classrooms to see a helicopter land on the parade grounds just outside the school. Out of the chopper came Nehru and his daughter, Indira. They spent forty-eight hours in Dehradun, staying one night at the house of the governor of Uttar Pradesh; then they returned to Delhi, where Nehru died of a heart attack during his sleep.

All of India was in shock. Members of the parliament were openly crying, and 250,000 people passed his body in an endless line of mourners. The governor of Uttar Pradesh sat in his house in Dehradun, inconsolable, somehow blaming himself because Nehru had fallen ill in his house and died the next day in Delhi. Shri Maharaji drove to his house with Charan Anand and Ramanand and asked them to speak to the governor to try to console him.

In the meantime, while Shri Maharaji's meetings across India kept growing in size, he managed to stay close to his students. He considered them to be members of his extended family, and occasionally he even showed up unannounced at their doors. Mr. V. N. Khare, who heard his doorbell ringing late one night, recalls, "I was irritated that someone was showing up so late with no warning. But when I opened the door to see Shri Maharaji standing there, I was overjoyed at the unexpected sight of his magnificent smile."

He invited Shri Maharaji inside, offered him food, and gave him a wooden cot so he could sleep on the roof where it was cooler.

Mr. Khare recalls Shri Maharaji standing on his cot to address a group of people who had spontaneously gathered on the roof. It was the season of the colorful *Holi* Festival, which is celebrated in most parts of India during February and March. The celebrations vary depending on regional and local traditions, but the common practice is spraying colors from one person to another to celebrate joy in all its colors. That night, Shri Maharaji and the people on the roof threw buckets of colored water all over one another amid laughter and noise as everybody became colorfully drenched from head to toe. The neighbors were surprised at the celebration but were not upset. In fact, they were all invited and complimented Mr. Khare on the beauty of his spontaneous celebration.

Shri Maharaji returned to Mr. Khare's house several times during his travels, and each time he was welcomed with open arms. He slept on a simple string bed, ate whatever the family had to offer, and left in a rickshaw the following day to reach the train station and his next destination. Nothing, neither hardship nor illness, would convince him to leave a tour in the middle—except the sincere pleadings of his youngest son.

A month or so before Shri Maharaji left on a tour to distant Punjab, Sant Ji had a private talk with his father. He had a sincere wish to grow as a student, he assured Shri Maharaji, but his schoolwork took so much effort and time, he missed listening to his father's talks.

"If you want an event here where we live," said Shri Maharaji, "why don't you put it together? If you do, I'll speak."

Sant Ji was overwhelmed. He was eight, hardly an organizer, and he had no idea what to do first. It felt like a huge mountain to climb, but he said, "All right, I'll do it."

After his father left the next morning, he recruited an experienced instructor to help him plan the event. They reserved the parade grounds next to the school for June 11–13. After he meticulously created handwritten invitations, he met with his school principal. "My father will be speaking here in Dehradun," Sant Ji said, "and I'd like your permission to give each teacher an invitation." With the principal's blessing, he walked from classroom to classroom, personally inviting all the teachers and his fellow students.

Shri Maharaji was touring in Punjab, an eight-hour drive from Dehradun, accompanied by Charan Anand and several other instructors, when he was surprised to see a messenger from Dehradun standing at his door. "Why are you here?" he asked him. "You have traveled a long distance to see me."

"Sant Ji sent me," the man said, holding out a letter. "He sent this to you. He wants you to speak at his event in Dehradun."

"But if he is there speaking, I don't have to come," said Shri Maharaji.

The messenger waited while Shri Maharaji read the letter, which contained such a humble, heartfelt request for his presence that he could not deny it. His son wrote, "You said to put something together and I did. Will you please come back and speak?"

Since Shri Maharaji had encouraged Sant Ji, there was no way he could *not* show up. But he was about to begin a three-day event there in Punjab, with a large number of people anxious to listen to him. He called Bihari to his room. "I have to go to Dehradun for Sant Ji, but we can't leave here in the light of day," he said. "Too many people will be upset. Come to my room late tonight after everyone has gone to bed, and we'll sneak out. If we drive all night, we can be there in time."

Shri Maharaji and Bihari ate a light meal, went to their rooms, and closed their doors as usual. At 1:30 a.m., Bihari went to Shri Maharaji's room, but before he could knock, the door opened and Shri Maharaji quietly stepped out. The two men walked swiftly down the stairs and into the cool night. All was going as planned until Bihari noticed something sticking out from under the car—a pair of beat-up sandals, connected to feet and legs. One of Shri Maharaji's female students was sleeping under his car, making sure she would see him if he went anywhere.

She heard the men's footsteps and slid herself out from under the car to face Shri Maharaji in the moonlight. He thought quickly and said, "Go to my sitting room and practice Knowledge. Do not tell anybody that you have seen me and Bihari Singh."

The student was so overwhelmed that Shri Maharaji had invited her to practice Knowledge in his quarters, she agreed with no hesitation. Off she went, and the two men quickly got into the car and took off. Bihari drove all night, and they arrived in Dehradun by midmorning. But later in the day, Shri Maharaji was surprised to see that a group of his students had pooled their rupees to charter a bus from Punjab to Dehradun when, upon waking, they'd discovered that he was gone.

Sant Ji had taken great care with every detail for this event. The audience included his teachers and fellow students, as well as prominent citizens from Dehradun. It was after dark when everyone gathered under the moonlight, anxious to listen to Shri Maharaji. But it seemed that the boy had invited more than he realized. When they were leaving the house for the grounds, Shri Maharaji told his eight-year-old son, "You speak first in Hindi. And then speak in English."

Sant Ji was shocked. This was more than he had bargained for. True, he was accustomed to talking in front of crowds. He'd been opening for his father for many years, but not this close to his school or in front of his teachers and schoolmates. And never in English. A moment of fear overtook him. What if he made mistakes with his teachers listening? All the members of his family were there, as were his friends and people from all over Dehradun. What if he made a fool of himself?

Today, Maharaji explains that after his initial shock, he was not nervous when he arrived at the event, because he realized this was not about performing. Rather, it was a beautiful opportunity to express what was in his heart. He got up on the stage, and the next thing he knew, he was speaking English to the people who knew him best. He began, "Today I am very glad to see you here. I have to know God, and you also have to know God. God is in your heart. There is a bhajan in Hindi that says God is very, very kind. He is so kind that I cannot describe His kindness. He gave us everything that we need. He gave us eyes to see, ears to hear, mouths to speak and to eat, hands to work, and feet to walk."

Sant Ji was hitting his stride as he let the words flow easily from his heart. "I've told you that everything you need, He has given to you. Never think that you cannot know God. He is in your heart. He is everywhere. Just like the air, which you cannot see but is everywhere, in the same way God is also everywhere. Know God. Don't waste time. The time you are wasting will never come again.

"India is such a nice country," the child continued, "but today, India is begging to America, Japan, Russia, and other countries of the world. How long are you going to depend on foreign aid? You have the resources, and you need to work together to develop this country. But first you have to educate your people and learn to work together. Material development alone, however, is not going to bring happiness and fulfillment in your life. Don't forget the ancient wisdom. Without that, one leg will be long and the other will be short."

Sant Ji was referring to a well-known Indian metaphor in order to describe the difference between Western and Eastern culture. It says that both cultures walk with a limp. In the West, the material leg is long and the spiritual is short, while in the East it is the other way around.

Shri Maharaji spoke next, after which bhajans were played, expressing the words of great sants such as Kabir and Brahmanand. The 16 mm footage shows Shri Maharaji suddenly turning to look at his son, and as if he could feel the gaze, Sant Ji turned to face his father. As two immense souls looked each other in the eyes for a few seconds, it felt as if two great oceans were merging.

You people are looking at my body, but I'm not just my body. After knowing that power which is within me, there is no need to know anything else. I and all of you have this beautiful body. Don't waste it.

MAHARAJI
Dehradun, India, 1966

What is this practice? It is like an electric current. It keeps flowing from the consciousness continuously like a current.

MAHARAJI,
DEHRADUN, INDIA,
DECEMBER 1, 1965

Maharaji in the arms of his father, Shri Maharaji, Prem Nagar ashram,
Haridwar, India, 1958.

Shri Maharaji and Maharaji, age two, sitting on stage.

Family portrait, Dehradun, India, 1959. From left: Badhi
Mataji (Older Mother), Bhole Ji, Raja Ji, Shri Maharaji,
Maharaji (Sant Ji), Bal Bhagwan Ji, Mataji (Younger
Mother).

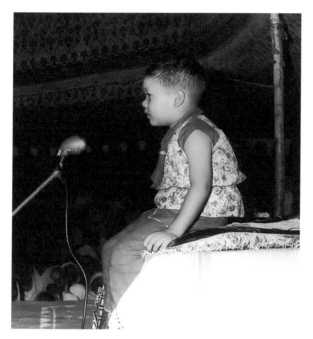

Maharaji speaking at an event before Shri Maharaji.
This is believed to be in Nasik, near Mumbai, the first
event where Maharaji addressed an audience at three
and a half years of age.

Ready for school, at age five, Dehradun.

Speaking in English, at age eight, at an event on the Parade Ground, Dehradun, June 1966. Maharaji organized the event himself, with help from an instructor. He invited his teachers and his father, who was away on tour. Shri Maharaji traveled all night to return in time.

Shri Maharaji singing his favorite song at the time, which said, "Human being, this life is a two-day festival," a short time before he passed away, Satlok ashram, Meerut, India, July 1966.

Thirteen days after Shri Maharaji passed away, Maharaji was formally acknowledged as the new master. He wore a ceremonial crown, and Charan Anand put a tilak (traditional mark given on special occasions) on his forehead, Prem Nagar ashram, July 31, 1966.

Eight-year-old Maharaji speaking at an event in August 1966, shortly after he took on the responsibility of spreading the message of peace. His head had been shaved when his father passed away, according to the custom.

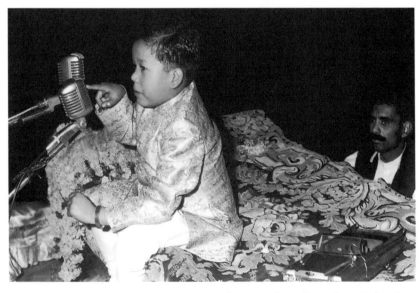

At an event in 1966. He is wearing princely attire from Rajasthan. Behind him is one of his toy cars.

Wearing garlands and ceremonial crown, Maharaji walks among students, most likely at Satlok ashram, 1967. To his right is Bihari Singh; behind him is Sampurnanand; to his left is Bhole Ji.

A young Maharaji with an unidentified Westerner in India, 1968.

At age twelve in his St. Joseph's Academy
school uniform.

Speaking at an event in Jodhpur, India, at age eleven, June 1969.
Maharaji would go to school during the week and attend events
on weekends or during school vacations.

June 17, 1971: Maharaji arrives at Heathrow Airport, London, for his first visit to the West. Accompanied by an airport press officer, he makes his way through hundreds of people gathered to welcome him. Some had garlanded him as he exited the customs and immigration area.

Small event in a home in Leicester, England, June 1971. Bihari Singh and Charan Anand are to the right. The room is full, and people are looking in through a window.

Maharaji was supposed to return to school in India after two weeks in England, but instead accepted an invitation to fly to America. Here, on July 17, 1971, at London's Heathrow Airport, he holds an impromptu meeting before departing for the United States.

In the living room at the Alta Loma Terrace center, Hollywood, California, 1971.

Tens of thousands of Indians and hundreds of Westerners who had come on the first chartered jumbo jet welcome Maharaji back to India from his first trip to the West, at a reception at Delhi airport, November 7, 1971. Maharaji and family members are in the open convertible decorated with garlands.

Speaking at Ram Lila Grounds, Delhi, in November 1971. Some of the Westerners who came on the jumbo jet are sitting on a nearby section of the stage.

Answering questions from Westerners on the roof of Prem Nagar ashram, November, 1971.

Maharaji is interviewed by the media upon arrival at
Los Angeles International Airport in 1972.

At the controls of a Piper Arrow, Leavesden Airport, England, September
1972. Bill Bach, Maharaji's flight instructor, is seated in the copilot's seat.
Maharaji flew almost daily.

Meeting with students in South Africa, 1972.

At a press conference upon his first arrival in
Australia, Sydney Airport, October 5, 1972.

Maharaji speaking at an impromptu gathering in the rear garden of the house at 3 Woodside Avenue, Highgate, London, June 6, 1973.

Thousands of people gathered in Trafalgar Square in London before attending an event at Alexandra Palace, July 13–15, 1973. More than 11,000 people attended the event.

On *The Merv Griffin Show,* at age fifteen, November 28, 1973. Maharaji told Merv Griffin, "I am the richest man in the world probably. Because you don't have to be rich in money to be rich. You have to be rich in heart."

Councilwoman Erma Henderson, the first African-American woman on Detroit's city council, presents Maharaji with a commendation recognizing his "continuous efforts in advocating peace." Maharaji was also given the keys to the city. Detroit, Michigan, August 7, 1973.

Eternal Meditation

By the time Shri Maharaji was sixty-five, his students noticed that he had become increasingly ecstatic. He was often up late at night, or even all night long, celebrating the glory of life, singing and dancing with his students, moving from one day into the next with little or no sleep. People talked about him being in a state of "divine intoxication."

Charan Anand says, "He always carried a long wooden walking stick with him, and he'd put the walking stick on his shoulder and dance." (In India, four people traditionally carry a corpse over their shoulders during cremation rites.) Shri Maharaji did his "stick dance" to the music and words of one of his favorite Brahmanand bhajans, which said, "This world is like a two-day festival. When you die, nobody will go with you."

After the annual *Guru Puja* Festival on July 1–3, 1966, at Satlok ashram, Shri Maharaji went home to Dehradun to be with his family, but he did not attend the usual weekly event in Dehradun the following Sunday. He said, "Sant Ji can go instead of me." It seemed that Shri Maharaji had developed a strong conviction that his son was the one to continue bringing the message to the world, and he was starting to give some hints about it. But this was a conviction that his wife, the child's mother, did not share.

Months prior, while Shri Maharaji was on tour and was about to return home, he sent a letter to the family in which he wrote, "I send my blessings to Mataji and the three eldest brothers and my full prostration to my youngest son."

When he got back home, his wife asked him, "Why did you write that?"

"You do not recognize who Sant Ji is, do you?" he said. "But I do."

A pundit once asked Shri Maharaji, "Why don't you send Sant Ji to Sanskrit school?"

"Why?" asked Shri Maharaji.

"So he can learn the scriptures," said the pundit.

"He doesn't need to learn scriptures," said Shri Maharaji. "When he grows older, scriptures will be created when he speaks."

On Saturday, July 16, 1966, Shri Maharaji took his family on a picnic to one of his favorite spots—Camel's Back, at Mussourie, a beautiful area with a clear view of the Himalayan mountain range. They sat on the lush ground, eating, laughing, and having fun, until Shri Maharaji spoke clearly and directly, addressing each family member one by one about the future. Bihari remembers that Shri Maharaji told the other family members that Sant Ji was going to take his message to the world. "He doesn't need anybody's help." To his oldest son, Sat Pal (Bal Bhagwan Ji), he said, "Try to support your brother in what he will do, but don't disturb his work."

The next morning at 4:00 a.m., Shri Maharaji left Dehradun for Alwar, Rajasthan. Some mahatmas, including Charan Anand, had left the day before to set up an event there. Thousands of people, including the governor of Alwar, were waiting for Shri Maharaji. But when he arrived after eight hours on the road, he was not feeling well. He called Charan Anand to his room and said, "You go to the stage and convey my message and my blessings to the governor and all the people. Tell them I'm not feeling well but I'll see them all in the morning."

At 3:30 that morning, however, he felt so poorly, he decided to return home to Dehradun. He let the instructors know he was leaving and that they should carry on for him. Bihari helped Shri

Maharaji into the car, making him comfortable in the backseat. Some hours later, just after they had passed the cutoff to Delhi on the road to Dehradun, Shri Maharaji ordered Bihari to turn around. "We will not go to Dehradun after all," he said in a thin voice. "We will go back and stay in Delhi instead."

Bihari protested, "It's too hot in Delhi. Dehradun is only a hundred and fifty miles away. It's cooler and you have family and doctors there. They can help you. Please let me drive a little bit longer while you rest."

"No," said Shri Maharaji, "there is nothing a doctor can do for me. We are going to stay in Shakti Nagar." He was referring to his house in Delhi. They pulled in to Shakti Nagar early in the morning, and Shri Maharaji asked for his bed to be removed from the bedroom and placed in a small room near the house's front gate. He told Bihari, "You have been driving constantly and have not slept for the last two nights. Go eat and take some rest."

Shri Maharaji sat down to meditate, and Bihari went to eat something. However, when Bihari lay down in another room, he could not sleep. He was so concerned that he crept quietly into Shri Maharaji's room and sat on a blanket on the floor just behind him, in case he needed anything because he had taken no food or water since the night before.

Shri Maharaji sat in meditation all day, not stopping to eat or drink. Anyone who opened the door saw him sitting with his legs crossed, his back straight, his awareness deep inside himself. When the sun set, Bihari went to the kitchen and brought Shri Maharaji a glass of water. He drank half of it, but when Bihari took the glass from him, he saw that Shri Maharaji's hands were hot and sweaty, his face pale and weary. "I'm going to call a doctor," Bihari said.

"No," said Shri Maharaji. "There is no need. Just tell the people outside the gate if they come to see me today, that I'm not feeling well. Tomorrow I will be better and everybody can come to see me."

Bihari was not convinced and called a local physician named
Dr. Gupta. The doctor arrived quickly, gave Shri Maharaji two
capsules, and told Bihari not to worry. "He'll be all right," Dr.
Gupta assured him. "In a few hours, give him two more capsules
and his fever will be gone."

"See?" Shri Maharaji said to Bihari. "I told you there was no
reason to worry."

In several hours, though, after taking the two additional capsules, Shri Maharaji's fever had spiked dramatically. Bihari called
Dr. Gupta again, but when the doctor saw how Shri Maharaji's
condition had deteriorated, he stood there helplessly. "Why did
you wait so long?" he asked Bihari. "He needs a specialist."

He called another physician, named Dr. Chatterjee, who arrived quickly. However, like Dr. Gupta, he had no idea why Shri
Maharaji's fever was so high or what to do about it. "Bihari,"
the two doctors said in hushed tones, "we have to take him to a
hospital."

When Shri Maharaji refused to go, Bihari located several
students, telling them that Shri Maharaji was ill and that they
should bring any doctors they could find. Several of his students and a doctor arrived within the hour, while Bihari and the
two attending physicians waited impatiently. All the while, Shri
Maharaji remained where he was, sitting in meditation, acknowledging no one.

Someone eventually knocked on the door with yet another
doctor, but he was too late. A moment earlier, Dr. Gupta had turned
to Bihari and said, "You can send everyone back home to bed."

"Why?" asked Bihari.

"Because Shri Maharaji is gone."

"What do you mean?" asked Bihari. "He is right here in front
of us, meditating." He gestured frantically toward Shri Maharaji,
still sitting upright with eyes closed.

"Yes," the doctor said, "he is here, sitting in meditation pos-
ture; that is true. But he is not in his body any longer."

Bihari Singh passed out, falling to the floor, and someone took him to another room to recover.

༄

Back in Rajasthan, Charan Anand and his fellow instructors were concerned as to why Shri Maharaji had suddenly abandoned the tour. But they finished the gathering in Alwar, just as Shri Maharaji had asked them, and went on to the next one in Jaipur, hoping he would rejoin them there.

It was a lively event, with people asking many questions, some of them too intellectual for simple mahatmas. They fulfilled their obligation, though, making apologies for Shri Maharaji's absence and answering questions from their hearts as best they could. They taught the techniques of Knowledge to people who were ready and helped them to understand the message. But all the while, they were deeply concerned about Shri Maharaji, wondering what was keeping him away.

On July 19, early in the morning at Shakti Nagar, Bihari was resting in the small cubicle adjoining the room where Shri Maharaji's dead body was still sitting upright. Bihari was so bereft and stressed that he wanted to be alone—until he heard someone talking about calling a taxi. "Why are you calling a taxi?" he asked them, coming back into the room where the master sat, forever silent.

"To take his body to Dehradun," was the answer.

"What's wrong with my car?" Bihari wanted to know.

"Nothing. But you can't drive. Not in your present state."

Bihari pulled himself together and said, "For nine years I drove him when he was alive. Today he has left his body, and I will be the one to drive him back home."

They placed several blankets in the backseat of the car, where they sat Shri Maharaji between two men. For the next five hours, Bihari Singh drove, looking into his rearview mirror to see Shri

Maharaji, his body frozen in an upright position, his eyes closed. It appeared that he was in a meditation that would never end.

"A perfect master never lies," Bihari Singh thought. "You told me you would have me with you for your whole life. Now you have left, but I am still driving your car. I don't understand."

His confusion would be cleared up faster than he could have ever imagined. But he also struggled with a question that was far more immediate and compelling: How would Shri Maharaji's family react to the news that their beloved husband, father, and master had passed away and would not be coming back?

Many people quote the Bhagavad Gita *where it is written, "If you think of me at the last moment, you will find me." So you say you will meditate at the last moment. But if you don't know how to meditate now, how will you meditate at the last moment?*

MAHARAJI
Dehradun, India, April 1965

Part Two
1966–1971

Don't cry. You don't have to cry. That which you loved about Shri Maharaji will always be with you. Nobody can take that away from you…. The same Guru Maharaji is within me. He is within you. He is within everybody. We must understand that it is Guru Maharaji himself speaking now.

MAHARAJI,
HARIDWAR, INDIA,
JULY 30, 1966

The Succession

Bihari Singh debated with himself all the way to St. Joseph's. The night before, he had returned Shri Maharaji's body to Dehradun. This morning, he was filled with grief and disbelief, and it was difficult to make a decision. Should he tell Sant Ji and his brother Raja Ji the real reason he was picking them up from school early? Or should he just drive them home and let them see for themselves?

When Bihari appeared at the door of Raja Ji's classroom, his face told a painful story. He whispered something in the monk's ear, who then waved Raja Ji from the room. Together, Bihari and Raja Ji walked down the hallway to collect Sant Ji.

"Why did you come to take us out of class?" Raja Ji asked Bihari. "I thought you and my father were away on tour. Is Shri Maharaji home? Does he want to see me? Did he come back early?"

"He is back," Bihari Singh said.

Sant Ji was allowed to leave his fourth-grade classroom, and the three of them drove in silence to the residence. The boys had no idea what had happened or why Bihari was crying. But they knew something was wrong the moment they got out of the car, as everybody was milling around outside, crying and speaking in hushed voices.

Sant Ji went directly to his father's room. There sat Shri Maharaji in eternal meditation, his eyes closed. Sant Ji approached his father's motionless body, touched his feet, spent a few moments in silence, and walked outside. "I wanted to feel him one last time," says Maharaji. "And I was filled up. It was a beautiful experience, and yet it was terrible, too. Like it was the end of the world. Afterwards, I realized that something had just sprouted within me, that the beautiful fountain was really within me. The world had ended, but it had also begun, and everything was different."

Maharaji recalls crying for several days without stopping. He loved his father/master more than he could possibly say, and the loss was deep and substantial. At the same time, his mother was beside herself, lamenting, "Why didn't he give any indication? He wasn't even sick!" She ordered Shri Maharaji's body to be packed in ice, a customary practice in the heat of India to preserve a body until the cremation. However, the truth was, she believed that maybe her husband was not really dead, but rather was in a deep meditation and eventually could be revived. Was it denial or her belief in the extraordinary powers of the man she had married? No one can say for sure, since shock and grief can cause people to think and act in unusual ways.

Early the next morning, Shri Maharaji's body was placed in the top section of a van and driven to Prem Nagar, his final destination. Word had traveled quickly that Shri Maharaji had died and would be cremated at Prem Nagar. Hundreds of stunned and grief-stricken students were hurrying there to pay their last respects. When they arrived, they began searching for fragrant sandalwood (not readily available in stores) on which to cremate the master's body. In the twenty-four hours from the arrival of Shri Maharaji's body to Dehradun to his cremation the next morning in Haridwar, people managed to collect forty pounds of sandalwood by gathering a little bit here and there.

On the day of the cremation, Sant Ji stayed home with his mother. In Indian tradition, those present at the cremation poured coconut oil and *ghee* (clarified butter) over the pyre just before they set it on fire. As Shri Maharaji's body burned and smoke rose to the heavens, his students had various reactions—from sobbing and covering their eyes to feeling a beautiful peace.

According to Hindu custom, a mourning period of thirteen days was prescribed, during which time the male family members shaved their heads. On the thirteenth day, the mourning would end. There was a general anticipation among the mourners because they hoped that when the mourning was over, it would be clear who the new master would be.

As the days passed, more and more people arrived at Prem Nagar full of anticipation. Shri Maharaji's students needed someone to take his place, someone who could guide them and inspire them, but there were no preset rules as to how the next master should emerge. Shri Maharaji's master, Swami Swarupanand, had not left behind written instructions, which had led to the various opinions and ensuing confusion as to who should succeed him. Shri Maharaji *did* succeed him in the eyes of a few, but because the others were not clear that he truly was the one, he had to start his work from scratch. And just like his master before him, Shri Maharaji had left no written instructions before he died.

"When my father was about to die," says Maharaji, "he did not sit down and write a will. He did not dictate to somebody what should happen next. He did not call anybody into his room and tell them, 'Ah, you should do this, and we should be doing this, and I wish I could do this.' He simply went into a room, sat down, and practiced Knowledge."

When Shri Maharaji died, Sampurnanand, like Charan Anand and other traveling mahatmas, was on tour, returning only after the cremation was finished. He was bereft when he learned that Shri Maharaji was gone, and he was crying in the backyard of the residence when he saw Sant Ji.

"Why are you crying?" the young boy asked.

Sampurnanand was so devastated, he could not answer.

Sant Ji soothed him. "What are you worried about?" he asked. "Do you think Shri Maharaji has gone? You don't have to worry about anything. Knowledge is my responsibility now, and I know how to spread it. You will never see me *not* being able to do that. I'll take care of it."

When Sampurnanand heard the boy speaking with such confidence and faith, he was taken aback. He recognized the new Guru Maharaji speaking. In fact, he felt certain of it, as he remembered the subtle hints from Shri Maharaji about his youngest son being the next master. When Sant Ji later took Sampu into a room, together with Charan Anand, Bihari, and others, and talked tearfully about times and places where he would be going on tours to continue his father's work, it was clear to those gathered that Sant Ji, despite his young age, was the one.

The family and the senior members of the organization, however, did not feel that Sant Ji could succeed his father. They seemed to have forgotten Shri Maharaji indicating that his youngest son would be the one to someday carry his message. Or perhaps they held too many entrenched ideas that didn't allow them to accept this possibility.

On the eve of July 30, the twelfth day of the thirteen-day mourning period, people gathered in the large meeting hall at Prem Nagar. Sorrow and grief hung heavy in the air, and no one stepped onstage to speak because no one knew what to say. Instead, in a back room, Mataji and her eldest son, Bal Bhagwan Ji, were meeting with senior instructors and organizers, trying to decide who would succeed Shri Maharaji.

Charan Anand and Sampurnanand were purposely not included in the meeting, even though they had been prominent in Shri Maharaji's work. Charan Anand was probably seen as too uneducated, and Sampu was, as usual, taking care of Sant Ji, who was riding on his shoulders, commanding him to go here and there. When Sampu and Sant Ji approached the room where the succession discussions were going on, Sant Ji told Sampu to open the door. But when he did, Sant Ji's family stopped talking immediately.

Mataji had been pushing her favorite instructor, the organization's treasurer, to advocate her case. "Mataji is the one to lead us now," he had said, but that did not meet with general approval. A woman as master? That would be much too controversial. Even though Shri Maharaji had appointed as many women instructors as men, he had received his share of criticism for this, both from traditional religious groups and from Arya Samaj. The idea simply did not fly.

The people in the room were behaving as if the master's family or the organization that had supported him owned his work, as if the master's title, like some deed of trust, could be passed on through administrative criteria such as precedence and seniority. But soon enough, they would be reminded that the master's ways defied worldly logic and predictability.

Out in the great hall, thousands were waiting in anxious anticipation, feeling the profound contrast to what usually happened there. Whenever Shri Maharaji had spoken there, the hall had been filled with inspiration and devotional singing. Now, many people were crying openly, and others talked in hushed voices.

Behind the stage, Sampu took Sant Ji to a little window where he could watch the crowd, unseen. By this time, one of the organizers in the back room had named fourteen-year-old Bal Bhagwan Ji as successor, and Mataji was beginning to accept that outcome. But in the meantime, when Sant Ji saw the people's sadness and sensed the huge void, a desire to comfort them overcame him.

And so, while his mother, his eldest brother, and all the "important" people huddled in the meeting room behind closed doors, arguing and planning the organization's future, Sant Ji walked out onto the stage and sat in his father's chair. Behind him was a large picture of Shri Maharaji looking straight ahead with eternal serenity, decorated with flowers.

Sant Ji sat for a little while with his eyes closed while the audience quieted down. "In that one moment of my life," he recalls, "everything changed. The only thing I could do was close my eyes and listen to the words of my teacher, my father. And believe me, his words echoed and echoed as if he was standing on that platform telling me exactly what to do. There are rationales I could have gotten into, but I didn't give myself a chance. I went for it. I have absolutely no doubt in my mind that my destiny was changed in that moment. Absolutely."

"Don't cry," were his first words to the thousands of mourners. "You don't have to cry. That which you loved about Shri Maharaji will always be with you. Nobody can take that away from you."

Silence filled the hall as Sant Ji continued. "I feel that Guru Maharaji is here. After all, what is in me? I have only flesh, nerves, blood, and bones. And I do not have anything more. But I have got the same soul. The same Guru Maharaji is within me. He is within you, too. He is within everybody. We must understand that it is Guru Maharaji himself speaking right now."

Sant Ji pointed to the photograph of his father and said, "You are looking for him in the picture, but look in your own hearts, and then you will understand." People were crying again, but their tears of sorrow had become tears of relief. When Sant Ji finished speaking, people filed slowly out of the hall, feeling that a seed of hope had been sown.

The next morning, on July 31, 1966, people gathered early in the great hall. Sampu, as usual, was carrying Sant Ji around on his shoulders. The family remained stubborn. Even after they heard about Sant Ji's appearance onstage and how the people had reacted, they were still involved in discussions about the future.

As the large meeting hall filled up, Mataji asked Charan Anand to say something comforting. But when the PA system failed, Charan Anand passed the job to Sampu, whose powerful voice could reach the back of the audience. Sampurnanand asked the people why they were so impatient. Hadn't they heard what Sant Ji had said the night before? Mataji was not happy with his words, but she couldn't or wouldn't stop her youngest son from stepping on the stage next.

Suddenly the PA system began working, and Sant Ji said, "Look, good people. This is not an occasion for celebrations, because at three in the morning of the nineteenth, Guru Maharaji left his mortal body. But I feel that Guru Maharaji is still here and always will be. Guru Maharaji is not here anymore in his old body. However, I shall explain everything to you. A guru is never born and never dies. Guru Maharaji is and always will be present."

People started to shout, "Bolie Shri Satgurudev Maharaj Ki Jai!" This meant "Glory to the master!" and was a greeting of jubilation called out in the presence of Shri Maharaji. Others picked it up, but some started talking amongst themselves or shouting remarks until Sant Ji said sternly, "Listen. You must open your ears and listen. If you don't listen, then I will have nothing to do with you."

The hall fell silent again. "When Guru Maharaji was here," Sant Ji said, "what did he do? He gave Knowledge to everyone, and he gave of himself as if it would never end. Everyone kept taking from that endless treasure, and now he has passed so much power over to me. He told me to do his work, and Guru Maharaji is in front of us. He is within my heart and everywhere."

In the back room, senior officers of the organization were preparing to come out and announce Bal Bhagwan Ji as the next master—until somebody burst into the room and told them what was happening. They rushed out just in time to see Charan Anand putting the tilak on Sant Ji's forehead while Mataji looked on in surprise. Thousands were shouting for little Sant Ji, his shaven head covered by a piece of white cloth as he sat in the master's

chair while Sampurnanand, Charan Anand, Bihari, Gyan Bairaganand, and several others improvised a ceremony to crown him.
After Bihari put a crown on Sant Ji's head, never again would the
students call him Sant Ji. For them, he was now Guru Maharaji.

When Mataji and Maharaji's brothers touched his feet as a
sign of respect, he garlanded each member of his family, including
Older Mataji and Didiji. But while most of the audience were ecstatic, some were still not yet convinced. Maharaji told everyone
that the next day he would show them proof that "Guru Maharaji
never dies."

The next morning, on the first of August, in front of a full
hall, Maharaji told the attendees, "When I was in Dehradun, I was
asleep in bed, and I felt that a man was there. I touched him with
my hand and saw that it was Shri Maharaji. We spoke to each
other for a long time. Guru Maharaji is right here; he is not gone.
If you want me to prove it, I shall prove it to you. Tonight, you
shall see Maharaji right before you."

That night, eight-year-old Maharaji stood up and began to
dance and play the *manjeeras*, the small cymbals that his father
used to play. Within a few minutes, the people in the hall witnessed the same radiance they had seen and felt in Shri Maharaji.
Here was Shri Maharaji himself, they decided, dancing before
their eyes, with the same radiant grace, glorious smile, and shining eyes.

What really occurred that evening remains a mystery, something that words cannot describe. People say it was as if father
and son were one and the same in front of them, as if time and
death had been suspended for a moment and life was manifesting in an eternal moment of glory. When the dance was done, the
new master asked his eldest brother to come onstage and speak,
telling the people that he had been looking forward to listening to
Bal Bhagwan Ji with much anticipation. Did Maharaji know what
they had plotted behind closed doors? Did he know when he had

been crowned that some had already chosen his eldest brother as master? It was likely that Maharaji, in his innocence, was unaware of this until several years later when his eldest brother and mother turned against him and embarked upon an organized effort to harm his reputation and push him aside.

When Guru Maharaji was here, he gave himself to
spreading Knowledge to everyone, never stopping.
I came for this purpose. I need his grace to do this work.
Guru Maharaji is within my heart.

MAHARAJI
Haridwar, India, July 30, 1966

We will spread Knowledge throughout the whole world. The spreading of Knowledge is beneficial for all. That is why we should not waste time. We have to give even our last breath for the good of others.

MARARAJI,
HARIDWAR, INDIA,
JULY 29, 1966

A Double Act

The day after Maharaji was crowned, his mother awakened him at 5:00 a.m. to do his homework. By 6:30, he was in his school uniform, and by 7:00, he arrived at school for his first class. Now he was a fifth-grade student by day, and on the weekends and holidays he was a traveling guru who inspired thousands.

"It was a double act to be with my friends in school," Maharaji recalls. "Everybody knew who I was and who my father had been. They would ask me questions about what I did on tour, and I'd say, 'I'm not going to talk about this. This has nothing to do with you guys. I'm your friend, just another schoolmate, so let's get on with it.'"

It appears that Maharaji accepted his schooling as a necessary responsibility and did the best he could, which is definitely in character with the rest of his life. Even back then, he did his best to reconcile the fulfillment of worldly obligations with those of the heart. And he was eager to excel in both. In fact, he developed so much affection for his science teacher (science was his favorite subject) that when he returned to India from the West in 1972, he brought with him an 8 mm movie projector as a gift for the elderly gentleman.

Maharaji struck up two close friendships in his school days— one with a Muslim boy and the other with a Christian boy named Mercy who was born into what the Hindus considered the lowest caste, commonly called the *untouchables*. Mataji disapproved of both friendships and barred the Christian boy in particular from

coming to their home. "But he's my friend," Maharaji argued
with his mother. "Can't you see he's a human being?"

By this time, Mataji and Bal Bhagwan Ji had accepted Maharaji's role as public speaker and figurehead. They regularly es-
corted him to events, but they were still convinced they were part
of a family collaboration. On the weekend of October 28, 1966,
Maharaji attended his first large event as master, outside of his
familiar surroundings of Dehradun and Haridwar. The mayor of
New Delhi inaugurated the event, which inspired eight-year-old
Maharaji to say, "We just heard Mr. Mayor speak. I don't know
his name, but I liked what he said very much. Until today, I have
not heard anyone say what Mr. Mayor said. He said that we must
love God implicitly. And God, too, loves us implicitly. God loves
all. God made you all, showered His blessings upon you, but He
tests you to find out whether you have the devotion, the flame of
love within you."

In late December, Maharaji had just turned nine, and his
mother accompanied him on his first long tour to Bihar, several
days' drive from Dehradun. Patna, the capital of Bihar, had been
an important venue for his father. One of the most desolate states
in India, many indigent people there had followed Shri Maharaji
all their lives, always welcoming him with warmth and appreciation whenever he visited them.

Now posters of Maharaji were nailed up all over the city, featuring a photo of him wearing a white Kashmir cap like his father
had worn. The inscription read, "Nine-year-old Balyogeshwar [child
master of yogis], Sant Ji Maharaj is coming to address us." (Balyogeshwar, one of the various titles given to Maharaji, became his
prominent name in India during the next decade or two).

Before the event, the press in Patna arrived at a building close
to the grounds where Maharaji was staying. They were anxious to
meet and interview the boy guru, but he kept them waiting for
close to an hour while he rested from the grueling trip over unpaved,
dusty roads. When his mother went to fetch him and saw that

he was sleeping, she did not have the heart to wake him up. The press waited, and finally, Maharaji showed up.

Rajeshwar, a local judge who had been close to Shri Maharaji, remembers that press conference very well, even though it took place nearly forty years ago. According to him, when Maharaji entered the room and sat on a beautiful sofa, a reporter looked at his watch and said, "Balyogeshwar Ji, you asked us to come at a particular time, and do you see how late it is? We have been waiting for you for a long time. Don't you have respect for our time?"

"I'm a little child," Maharaji said quite innocently, "and I was taking a nap. Besides, I did not invite you."

"But your followers invited us," the reporter said.

"Then I am sorry for my delay," Maharaji said.

Someone else asked, "Balyogeshwar Ji, how old are you?"

"I was born on December tenth, 1957."

The first reporter said, "Do you know that some of us are forty and fifty? Balyogeshwar, you are so young, and all of us are senior to you. And you are sitting on a high chair, and we are sitting on the floor. Is it befitting that a small boy should sit on a high pedestal?"

Maharaji replied, "Have you ever seen an elephant sitting on the back of a human being? No. But I am sure you have seen a human being sitting on the back of an elephant."

Someone asked, "Do you smoke, Balyogeshwar Ji?"

"No," Maharaji answered with a big smile. "I don't smoke. Why should I smoke?"

"Do you drink alcohol?"

Maharaji laughed. "I am nine years old," he said. "Do you think I should drink at this age? Of course I don't drink."

Rajeshwar recalls that the reporters were amazed that the young boy was so calm and witty in the midst of their questioning. When someone said, "We are not going to publish any news about you in our newspaper," others nodded in agreement.

"Ah," said Maharaji, "I know why you are not going to publish any news about me, even if you don't know it yourselves. It is because whatever I have to do in this world, you cannot help me. The newspapers you publish are lifeless, but every one of my students is a living newspaper, and they will help me. You people are businessmen, and you always want to make money. So I tell you that if you print my photograph and my exact words and what my message is, then you can go and print twenty thousand extra copies because every person attending the event here in Patna will buy one, and you will make lots of money on this one night."

"I tell you," Rajeshwar says, "they didn't know what to think, but they were nailed."

Toward the end of the interview, a reporter asked, "Okay, Balyogeshwar Ji, what do you have to say? What message do you have for the people of Patna?"

Maharaji became serious and said, "This should have been your first question: What do I have to say? What message do I have for the people?" He gave a short speech, and they left.

Rajeshwar had known Maharaji since he was very small, having held him in his arms many times. Now, at nine years old, Maharaji was holding his own with senior journalists in Patna, and Rajeshwar thought, "Oh, he is getting bigger and bigger. I will never hold him in my arms anymore."

When Maharaji started to go upstairs, Rajeshwar and some others followed him. But Maharaji turned around and said, "All of you should go down. Rajeshwar, please come with me." He took Rajeshwar to the roof and asked, "Would you like to hold me in your arms and show me Patna?"

"I lifted him up," Rajeshwar remembers, "and he was so light, like a small baby. He looked towards the east and asked, 'What is that?' I told him, 'Maharaji, that is Gandhi Maidan, where we will have the event tomorrow.'"

Maharaji asked Rajeshwar to take him to the north side of the roof. "What is that?" he asked.

"That is the Ganges," Rajeshwar said.

"And that?" asked Maharaji, pointing toward a round, architecturally unique building.

"Golghar," Rajeshwar said.

"Who made it?" asked Maharaji.

"Emperor Ashok made it fifteen hundred years ago," said Rajeshwar. When Bihari arrived, however, Maharaji said, "Okay, put me down." It seemed that although Rajeshwar had said nothing, Maharaji had granted his wish to carry him in his arms one more time.

∽

When school closed for the summer, Maharaji spent an entire month on tour around India, a pattern that would repeat itself for the next three years. Summer was the hardest time to travel due to the paralyzing heat, but Maharaji's desire to spread his message across the country was stronger than his need for comfort.

Maharaji recalls the asphalt being so hot one weekend that the car tires sank into it, and everyone had to get out and push the car. In fact, the heat was so debilitating, they often traveled in the somewhat cooler nighttime, just as Shri Maharaji had done. Maharaji remembers that in one town, they put his bed on the roof of the home where he was staying, and it was still too hot to sleep. "They got a huge block of ice," he recalls, "and put it under my bed. When it was still too hot, I wet down my bed with a hose and put some ice on top."

Around this time, Maharaji fell ill with jaundice and liver problems. No one is sure at what age the illness took hold because Maharaji seldom speaks of it. But he apparently missed several months of school, all the while working diligently on his studies at home during the course of his sickness. Even breaking his arm by slipping on a waxed floor didn't slow him down. In fact, he broke the plaster over and over again, visiting the doctor who continuously retaped it and asked Maharaji to slow down long enough to heal—a tall order for the eager young boy.

No matter his circumstances, Maharaji got excellent grades, especially in English, and he remembers being fascinated with a fellow student in his school. "I was in the fifth grade when a boy from England was enrolled. I would listen to him speaking English fluently, and I marveled at his ability. I thought he was smarter than I was, and I stepped up my studies, but I didn't take into consideration that English was his first language, not his second like it was for me."

☙

In 1967, at nine years old, Maharaji was already addressing large audiences, inspiring people to seek peace within and offering to show them Knowledge. Life, he said, was meant to be lived in peace, and peace was to be found only in the heart.

This era saw young people all around the world avoiding the military draft and looking for alternative lifestyles, wearing buttons that said, "Make Love Not War." While the "Summer of Love" was unfolding in San Francisco, Maharaji spoke in New Delhi. "In this human body exists the love we have to discover," he said. "Love is the essence. Inside us there is something that can spread peace upon the whole world. I feel it is a peace bomb. Like an atom bomb can spread terror and kill people, there is something that can bring peace. But until we know its mystery, we cannot achieve it. One has to realize that secret."

A year after Maharaji's first press conference in Bihar, he gave another in the Indian capital of Mumbai, about a thousand miles from Dehradun to the south. It was the beginning of 1968, a troubled year marked with the political assassinations of Dr. Martin Luther King, Jr. and Robert Kennedy, the brother of President John F. Kennedy. In Paris, France, dissidents conquered the Latin Quarter, home of the old and famous Sorbonne University, and held it for a month. Marc Levitte, a member of this same inner circle of rebels, would later become a student of Maharaji's and would help spread Maharaji's message of peace in France among his revolutionary friends.

On the other side of the Atlantic, there was a growing resentment toward the war. Rebellion against excessive consumerism and a growing desire for radical change marked the Democratic Party's National Convention in Chicago, which attracted young demonstrators from all over the country. The ensuing riots led to a radical group of men, notoriously called the "Chicago Seven," being charged in a political trial. In 1973, Maharaji and his message would captivate Rennie Davis, one of the main organizers of these demonstrations. Change was rampant all around the world, even in China, where the "cultural revolution" was in full swing, with hundreds of thousands of young people battling to establish a new social order.

In this shattering global climate, ten-year-old Maharaji held a press conference in Mumbai in a living room with about ten reporters and his staff; family members; and instructors, including Charan Anand, Sampurnanand, and Ramanand. Charan Anand recalls that the press barraged Maharaji with questions, obviously attempting to rouse him into anger and debate.

"I've heard you speak," said a reporter, "and I'm impressed by your eloquence. May I ask exactly how old you are?"

This was an implied suggestion that he was older than he was admitting. In fact, throughout his childhood, rumors would keep surfacing in the media that Maharaji was as old as sixty or more, which is quite comical considering that he is not yet fifty at the first printing of this book.

Maharaji answered, "I have two things: body and soul. If you ask the age of my body, then it is ten years old. If you speak about my soul, it is ageless."

"How do you speak so well?" another reporter wanted to know. "Do you prepare your speeches?"

"I speak from my heart," Maharaji assured them. "I don't need to prepare or memorize a speech. What I say is based on my own experience and understanding."

When a local journalist asked him why he was so focused on learning English, he answered boldly, "If I don't study English, how can I go to places outside India, like England, Australia, and the United States? Speaking Hindi does not work there, and I have to awaken them."

A reporter asked him if he valued politics, and he said, "I do, but politics have drifted away from the world. In its place, the rule of disorder has come in and righteousness has disappeared."

The next day, a journalist from the Mumbai edition of the *Times of India* reported that "after his studies, Balyogeshwar will set out on a world tour to spread the message of peace." The local edition of *Nav Bharat Times* ran a short report:

TEN-YEAR-OLD BALYOGESHWAR

On Saturday, in a press conference ... various religious topics were discussed with Balyogeshwar. This 10-year-old sant is the student of Class V of Saint Joseph Academy of Dehradun. He said that he is studying English because he wants to promote his message abroad. First and foremost, he claimed that the knowledge of the self is to be realized through a guru.

(*Nav Bharat Times*, Mumbai, January 7, 1968)

During his talk that night, Maharaji answered a potent question: "Must one renounce the world in order to achieve enlightenment?"

This question, which would be asked of him in many forms in the years ahead, allowed him to elaborate that finding peace within was and always would be compatible with and independent from belief systems, philosophies, or religions. Ten-year-old Maharaji put this in very simple and direct words, in a statement from which he would never stray, when he said, "The peace belonging to the heart exists in the heart, and the peace belonging to the outside world is outside. Some people may be thinking that one has to abandon everything, that one must practice and achieve renunciation. But I say that it is possible, even without renunciation."

Maharaji, like his father, had no qualms about challenging centuries of Indian tradition. Throughout the ages, candidates who wished to receive the guru's initiation had been expected to perform hard labor every day for years at the ashram. If the master was pleased, the student might eventually be initiated and was then expected to renounce the world and live in the ashram for the rest of his life. Maharaji, however, assured people that renunciation was not necessary for self-realization and neither was ashram life.

After the event, Charan Anand met with a group of people who refused to believe that a ten-year-old child could speak so eloquently. Some said that Maharaji had mouthed the words to a prerecorded speech scripted by his mother. Charan Anand defended him, but it would be some time before many people perceived Maharaji as a man and a master in his own right.

Later that night, after speaking and answering many questions, Maharaji visited a man named Ramakrishna Dalmia, who was too ill to attend the event. One of India's richest citizens and a friend to the leaders who had secured India's independence from British colonial rule in 1948, Mr. Dalmia had always been controversial. Despite being born into a poor family, he had been instrumental in the rapid expansion of several industries in India in the 1930s by taking advantage of textile manufacturing, banking, agriculture, and transportation opportunities. Now, the first native owner of the *Times of India* and an ex-con who had spent a year in prison for fraud, he was dying in his opulent mansion on famous Marine Drive in Mumbai, bordering the Arabian Sea.

When Maharaji initially received the invitation, he refused it, unable to envision what he could do for a rich, dying man. But when he understood that the man was sincere about wanting to open his heart, he changed his mind. A Mercedes came to pick Maharaji up and drove him to Mr. Dalmia's private home, an eight-story apartment building on the beach that had a two-story parking garage for his many luxury automobiles. Each level of the residence was dedicated to a different room: one floor for the kitchen, one floor for the dining room, and so on.

Maharaji ascended to the upper levels in a silver-studded elevator that opened onto each floor of this extravagant residence. When he caught sight of the plush wall-to-wall carpeting, the gold fixtures, and the priceless artwork and sculptures, he could only imagine how opulent the bedroom would be. But when he arrived at the top level of the building, Mr. Dalmia was not in the master suite. Rather, he languished in a tiny room at the end of the hall on a metal hospital bed with a bedpan on the side table. A Hindu pundit stood beside him, waiting to turn him over since he could no longer do it for himself.

Maharaji stood before the dying man. Mr. Dalmia, propped up on pillows, squinting with pain and groggy from morphine, asked Maharaji, "Tell me how I can get to heaven."

"You are already in heaven," Maharaji answered. "Where do you want to go? You're missing it right here."

The pundit was angry when he heard these words, which he felt meant absolutely nothing. But Mr. Dalmia was listening carefully.

"Whatever is in this life," said Maharaji, "we go through it. But there is a beautiful experience of love that we can have right now." The two communed from heart to heart, and Mr. Dalmia thanked Maharaji for his wisdom and kind words.

When Maharaji returned to his bungalow, a group of people were waiting to see him. "Mr. Dalmia has bathrooms with marble floors, golden faucets, and double sinks," he told those around him, "but what good does it do him when he is so miserable, he can't use or appreciate them?"

By the time Maharaji turned eleven, the number of people attending his events was on a steep rise. The instructors were going out on speaking tours and teaching the techniques of Knowledge, and most people did not realize that much of the work done in Maharaji's name was not always according to his own desires and opinions. He did not appoint the instructors, and he was not given information about the organization's legal and financial dealings. At that point in time, he did not even decide where or when he would speak.

One afternoon, Maharaji discovered that Mataji had bought two tickets to Patna for that year's Guru Puja Festival (a festival where students honor the guru). She would be going with her attendant. But she had purchased no ticket for Maharaji, whom she wanted to stay in school.

"Mataji," Maharaji said, "what is the meaning of Guru Puja if the guru stays in school? Without Guru Maharaji, how can there be Guru Puja in Patna?" Mataji had no acceptable answer, so she reluctantly bought additional tickets for Maharaji and Bihari to attend the festival. If Maharaji had not insisted, this would have been the very first Guru Puja where the guru's mother was the guest of honor and main speaker.

Mataji, Bal Bhagwan Ji (now seventeen), and some of the organizers and instructors were promoting the event quite aggressively, plastering posters all over the city. But several wild claims about Maharaji and Knowledge angered people of different religious beliefs. Contrary to what Maharaji had told people, his message was erroneously perceived as incompatible with traditional Hinduism and Sikhism. Perhaps, then, it was inevitable that a series of riots and disturbances would occur at Maharaji's events during the years 1969–1971. More than once, Maharaji's students had to defend themselves against violent attacks, and Maharaji and his family were sometimes forced to flee in cars to avoid angry mobs.

One such riot was in the works when Maharaji and his family arrived in Muzaffarpur in Bihar early in the morning. From the moment they arrived, it was clear they were not wanted—members of Arya Samaj had distributed posters all over the city, denouncing Maharaji and his teachings.

Sampurnanand, who had arrived ahead of time to set things up, approached Mataji and Maharaji. "We should leave here," he warned them. "There is too much negativity, and tonight's event should be cancelled."

They both agreed with him, and Maharaji declared that the event absolutely would not occur. But what about the thousands of people who had shown up? Despite Maharaji's declaration, Mataji began to waver in her decision to leave, as Bal Bhagwan Ji kept repeatedly chiding her, "We are *rajputs*. We were born to fight. If we leave, we are cowards." He was referring to the Rawat family's formal membership in the royal warrior caste.

At 3:00 p.m., while preparations were being made for their departure, Mataji decided that she and her attendant would put on ceremonial saris and visit the grounds. Once they took a look at things, they could make an educated decision whether to leave or stay. Bihari drove them to the site, and when Mataji stepped onto the stage, the audience began signaling that they were waiting for Maharaji to come and speak. How could Mataji have known that they had gathered rocks, intending to throw them at her son? She assumed that since they seemed to want to see him so badly, they would be quiet and respectful when he arrived. Mataji ordered Bihari to bring Maharaji to the grounds, but the moment he drove away, people began shouting, climbing onto the stage, and destroying the sound system.

Mataji and her attendant were hoisted onto the backs of two men and sent over the wall at the back of the stage. They landed safely on the ground and walked for two blocks before they flagged down a rickshaw, directing the driver to the bungalow where they were staying. There sat Maharaji in the car, waiting for Bihari to drive him to the event area.

"Stop!" Maharaji heard his mother yelling from the approaching rickshaw. "Do not go back there."

He got out of the car and said to his mother, "I told you this event was not going to happen."

They went inside, walked upstairs, and Maharaji sat cross-legged on his bed while boisterous crowds from the event grounds began arriving at the bungalow. Mataji paced back and forth, and Maharaji remained in his position as they heard people threatening from the ground below, "We're going to kill you!"

Outside and down a long flight of stairs, a brave man named Fulsing stationed himself in the doorway with a big stick in his hand. He told the angry crowd, "Life is immortal. Death I am not afraid of. If you touch this stairway, I will break your head, and there will be a dead body in front of the door." He then began to sing.

The crowd started throwing stones at the house, breaking windows. The frightened Rawat family sat in a room, the eldest son no longer so eager to fight it out, despite earlier claims of the family's heritage as royal warriors. Maharaji, still sitting calmly on the bed, said, "Don't worry. At about nine or ten, it will be over."

Close to 9:00 p.m., the skies opened, rain poured down, and while Maharaji never left his bed, the rioters dispersed. The family quickly got into several cars and fled the city, so scared that they did not stop for hours, even for a drink or a meal. In the backseat, eleven-year-old Maharaji couldn't resist teasing his elder brother by saying, "We are rajputs, aren't we? So why are we fleeing?"

⌒

One morning, when the family had returned home late from an event the night before, Maharaji wanted to stay in bed instead of going to school. But Mataji insisted he get up. "Your teacher will be very angry," she said. "You are already several days late, so go to school."

Maharaji dragged himself out of bed and showed up at school. But when Bihari arrived at the end of the day to pick him up, he noticed that Maharaji looked upset. "What's wrong?" he asked him on the drive home. "Did you fight with the other kids?"

"No," he said, reluctant to complain. Finally, Bihari dragged the truth out of him. "My teacher was upset," said Maharaji, "because I was gone for so many days, and she made me move my chair to the back of the class. But the teacher is the teacher, and I don't know what to do."

That afternoon, Bihari told Maharaji he was taking the car for a tune-up to the family mechanic—Maharaji's teacher's boyfriend. Ten minutes after Bihari got to the auto shop, Maharaji's teacher arrived. Over tea and samosas, Bihari asked her, "Do you know Prem Pal?"

"Yes," she said, "he's my student. Is something wrong?"

"What happened today?" Bihari asked.

"He was gone for a long time," she said, frowning, "and I was so angry, I put his chair at the back of the room."

Bihari gently told her, "Do you know how many people travel long distances to see him?" He told the teacher about Maharaji's message and his demanding traveling schedule. When the car was ready, Bihari left the shop, and the next morning, when Maharaji took his new seat at the back of the room, the teacher placed his chair in the front row. "I like seeing your smiling face," she said, "so please don't be mad anymore."

Rich or poor, highborn or lowborn, he, too, can see. The ocean is impartial. It does not see that this one is rich, this one is poor. What we see in front of us as green, equally everyone sees it the same way. Likewise, that thing within our hearts is also the same for everyone.

MAHARAJI
Mumbai, India, January 6, 1968

I remember, I came home from school, and they told me some Westerners had arrived in a van. They had driven from England. I was, of course, quite curious. "Who are these people? What do they look like?" Sure enough, there was a green van with a white top, half corroded—parked right there. I opened the door, and I looked inside, and they were looking at me, and I was looking at them.

MARAHAJI,
WEMBLEY, ENGLAND,
JUNE 13, 1998

Invasion from the West

Among the cultural front-runners in the West, particularly for those looking for mysticism, spiritual growth, and alternatives to the way things were, the needle of the compass was pointing increasingly toward India. In spring 1962, the celebrated American beat poet Allen Ginsberg wandered through northern India with fellow "beatniks" in search of gurus, mantras, and yoga. Five years later, in 1967, the Beatles surprised the world by becoming disciples of Maharishi Mahesh Yogi, suggesting that the East held the secrets to the hippie dream of discovering and living in a "higher" consciousness.

In an overt departure from the tight-laced demands and dogma of the '50s, these youngsters or "hippies" were occupying a prominent place on the world stage. In London, as in San Francisco, they were breaking through the status quo to demonstrate an alternative set of beliefs and lifestyles in what was called the "counterculture." While the press projected images of young, unwashed, barefooted individuals smoking pot and begging for loose change, there was another aspect to this group of self-declared pacifists. They were courageous individuals, standing firm in their belief that fighting and killing one another was unacceptable. They wanted to change the world, and they believed, naïvely perhaps, that if they banded together, they could.

Out of this counterculture emerged the first travelers to arrive in Dehradun to meet Maharaji. In contrast to the Indians coming to hear him speak, who were from all walks of life, from the most learned and established to the humblest, the first visitors from the West were hippies. In later years, Westerners from all levels of society, including many with high-powered careers and great worldly success, would be listening to him. The peace-loving soul searchers who first met him in the late '60s found themselves magnetically drawn together in one place at the same time in order to fulfill a hope they all shared. Maharaji's first group of Western students began their respective journeys from 1967 to 1970, all arriving in India before 1971.

In 1967, eighteen-year-old Joan Apter, a slender, pale-skinned, red-haired American woman from Washington, D.C., began her long journey to the East. "I left America," she says, "when my friends were fleeing to Canada to avoid the draft. America felt like a sinking ship, and I had a vision of finding a way of being that would feel like home. I really didn't know I was looking for a teacher. I just wanted an internal experience that was different."

Although Joan started out before any of the others, her journey to the East was slow, as she spent time performing on the streets of Amsterdam, wearing a bear suit, and begging for money. "I never intended to return to America," she recalls. She stopped in Afghanistan for a while, where she stayed in the Bamiyan Valley, home to the enormous, ancient stone Buddhas that the Taliban blew up months before the World Trade Center attacks in 2001. But after studying medicinal herbs with the Afghanis for a while, Joan felt compelled to get back on the road. By 1969, she had been on the road for two years.

Brian Kitt, a young Englishman, began his journey to the East in the spring of 1968. "In my mind's eye," he said, "all of Europe looked dark, but as I looked eastward, a glow of light seemed to hover over India." Brian left his job washing dishes in a luxury hotel to pursue his dream of finding the truth.

He asked his friend Glen Whittaker to join him, but Glen was not so anxious to drop everything and just take off. "In 1968," Glen says, "I was an Oxford-educated hippie in London, kind of a weekend dropout with a pretty good job, nine to five, Monday through Friday. An American cousin was staying with me to escape the Vietnam War draft, and we went to visit Brian in his flat in Ladbroke Grove. He told us that the next day he was setting off to India because he was sure the truth could be found there and asked if I wanted go with him. But I said, 'I feel if the truth is around now and if it is in India, then it will come to the West because this is where it's seriously needed.' And so I declined."

A flamboyant figure on the London psychedelic scene, Brian viewed himself as a mystical poet, a *sadhu* (holy man), and a seeker who was well-versed in the life of Krishna. Once he arrived in India, he studied yoga, visited a number of teachers, and began to dress in white robes. But so far, he had not found what he was looking for. He'd been staying at a pilgrim's hostel in the holy city of Rishikesh in the Himalayas, where he was getting sick, weak, and undernourished, when one day, his prayer was, "I came to find you, but it has ended in failure. If I do not receive a sign that I should continue, I will start back to England tomorrow."

Just before Brian opened his eyes, someone tapped him on the arm. He turned to see two well-dressed Indian men who wanted to know what he was doing. When he told them he was trying to meditate, they said, "But meditation is a happy thing." They recommended he join them to visit Balyogeshwar, who lived a two-hour drive away. Brian looked at a photograph they had of the eleven-year-old boy, who was beaming with happiness and good will.

"Somewhere inside," says Brian, "I felt he was the one I was looking for, but when I asked if they thought he might accept me as a student, they were doubtful. Apparently, two Westerners, one from Germany and the other from America, had been the first to visit Maharaji, but they had left and lost touch."

The two men took Brian on a bus ride to Maharaji's residence anyway. Hiring a *tonga* (bicycle rickshaw) at the bus station in Dehradun, they brought some fruit as an offering and set off to 13 Municipal Road. "As we entered the gate," Brian says, "I caught sight of Maharaji and his brothers riding bikes. They sped off, and his mother met us and invited us to sit on the front porch and have tea."

In a few minutes, a windswept Maharaji jumped off his bike and approached to ask Brian why he had come to India.

"To find God," he answered.

"Then you have come to the right place," a smiling Maharaji said.

During the next half hour or so, Maharaji and Brian conversed. In the end, Maharaji invited the Englishman to stay, sharing a room with a mahatma, and agreed to talk with him every morning. The next morning, Brian looked in a mirror and saw that the whites of his eyes were yellow. It was unmistakable—he had hepatitis.

When a radiant Maharaji arrived on the front veranda to speak with his visitor as promised, Brian warned him of his contagious disease and regretted that he would have to cancel their meetings. Maharaji sympathized and made arrangements for Brian to go to Prem Nagar to be attended by an ayurvedic doctor. He assured Brian they would fill him up on papayas and buttermilk, which were both good for his condition. Mataji accompanied the sick young man while Bihari drove.

A month later, after Brian recovered, the talk that Maharaji had originally promised finally took place. "The most wonderful moments of my life," says Brian, "were probably those spent around an eleven-year-old Maharaji in his own playroom, talking about the universe, God, life, and the path to enlightenment." Brian attended a series of Maharaji's events in February 1969, and at one festival, he was stunned to see that tens of thousands had gathered. "They came by train, oxcart, and on foot," he says.

Early one morning, in Faribadad, a large industrial city to the south of Delhi, Brian sat at Maharaji's bedside, waiting for him to wake up. "What do you want?" asked a sleepy Maharaji when he spotted Brian.

"Knowledge," said Brian.

"Not a shirt?" asked Maharaji with a smile, noticing that the Englishman's arms were covered in mosquito bites.

"I want Knowledge," he repeated.

"How about lots of fruits?" teased Maharaji.

"I want your Knowledge," Brian said.

Maharaji arranged for him to receive Knowledge from Charan Anand the very next day while he was at school. After practicing for a week, someone asked Brian how it was going. He said, "These are not simply techniques. They are the truth itself."

Soon afterward at Shakti Nagar in Delhi, Brian dreamt that he needed to seek out other Westerners who were already in India. He took the bus to Connaught Circus, in the heart of Delhi. "I saw no one I knew there," he recalls, "but a Sikh became interested in my story and offered to take me to a sort of cellar club with Jimi Hendrix songs on the jukebox." The Sikh showed him to a table at which sat Sandy Collier, Ron Geaves, Michael Cole, and David Beales. Brian would soon be responsible for guiding the group to Dehradun.

In 1968, Sandy Collier, a twenty-one-year-old Englishwoman of delicate constitution, was in what she called "a sorry state" when her boyfriend, Ron Geaves, visited her in the hospital in London. Unlike so many others, they were not heading East in search of the easy, drug-fueled lifestyle so common at the time. "I had a desperate longing to discover the truth about creation and other such things," says Sandy, "and so did Ron. He and I had been searching for a long time, which was how our friendship started in the first place."

Sandy was born into a working-class family. She had left school when she was fifteen and worked in an insurance office before embracing the hippie dropout lifestyle. Ron was sixteen when he dropped out of school, and the day after he met Sandy, he had a dream in which he was climbing a ladder with a yogi standing at the top. When he looked back, Sandy was on the rung just below him. Now, as they made plans to embark on the long journey to India together, they had somewhat similar goals. Ron envisioned himself as a renunciate, traveling far and wide to merge with the "divine," while Sandy set her sights on the vast foothills of the Himalayas, renouncing the world there and discovering the truth.

And so, late in 1968, they stuck out their thumbs, carrying with them a few simple belongings as they began to hitchhike across Belgium, Austria, Romania, Istanbul, and Turkey. In eastern Turkey, caught in a freezing downpour in a forest with inadequate sleeping bags, they were forced to postpone the rest of their journey until the weather eased up. They then traveled through eastern Turkey, Iran, and eventually Afghanistan, where they settled for a month before moving through the Khyber Pass into Pakistan and onward to India. The entire journey took them five and a half months, and they arrived in Old Delhi in the early morning in April 1969.

❧

Michael Cole and David Beales, two British music entrepreneurs with cheerful, cockney approaches to life, left London together in 1969. Milky (a childhood nickname for Michael that stuck), tall and handsome with boyish charm, quit school at sixteen to work in his father's business for a couple of years. Soon afterward, he began managing several bands. He also had a desire to travel to India. "I wanted to search for what I considered 'the secret of life,'" he explains.

David, born in the poor East End of London, was a teenage champion swimmer who broke the British record for the backstroke. But he quickly became disillusioned when he was overlooked for the Tokyo Olympics. It seemed that six months after his record-breaking swim, the team chose a less able but wealthier swimmer, as the sport was known for its elitism. "I was from the wrong side of the tracks," he says.

Intensely disappointed, David became a dropout, growing his hair long, taking drugs, and working as a roadie for musical groups. During his travels with various bands, he met Milky. When they exchanged stories, they realized they both wanted to go to India to find "the truth."

Milky bought a sleeping bag and a rucksack and joined the YMCA so they could find cheap places to stay along the way. "A harrowing six weeks later," said David, "we arrived in India, dirty, hungry, and broke."

In a ramshackle Delhi hotel called The Crown, they met Ron and Sandy, who were staying in an adjacent room. The next morning, the four of them walked into a café that was streaming Bob Dylan into the street. There they met Brian, who told them about Maharaji. Soon after, the five headed off together to Shakti Nagar ashram to meet the boy guru.

They were welcomed at the Delhi ashram and offered rooms in the garage, which had been converted into a dorm. They were given clean clothes and good food, something of a rarity during their travels.

Maharaji was not at the ashram when they arrived, but Charan Anand invited the Westerners to join the tour across northern India where Maharaji was going to speak. All got on the train with Charan Anand, but Ron hung back. In his opinion, the Indians he had met at the ashram did not fit his preconceived concepts of holy men (they dressed like the middle class, not like sadhus), so he decided to continue searching on his own.

The foursome first heard Maharaji speak in Bareilly, a large industrial city in northern India, where Maharaji stayed in a small house and talked to the Westerners. They followed Maharaji's tour from city to city in third-class train compartments, and Milky was getting sick and frustrated at not yet having received Knowledge. Upon arriving in India, he and his buddy David had expected to immediately find the master, receive his initiation, become enlightened, and then go straight back home to England to live happily ever after. But things were not going according to their plans.

In Chandighar, located on the fringes of the Shivalik Range in northwest India, the four Westerners were invited to live in the house where Maharaji was staying. When the event was over, Maharaji invited Sandy to drive back to Dehradun in the family's Ambassador car with him, Mataji, Raja Ji, and Bhole Ji, and she enthusiastically accepted.

The Ambassador was one of the first cars ever manufactured in India. A hardy vehicle suited to India's dire conditions, it was easy to keep running on India's extraordinarily bumpy and broken-down roads. But Sandy, driving along with Maharaji, his brothers, and his mother, had no interest in the car or the road's condition. She was going to live with Maharaji and his family. That was all that mattered.

When they arrived at the residence, Sandy took a room in the main house while Milky, David, and Brian—who arrived by train—were put in the guesthouse. "Three days later," says Milky, "Maharaji turned up for tea. He talked to us and made us feel very comfortable. He showed us around the grounds, and he showed me his hobby room."

Among the four Britons, it would have been difficult to find more varied personalities. Brian was proud, highly communicative, and moody, and he had a strong spiritual ego. Sandy was gentle and earnest, with a calm and frail demeanor. Milky was a joker, a quick-witted, easygoing cockney who was playful and boyish, which appealed to Maharaji, who had the same lively qualities. By contrast, David was a self-effacing person who, when asked by Maharaji what he really wanted, answered in a heavy cockney accent, "To be 'appy, innit?"

Every day they asked Maharaji for Knowledge, and he answered, "Oh no. Not yet. You're not ready yet." But after a few weeks, when Milky asked the usual question, Maharaji surprised him by saying, "Okay. Today's the day."

Before dinner, someone had prepared a small room up in the guest quarters with incense, candles, and lovely cloths. "Sampurna-nand gave us Knowledge," Sandy recalls, "and some other people were watching. Everyone treated us in special ways, just because we were from the West. Maharaji didn't, though. In every interaction I had with him, he managed to say the perfect thing to help me, whatever the problem was.

"Even at eleven years old, he wasn't impressed by us being Westerners. He simply responded to what was going on, whether it was our arrival, our requests for Knowledge, or the meetings we all had with him. He behaved like a master, and he told us what he felt was the truth, just like he does now."

Sandy slept in a small room right next to Maharaji's and Mataji's rooms, adjacent to the veranda. She was practicing Knowledge there one day when Mataji asked her in Hindi how she was getting on with her practice. Maharaji came in to translate and told Sandy that Mataji had said, "So what are you experiencing?"

Sandy was shy, overwhelmed by having mother and son in her room asking her questions about her practice. "My jaw dropped," she says. "When Maharaji saw this, he told me in English, 'Well, so tell her you experience this and that.'"

When Sandy said nothing, he told his mother in Hindi, "Yes, yes, she's experiencing this, and she's experiencing that." Sandy realized he was covering up for her. "When Mataji left," says Sandy, "I was in a state of awe. Maharaji, at eleven years old, cut through it by suddenly saying to me, 'You know, scientists in America have invented a new toothpaste that's even better than Colgate.' And he gave me a mischievous smile."

"Oh," was her only answer. She felt that Maharaji, in his own way, wanted her to know that everything was okay.

Every day, Sandy sat under a tree in the garden and practiced. "It gave me a new energy and an enthusiasm for life," she says. "I found answers within me that didn't necessarily come from my personal knowledge or my understanding. They were just inside of me, and Knowledge showed me a simplicity, a silence, and a contentment that I had never experienced before. I knew my life would never be the same again."

Ron returned to Shakti Nagar some weeks later, and someone told him that Maharaji was going to Ghaziabad. They asked if Ron would like to go and see him or if he wanted to head back to Varanasi once again.

"This time," Ron said, "I'll go see Maharaji."

Ron remembers there were about 10,000 people at the event, which generated tremendous excitement. He was still "pretty wiped out," as he describes it, and Maharaji spoke in Hindi, which Ron did not understand. The heat was stifling, it was late in the evening, and still, Ron was moved.

"The thing that struck me about him," says Ron about his first encounter with Maharaji, "was his confidence. It was clear that he spoke with passion, commitment, and enthusiasm, and it wasn't a script. Even though I couldn't understand what he was saying, I was overwhelmed, and I cried. I knew that something exceptional was going on as this young boy spoke." Ron went on, "He spotted me, or someone told him I was there, and he asked to see me the following morning for a one-on-one talk."

When they met, Maharaji was trying to figure out how to

work the new tape recorder someone had given him. "His attention was divided between the tape recorder and me," says Ron. "He would poke the tape recorder, and then he would come back to the conversation, mainly in the form of questions. Penetrating questions. I was amazed at his ability to gently address personal issues that might otherwise have been confronting. He knew I was Sandy's boyfriend, and he began by talking about her. But then he said, 'What about you? What do you want?'"

Ron said something about wanting peace, and Maharaji asked, "What kind of peace? What are you really looking for?"

Ron recalls, "The more he questioned me, the more my answers sounded glib, like I was speaking meaningless words."

"Well," Maharaji said, "you're in India now. You've come a long way, so take advantage of it. Go off and search. There are loads of gurus here. There are loads of temples and holy places. Go search and see if you can fulfill yourself, but just hold me in reserve if you can't find it. I'm only eleven. I'll be around. You can take as long as you like and come back when you've used up all the other possibilities."

Ron was not keen on heading back to the holy cities along the Ganges, where there was so much sickness and terrible heat, so he said he didn't want to do that.

"Fine," said Maharaji. "If you're really sure about that, why not go back to the ashram? Ask questions. When all your questions have been answered, come and ask me for Knowledge. When I feel you're ready, I'll give it to you."

Ron did as he was told. He returned to the ashram and drove the instructors crazy with his questions. "I was such an annoyance to them," says Ron. "They went to the local university and brought back a professor (who was a student of Maharaji) because they couldn't deal with my intellectual questions anymore. Mataji spoke to me quite a lot, and eventually Charan Anand gave me Knowledge."

Ron recalls that initially he was bewildered. "Nothing really prepares you for the reality of that experience," says Ron. "I was weighted down with concepts concerning enlightenment and spiritual experiences, and I was expecting some kind of Buddha-type moment. But after I practiced, I felt the power of Knowledge and began to wonder what impact it would have on the lives of others in the West."

∽

"How much English do you know?" Maharaji asked Charan Anand some days later. "Do you know the meaning of these words—*Knowledge, experience, acceptance, practice?*"

"Yes," said Charan Anand, and gave him the Hindi translations.

"Perfect," said Maharaji. "You are ready to go to the West and prepare the way for me." Although those few simple words were the extent of Charan Anand's grasp of the English language, he was willing to leave, trusting that with Maharaji's blessings, he could do anything that was asked of him. A passport was arranged for Charan Anand, with a made-up date of birth since they kept no records in his birth village in Rajasthan.

At the same time, Mataji, who believed that Brian's knowledge of the English language would be an asset in spreading Maharaji's message, gave him the mahatma name Param Saphlanand (Joy of Completeness), and from then on Brian became known as Saph. However, Saph kept seeing himself more as a channel for some universal truth than as a mahatma of the young master and had no interest in relinquishing his hippie way of life.

A few days later, Charan Anand flew to England while Saph, Sandy, Ron, Milky, and David all headed back to England over-land. On their way home, when Sandy and Ron were hitchhiking back through Afghanistan, they ran into Joan Apter, the young American woman who had left the States early in 1967. When

Joan said she was heading for India, they told her about Maharaji and suggested she look him up. She had heard of him once before from a stranger, but she was on her way to Tibet, determined to walk three times around a sacred lake. The legends said that after doing this, a person was meant to reach enlightenment.

Once in India, Joan went by foot from one kind of ashram to another. A severe case of malnutrition stopped her in her tracks, but after she was hospitalized for a while, she continued her adventure until she reached the border of Tibet, only to learn that the border was closed. Devastated, she sought refuge in a nearby temple and began to fall apart. A self-declared emotional wreck, she had no idea what to do next, when she saw an Indian man camped out under a tree with a big tin gold-colored suitcase. He turned out to be one of Maharaji's instructors, and when he showed her a picture of the young master in his velvet coat and ceremonial crown, it was the third time she'd heard Maharaji's name.

"If you want practical knowledge of God," the instructor told her, "you had better go to Dehradun and see Maharaji." He handed her a letter of introduction and put her on a bus to Dehradun, where her life would change forever.

Everything can be done in two ways: one way is to command and demand, and the other way is to do it with love. I believe that if a person is made to understand with love, he will agree.

MAHARAJI
Haridwar, India, March 23, 1970

I was talking to people about Knowledge, and
I used to have to go to school, too. There was
such a big difference, because I was teaching
people and I was getting taught. And what
I always wanted was to make it as enjoyable
as possible, because a subject like
peace deserves that.

MAHARAJI,
LONDON, ENGLAND,
JULY 4, 2004

The Peace Bomb

When weary Western travelers, exhausted and sick with dysentery, jaundice, or hepatitis, showed up at the residence in Dehradun, Mataji graciously took them in and helped them heal. When Joan Apter arrived in a terrible state of health, both mentally and physically, she particularly appreciated Mataji's kindness. She still remembers clutching that letter of introduction when Mataji invited her inside and asked her to wait on the veranda until Maharaji got home from school.

"I was a wreck," Joan recalls, "but I remember somebody coming out and offering me a cup of tea, which really helped. Then I heard a gate creaking open, and a car sped into the driveway, screeching its tires. A young boy came streaking out of the car, as everyone in the vicinity literally hit the decks. I mean, they stretched out flat on the ground in full-body prostration, as was expected in Indian culture. I realized that blur had to be Maharaji."

She watched him tear into the house, and in a few minutes, he emerged in his kurta and pajama and sat in a chair opposite her on the veranda. "So," he said with his arms crossed, "now that you are here, what do you want?"

She burst into tears.

"Why are you crying?" asked Maharaji, smiling kindly.

"Because I'm lost," she said between sobs.

"Well," said Maharaji good-naturedly, "you can stop crying because now you are found." That was followed by another outburst of tears. Maharaji sat quietly, and when Joan was through sobbing, he said, "Okay, you go and take some rest now. We can talk again tomorrow."

Joan was shown to a room above the garage where she stayed for a month while she got better. She would show up on the veranda each afternoon with a yellow notepad filled with "questions of the day." Maharaji would get home after school, change out of his uniform, and sit with Joan. "Let's have it, madwoman," he would say with glee, and off they went as she barraged him with question after question.

Joan says, "I was negative, and I saw the glass as half-empty. But Maharaji was very good at getting me to see it half-full by making me laugh and loosen up. I would say, 'There is no hope and no such thing as truth.' And he would say, 'Yes, there is.' He once called me sophisticated, and I didn't like it. But then, an aha! would come. It was almost impossible to comprehend that I was talking to a twelve-year-old boy, so I ignored it. I developed a love and appreciation for him that was so strong, all I wanted was to be with him."

Joan looked forward to her daily meetings with Maharaji as her attitude began to soften and her health steadily improved under the personal care of Mataji. But when Maharaji wondered why she didn't ask for Knowledge, she had no answer. Why did she need it? She liked things as they were, since she got to have her private talks with Maharaji each day. She felt she had no other needs. "I felt so much love," she says, "but he kept telling me if I wanted a permanent connection, I needed to ask for Knowledge."

Up until 1971, Maharaji lived his double life, going to school during the week and touring India on weekends and holidays. He was fascinated with his Western visitors and envisioned future work in their countries. This must have made it difficult for him to go to school. For example, the forty-five-minute period devoted to woodworking seemed like an utter waste of time as he and his fellow students chopped wood and learned to use a planer and a saw. The teacher was a particularly bad-tempered monk who erupted with fury when a child forgot to bring his materials to class.

One morning, after Maharaji had been up late the night before talking with his Western visitors, he mistakenly left his piece of wood at home. "Why did you forget to bring what I asked you to bring?" the teacher raged at him. "Why aren't you taking this seriously?"

"Look," Maharaji said gently but firmly, "do you really think I came to this high-class school so I can chop wood when I grow up?" His blatant honesty was like taking a match to gasoline, but a few days later, the students were informed that woodworking was no longer required.

Maharaji believed that love, not authoritarianism, would inspire people. When his father had scared people with his thundering anger, a young woman who lived in the house heard Maharaji say to his father, "When I do it, I will do it with love." She also recalls Maharaji looking up at Shri Maharaji after he had scolded some people and saying, "You don't look beautiful when you're upset!"

In keeping with what he believed, when it was Maharaji's turn to be class monitor, he did not scold his classmates or order anyone around. Rather than bullying the kids to shut up, he told them, "Do whatever you want to do, as long as you keep quiet and what you do is in line with your schoolwork."

Maharaji did most of his traveling with his mother, who did not understand his role any more than she had understood her husband's. But she knew that Maharaji was the draw, the main attraction that would bring people in droves. One night, while thousands of people gathered in the audience, Maharaji was too tired to dance, talk, or do anything else. All he wanted was to sleep, but when he started to walk off the stage, Mataji stopped him. "Where are you going?" she asked him. "Don't leave the stage."

"Come on," he reasoned with her. "Give me a break. I'm just a kid. I'm tired, and I want to leave."

"You can't leave," she said, "because as soon as you do, everybody else leaves, too. If you need to sleep, then sleep on the stage." He did, and she never asked him to do it again.

Joan accompanied Mataji and Maharaji on tour. Their first event was in Delhi, where he spoke in front of more than 20,000 people. The sheer energy of so many like-minded, peace-loving people gathered in one place bowled her over. The next day they arrived in Chandighar, where 10,000 people attended. Inspired like never before, Joan asked Maharaji for Knowledge, and Sampurnanand gave it to her. But soon enough, her fears came back to haunt her.

Joan recalls Maharaji saying to her, "Now that you have Knowledge, I want you to learn about service."

"He sent me kicking and screaming to the ashram in Haridwar," she said, "where I was to help arrange talks for him. I never would have asked for Knowledge if I'd known he would send me away." But she had little time to complain because she was immediately given a huge task—to head public relations for the English-speaking press in India for a huge event in Delhi in 1970 called "the Peace Bomb."

One can only imagine the courage it took for Charan Anand, who knew virtually no English and had almost no money, to fly alone across the world to London, where he barely knew anyone. When he first arrived, he stayed in the beautiful home of an Indian man who had invited him, but when long-haired hippies arrived at the house each day to visit with Charan Anand, his host grew upset.

After a few months of the neighbors complaining, someone rented a small basement room for Charan Anand for five pounds a week at #17A Fairholme Road in West Kensington, London. During the next year, hundreds of Westerners were taught the techniques of Knowledge in that tiny room, which had only a single bed in the corner, threadbare carpets, and an electric meter that required constant coin feedings to provide light and heat in the cold nights of the English winter.

The flow of people was almost constant. One time, a girl and her long-haired boyfriend showed up, and Charan Anand had no idea who was who. He called them both "sister," and they were fine with that. An American, John Berzner, who would later be instrumental in helping arrange for Maharaji's first visit to America, received Knowledge from Charan Anand at that time.

One day, Glen Whittaker bumped into Saph (Brian Kitt), who was back from India. "Oh man," Saph told Glen, "I've met a twelve-year-old Indian master." He showed him a picture of Maharaji and took him to meet Charan Anand. Also present in Charan Anand's small flat was Peter Lee, a tall, thin, dark-haired man who described himself back then as "a hippie who was trying to squeeze something real out of life."

Both Glen and Peter thought that, against all odds, they had found what they were looking for when they met Charan Anand. They spent many evenings in the small room with him, feeding shillings into the electric meter when the heat or the lights suddenly went out. Charan Anand loved being with the English hippies he liked to call "happies."

Glen Whittaker had received his master's degree in history at Oxford in 1966. He had spent four years as a writer and public relations executive before heading to India to meet Maharaji. And Peter Lee had been a local government employee when he moved into a hippie commune in South London on 341 Upper Richmond Road. Living there at the time were Glen, David Lovejoy, Carol Hurst, and other future students of Maharaji. Glen and Peter had been doing TM (transcendental meditation), which they had learned from Maharishi Mahesh Yogi, but were not fully satisfied with their practice.

"When I first heard Maharaji's message," says Peter, "I felt a big yes inside of me. His message answered all my questions, and I knew it would satisfy the inner void I'd been feeling. I was twenty-five when I received Knowledge from Charan Anand in that funny little 'no-frills' basement room. There was a black-and-white photograph of Maharaji on the wall, and one small bed on which Charan Anand slept, ate, and talked to us.

"It was a day that put me in touch with my heart," Peter says. "It gave me a sense of myself and took me somewhere deeper than the vast cornucopia of drugs and religion had ever taken me. Knowledge showed me a simplicity, a quietness, and a sense of contentment that I had never experienced before. I knew my life would never be the same."

Glen, who received Knowledge at the same time, says, "What I thought was a wall, I discovered to be a doorway to a path that led deep within towards an inner infinity, where I could discover an ever-growing source of peace, wisdom, and joy."

Four months later, Peter sold his car, quit his job, and bought a minibus. Six friends headed for India with him in his minibus, including Glen Whittaker, David Lovejoy, and Suzy Witten. The seven-week journey was fraught with breakdowns and flat tires. Traveling in Istanbul, the brakes failed while they were going downhill. Miraculously, the driver avoided smashing into traffic by steering into the curb. In the end, Charan Anand would fly back to India, returning in time for the Peace Bomb event, but those traveling overland in Peter's minibus would miss it.

᎐

In 1969, nineteen-year-old Gary Girard, a handsome native Californian with hazel eyes and blond hair, was planning to adopt a sadhu lifestyle in India. The privileged son of wealthy parents, he had graduated from Beverly Hills High School the year before and was anxious to leave his current life behind and head east. At the same time, his friend Will Ganz, the son of a prominent Beverly Hills physician, was eager to do some seeking of his own. (Will would soon be called Sitaram, when he, like many Western seekers in India, acquired an Indian name that they felt more appropriately reflected who they were.)

"As the sixties progressed," Will recalls, "I found myself with few answers to my many doubts and questions. There was no place to turn, and instead of thanking God for the privilege of affluence, I questioned it and discovered that I was not who I thought I was. The real guy was buried somewhere beneath a mound of temporary identities. I needed to find a way back to myself."

Arriving in India in 1970, Will and Gary traveled from Kolkata (formerly called Calcutta) to Goa, where people from the West hung out on the beaches and enjoyed life under the palm trees. They began to thread through India on foot, going from village to village on their way to Khumb Mela, a Hindu pilgrimage that occurs four times every twelve years at specific dates set according to astrological configurations and attended by many sadhus.

Gary and Will, just like Brian and many Westerners before them, wanted to become sadhus—renunciates who leave behind all material attachments and live in caves, forests, and temples. The word *sadhu* derives from the Sanskrit *to practice* and refers to meditation. To this day, there are still about five million sadhus in India who are respected, revered, and sometimes feared for their supposed ability to cast curses on their enemies. But it was widely believed that their austere practices helped to redeem the community at large, and this inspired people to support them with donations.

Will went on alone to Prayag for Khumb Mela, where he met many sadhus. The crowds of sadhus—some half-dressed, some completely naked, some with their bodies painted or covered with ashes, and many with long hair and beards—were quite a sight. Some thirty years later, seventy-five million pilgrims would attend the same Khumb Mela, making it the largest gathering anywhere in the world.

While the Westerners were making their way to India and back, Maharaji enjoyed working at the family farm where they raised cows and grew basmati rice and sugarcane. There, he learned patience as he watched the farmers meticulously prepare the ground. "What will we do today?" he would ask a farmer impatiently. "Can we plant the sugarcane now?"

"Not yet," the farmer answered. "We have to make sure we get all the rocks out of the way before we start planting. The ground has to be prepared first."

Maharaji remembers walking through the fields with other workers, inspecting the earth and picking up small stones and rocks. A few months after the ground was cleared and the crop was planted, the sugarcane shot up tall and healthy. Maharaji would suck on the stringy end of a sugarcane stalk, filling his mouth with sweet liquid, and he would remember having meticulously cleared debris and creating a fertile field before planting. This process became one of his favorite metaphors for the preparation necessary for peace to manifest in a person's life.

⌒

Once Joan Apter was ensconced at Prem Nagar, she worked closely with Maharaji's oldest brother, nineteen-year-old Bal Bhagwan Ji, who was highly involved in organizing the Peace Bomb event, staying up for days on end, arranging things. Maharaji had come up with the expression "Peace Bomb" during a talk in 1968. Now Joan, in her role as liaison with the English-speaking press, was arranging for a hospitality tent and setting up interviews with reporters. Everyone jumped in to help, including some zealous mahatmas, who, unlike Maharaji and his father before him, were trying to publicize Knowledge as a new religion.

Maharaji had learned that it was essential to keep Knowledge separate from religion, but he was not yet able to ensure that the publicity for the event reflected that. Unbeknownst to him, one of the mahatmas put an ad in a Delhi newspaper just before the Peace Bomb event that proclaimed, "Knowledge is the one and only way to enlightenment, as talked about in the Koran." The mahatma quoted the holy book to make his point and challenged anyone who disagreed to come to the Delhi office to debate the issue with him on a certain date and time.

When Maharaji spotted the ad, he decided to show up at the office. He slipped in unnoticed and hid in the background, watching as a cultured Muslim gentleman arrived to talk to the mahatma. This man was so learned that the mahatma was completely outclassed in the discussion. Afterward, when Maharaji confronted the mahatma, he refused to admit defeat and claimed he had won the debate.

In 1998, Maharaji recalled this incident. "It showed me clearly," he said, "that Knowledge must be allowed to stand on its own, for what it is in itself." But in India in 1970, the prevailing tendency among the mahatmas and Maharaji's oldest brother was to try to prove its validity with quotes from the holy books of various religions.

On November 8, 1970, the largest peacetime procession Delhi had ever seen made its way through the streets, with people singing bhajans and playing manjeeras. According to Mahabir, one of Maharaji's young helpers at the time, Bal Bhagwan Ji was driving a Jeep in front of Maharaji, who was wearing ceremonial clothes and crown and sitting in a chariot. Every few hundred meters, Bal Bhagwan Ji would stop the Jeep, grab his megaphone, stand up, and point at twelve-year-old Maharaji as he shouted, "He is the incarnation!"

A sea of people paraded up and down the streets from 6:00 a.m. until 6:00 p.m., ending at India Gate, the venue for the Peace Bomb event. That night, Maharaji, with his hair neatly combed back from his head, addressed close to 100,000 people. "I feel such a power in me, I do not know where it came from," he said. "I feel as if I want to shake the world. And I will give you this peace because it is in my possession and I can give it."

"I tell you, the voltage was off the charts that night, and everybody felt it," Joan recalled. The atmosphere at the event brought everyone to tears, including the Westerners who could not even understand Hindi.

I declare I will establish peace in this world. But what can I do unless people come to me with a sincere desire in their hearts to know the truth?

MAHARAJI
Peace Bomb, Delhi, India,
November 8, 1970

When I was very young, about eleven or twelve years old, people used to say that I was very controversial. And I'd think about it—how controversial can an eleven-year-old child be? Some people used to say, "He is God." I used to tell people, "I am not God." I used to tell people clearly, and I tell them now as well, "My work is to take you to that place within you. That, I can do."

MAHARAJI,
DELHI, INDIA,
APRIL 12, 1998

Passport to the West

While one van with Maharaji's students had left England and arrived in India in time for the Peace Bomb event, Peter Lee, Glen Whittaker, and company were still traveling toward Prem Nagar when the event ended. They had run into so much car trouble along the way that they gave up all attempts at keeping a schedule and focused on just getting there. Despite the constant breakdowns, they had an easy time of it, except in Teheran when some men noticed the two women sitting in Peter's minibus. "Western whores!" they shouted, and rushed at the bus, which managed to pull away just in time.

The group drove through the night, traversing Afghanistan. As they traveled through Pakistan and neared India, Peter recalls being hit with the aroma of wood smoke and Indian cooking spices, a smell that was different from anywhere else in the world. Gratefully, they pulled up to Prem Nagar, a lovely, clean ashram with welcoming people and good vegetarian food.

The large three-story building, built by Shri Maharaji in the '50s, was constructed around a courtyard with thirty or so sleeping rooms as well as a large meeting hall erected in the '60s. At the top of the building was Maharaji's little rooftop apartment, and on the first floor was a ledge a few feet wide, where Westerners gathered in the early evenings to smell the jasmine and listen to the sound of bhajans drifting from distant ashrams, interrupted by the occasional whistle from a steam train. Gardeners were gathering roses when the tired minibus chugged up the driveway.

The thought of a good meal and a nap was enticing, but Peter and Glen were anxious to meet Maharaji, who had intrigued and inspired them from the moment they'd met Charan Anand. The minibus choked and wheezed out warnings all the way to Dehradun. When they finally drove through the gate, turned off the engine, and got out, a long column of black smoke belched upward from under the vehicle's hood. The engine sputtered like a drum roll, spewed a little more smoke, and died right there in the driveway. The gate closed behind them and there they were.

In the next moment, they heard the gate creak open once more, and in sped a chauffeur-driven Ambassador car, the now-defunct rounded Morris Major model. Out of the backseat jumped a boy in a school blazer and shorts. It had to be Maharaji, Peter decided. "I didn't know what to make of him. He was a kid, but his eyes didn't look twelve years old. He went right over to the minibus that was leaking green fluid."

"Is this what you came in?" Maharaji asked in his thick Indian accent.

Peter nodded. Glen was stunned by the boy's presence and relieved that he made no Biblical pronouncements. Instead, he was interested in the practicalities of the journey they had taken and the state of the car. Maharaji opened the door, looked under the hood, and checked the engine. In the next moment, he had hotwired the ignition, put it into gear, and was driving the previously dead minibus around the driveway, delighting and amazing the newcomers. With all that they had anticipated and hoped for, this kind of warm, casual welcome was greatly appreciated.

On December 10, 1970, Maharaji turned thirteen. He returned home from school that day (he was in the eighth grade) to find a hundred people in his garden. Charan Anand spoke in Hindi, at certain times gesturing toward the foreigners. Later the young Westerners found out that he'd said, "Look at these people. They were so full of passion for truth, they dropped their jobs, their home lives, everything, and came here all the way from England."

Maharaji's house looked like a fairyland, decorated with colors and lights for his birthday. The Westerners had made him a book, covered it with ribbons, and each person wrote something to Maharaji on an individual page. They had their pictures taken with Maharaji, who sat on a chair that was covered in a white sheet and surrounded with flower garlands. He became absorbed in the little book, and as he read the pages, he looked at the authors and smiled, while a line of students filed past him to pay their respects.

Present at the celebration were two young Englishwomen, Rosie Malcolm and Sue Ratcliffe, who had accompanied Charan Anand back from London. They would be the first Westerners to bring news of the young Maharaji to France. Sue was born near London and attended Cambridge University with the scientist Stephen Hawking. She later lived a beatnik lifestyle with artists, musicians, and poets in London and Oxford.

"I was living in a flat with an American seeker of truth who wanted us to go to Tibet," Sue says, "but I always felt that there was no reason for truth to be found in Tibet any more than on a football field. I always wanted desperately to know who I was—behind the façade and personality—my real identity. In Cambridge I'd argued endlessly with a group of scientific and literary students, to no avail. I'd read the basic scriptures of just about every religion, and everything seemed to be pointing to something, stirring an unidentifiable feeling within me.

"But I'd reached a nadir of depression where nothing meant anything and nothing had more or less value or truth than anything else. Then my friend, the poet Charles Cameron, came knocking at my door, saying 'I found it!' I accompanied him to a working-class, terraced house where a man dressed in saffron robes with a bald head and a huge smile opened the door. It was Charan Anand.

"I immediately felt a sort of magical love in me. And while I was there listening to him, who arrived but Sandy Collier and Ron Geaves. I couldn't believe it. I knew them from a few years prior in Oxford where I had lived, but I'd lost touch with them. Sandy walked in looking like an angel, and she told me, 'Sue, this Knowledge is really amazing.'"

After Sue received Knowledge and Charan Anand moved to Fairholme Road, she spent a great deal of time with him. She eventually flew with him on a one-way ticket to India with five pounds in her pocket to attend the Peace Bomb. Staying on in India after the event, she attended a school open-house party with Maharaji and joined him for weekend events in various villages.

Sue recalls, "He took me with him in the family Volkswagen bus to an event on the weekend, and we stopped at Ayodhya, a town with white marble buildings built on a lake. In this town, the lowliest workers lived next to kings. We had a picnic there, and we were attacked by a gang of monkeys who ate all our food. We laughed and scurried into the car to get away from them."

On this trip, Sue got a flavor of the family tension created by Mataji's dedication to Hinduism. When she insisted on visiting a temple dedicated to Rama and Sita that was located on top of a hill, Maharaji went along to keep his mother happy. But when she began throwing money at an ugly black statue and ringing bells, Maharaji turned suddenly and left, walking swiftly back down the hill.

"He was upset," Sue says. "It was the first time I witnessed how strongly Mataji was into Hinduism."

More interested in the life of Westerners than in anything his mother believed, Maharaji spent every weekend playing with his visitors, pumping them about the other side of the world. And they were learning from him, too, as they had no understanding of the master-student relationship, an alien concept in the West.

"This relationship," Peter Lee explains, "was harder for people in the West to accept than in India, where the culture revolved around that. But I had no problem with it at all. I can't say why. It just felt like the most natural thing because here was someone who was going to teach me and stop me from screwing up my life. I trusted him implicitly, and I still do, because he has always fulfilled every single promise he ever made to me. I can't say that about anyone else."

On the other hand, Saph had never really acknowledged Maharaji as his teacher or master. Saph toured England and the United States, telling people about Knowledge. However, his reputation for having a quick temper and being arrogant preceded him, and he turned many people off. He developed his own following, and he spent much more time indulging with them in the trappings of the hippie lifestyle than spreading the message of peace. Some time after Maharaji arrived in the West, he asked Saph to step down from being an instructor.

David Passes, a young man from London and one of the first people to learn the techniques of Knowledge from Charan Anand, remembers literally bumping into Maharaji one evening at Shakti Nagar when they were both leaving their rooms at the same time. But since David had not yet met Maharaji, he had no idea with whom he had collided.

"Do you like ice cream?" Maharaji asked him.

"Yeah, I do," David answered.

Maharaji headed back into his room and came out with a large carton of chocolate ice cream, which he handed to David. A few minutes later, when someone informed David that he had just met Maharaji, he was delighted and proceeded to share his treat with the other people in the ashram.

These were happy days for everyone. Peter Lee remembers the electrifying hours they all spent together asking Maharaji the most outlandish questions. The thirteen-year-old's sense of humor was apparent during these times, and he came up with some pretty creative answers. Peter, who would later drive Maharaji in England and Europe, saw Maharaji's wisdom shining through as he handled whatever was thrown at him.

"What was I in my last life?" a visitor asked.

"None of you had any past lives," Maharaji said with flashing eyes. "You all came out of cold storage. This is your very first life."

"Why don't we live longer?" asked Anne Lancaster, a tearful American woman who would later work for Henry Kissinger in the U.S. State Department.

"Why does my little finger end here?" Maharaji said, pointing to the digit on his hand. "How I would like my little finger to go on forever!"

"In the New Testament, what are the differences in aspects of the trinity?" she asked.

"Come above the language," he said. "God is one. Love is one."

Glen recalls, "We British guests were treated like kings and queens. At ten each evening, the *chai wallah* (tea server) came to our rooms and ladled ginger tea into our cups. In the mornings, we ate a wonderful breakfast of rice, curried vegetables, and chapati on round steel trays, crouching or sitting, using our fingers to mop up the plate. We washed the trays at the open tap with a handful of ashes, the water ran down into irrigation channels between cultivated areas, and the leftovers were fed to the animals. Nothing was wasted."

Life at the ashram was relaxed and productive, with plenty of free time. Between events each evening and doing various crafts and writing, Maharaji loved horseplay. David Lovejoy recalls, "We followed him out to the dunes by the banks of the Ganges and played King of the Castle, which was all about him pushing us off the top of the dunes. We liked rolling down the sandbanks, but we wondered what would happen when a Westerner came up behind Maharaji and heaved him down a large dune. The Indian students were ready to jump on the perpetrator, but Maharaji was on his feet in a second, happily calling out, 'No reprisals!'"

Those who have stayed connected to Maharaji since that time share a common trust and appreciation. They see him as their joyful companion. "Each time I sit down to practice," says Peter

Lee, "or when I'm out and about, I have this little flicker of re-membrance, thinking about Maharaji and how sweet life is. It's all about what is inside of me—that capacity for total joy and contentment. That is the one thing in my life that has not changed, and it never will." Glen Whittaker, who went on to spend many years heading the organization in the United Kingdom and has remained actively involved with Maharaji, comments, "Every day, thanks to Maharaji's gift and his influence in my life, I am contentedly in touch with the center of my being. It's impossible to separate the gift from the giver. Maharaji is like a polestar—a true and constant presence and guide." And according to Sandy Collier, now an instructor, "Maharaji has been a constant support to me, always putting Knowledge into a context that isn't conceptual or attached to a lifestyle, but is a pure experience that is always available to me."

On their momentous walk through India, Gary and Will met a man who didn't speak. In order to communicate, he wrote in the sand or on a piece of paper—in English. "Where are you going?" he wrote. "What is the purpose of your life? Why are you here in India when you could be back home?"

"He asked some very strange questions," Gary says. "We all walked around the village and the surrounding farmland and sugar fields, and he would write a question in the ground, like, 'Why are we here?' We spent all day having mini-conversations for a few minutes, two or three times in a day. Will left for the Khumb Mela, but I stayed. Then Will came back, and the man told us (or rather wrote down for us) Maharaji's name. So we left for Delhi."

At the Delhi ashram, Shakti Nagar, Mataji and her transla-tor spent the afternoon with Gary and Will, and after the young

men were fed and refreshed, they headed to Prem Nagar to meet
Maharaji. In early February 1971, they both received Knowledge
in New Delhi.

In that same session was a woman named Janet Wallace, an
art student from Halifax, Canada, who would later help prepare
for Maharaji's arrival in Canada in 1971. "I arrived in Calcutta
on December twelfth, 1970, with twelve others," she said. "We'd
traveled the world for a year as art students from Halifax, and
I met a British woman, Rosie Malcolm, on a train. She told me
she'd come from England to meet this boy who had shown her
peace. I thought I could use that, and I went with her to a modest
house in the Punjabi Bagh area, where Maharaji spoke. His presence was anything but ordinary. I stayed overnight, and the next
day, Maharaji invited me to talk with him.

"Maharaji said that life was like attending a party," recalls
Janet, "that we were all attending the party, but we did not know
ourselves, the other guests, or the host. Then he added, 'I can
show you these things so you can enjoy the party.'"

He asked Janet if she'd like to receive Knowledge. When she
said she didn't know, he said, "If you want it, you can have it."
Along with Gary Girard and Will, Janet received it a week later
from Charan Anand in a hut at Punjabi Bagh ashram.

Mataji's devotion to Hinduism, to which she steadfastly clung,
had intensified in the years after her husband died. It seemed that
without Shri Maharaji holding her religious concepts somewhat
at bay, her practices became so serious "we ended up doing a
ritual if an ant crossed the threshold," Maharaji says. But he tolerated his mother's beliefs out of respect, even when she moved a
Hindu pundit into the residence.

Maharaji respected the pundit as a nice enough human being,
but he would relentlessly question this man who swore he could

predict the future. "Pundit Ji," he would say, "will my teacher give me homework today?" The pundit would say, "Yes"—a pretty safe bet—and Maharaji would continue to ask him every day, until one day the pundit was wrong, and Maharaji gleefully informed him of that. When they discussed Hindu philosophy, Maharaji would pound a desk as if it was a podium and say dramatically, "How can *this* be? How can *that* be?"

"Because it is written," the pundit would say.

"But you merely accept these things you read in books as facts," Maharaji would persevere. "How do you know for sure?"

"Because it is written," he would repeat, and round and round they went.

The friendly struggles between the pundit and Maharaji were hot and heavy in 1969 when an astronaut landed on the moon. This was a contentious topic for the pundit because staunch Hindus believed that the moon was a powerful god. "The Americans landed on the moon in a spaceship," the boy baited the pundit. "A man walked on the moon. Do you believe it?"

"No," the pundit answered. "That is impossible. How can they land on the moon? The moon is a god."

"Well, Pundit Ji," Maharaji said, "that is what you think now, but you'll need to believe it sooner or later."

It seemed that Maharaji dodged a bullet when his mother and Uncle enrolled him in a prep course for a military academy, supposedly a step along the way to joining a division of the Indian army. Maharaji said it was a gift that he got out of it. "I took the exam," he said. "I had to, and I passed it. Boy, was I sweating. But the kid before me filled up their list. If one kid had flunked, I'd have been next in line. But it didn't happen, and was I happy!" A major obstacle to his going to the West had just been removed.

In January 1971, he began to ask the visiting Westerners to

think about going back to their countries. He was intending to follow them there, but one of them began to cry. "We aren't strong enough yet, Maharaji," she said.

"When you arrive home," he said in a gentle but firm voice, "you will find that you have the strength."

Some Westerners resisted at first, and for months, Maharaji kept suggesting they move on. They were happy with their gift of Knowledge, and they wanted to help Maharaji fulfill his wish of spreading the word. But they dreaded the prospect of not seeing him for years to come. One of the last holdouts was Joan Apter, who had vowed never to return to America. "I said there was no way I'd leave," she says, "but after the Baisakhi Festival in April, I finally told him I was ready to return to America. He said, 'Congratulations.' And I left the next day."

At the beginning of the summer of 1971, Maharaji toured the Mumbai area. In Nasik, he and Charan Anand were admiring the sunset from the window of a friend's apartment when Maharaji said, "What do you think about me going to England for a couple of weeks during my summer holiday?"

Charan Anand was enthusiastic. "That would be wonderful," he said, "because so many people there would like to meet you."

Back in Dehradun, Maharaji set the chain of events in motion. After they received phone calls, friends in England raised funds for two plane tickets, one for Maharaji and one for Bihari. And then, Maharaji needed to get a passport. But while he was still applying, his mother found out.

"I hear you are planning a trip to England," she confronted him.

"Yes, I am," he told her.

"That is not going to happen," she said. "You are so young. How can I let you go? And Bihari doesn't speak English."

Maharaji spoke respectfully to his mother. "Shri Maharaji wanted me to learn English," he reminded her, "so I could take his message to other countries. I did what he asked, and I feel this is the right time for me to go to England."

When Maharaji looks back, he recalls the irony of the Westerners wanting nothing more than to come to India and the Indians wanting to visit the West. He felt the pull from people there. He was ready to answer it, but his mother was adamant. "No," Mataji persisted. "I don't feel comfortable letting you go."

When Maharaji began to cry, however, he touched his mother's heart. Mataji turned to Charan Anand and said, "Do you think my son should go to England?"

"Yes," said Charan Anand. "This is a beautiful time for that. People there really want to see him, and you want to see that his message reaches other countries. This is the right time."

"Well, Charan Anand," she said, backing down from her initial position, "if you promise he will come back in two weeks, he can go."

"I promise," Charan Anand said. The deal was sealed, and Maharaji was excited when he finally got his passport. "I would look at the official seal and at my picture," he recalls. "When I got the ticket, I looked at it the same way. Up to that time, when someone talked about the other side of the world, it meant Delhi. Now it really *was* the other side of the world, and I had never really been anywhere."

In London, a large center was being established in Alba Gardens in a verdant area called Golders Green where people could come and hear about Maharaji. And so, while his original Western invaders were back home spreading the good news, Maharaji dreamt of the West, preparing for his own invasion as he met his destiny head-on. The young man was aware that a page had turned in his life, but neither his students nor his family members, and maybe not even he himself, grasped the magnitude of the seachange that was about to sweep over all their lives.

I have always had a vision. I have never seen a problem.
When I started off, I didn't even know where I was going.
I had no idea what England was going to be like. It just all
happened so quickly. I got a passport, and the next thing I
knew, I was in London. And then I just started traveling.

MAHARAJI
Kuala Lumpur, Malaysia, May 5, 2005

Part Three
1970s and 1980s

I have found the perfect Knowledge, and I have
come to London to give it to you—not to see
London, not to see these roads and these cars,
not to see the outward show of London,
but to give you that free-of-charge
Knowledge, a method that one applies
to receive perfection.

MAHARAJI, THIRTEEN YEARS OLD,
LONDON, ENGLAND,
JUNE 30, 1971

Culture Shock

Maharaji sat cross-legged on a king-sized bed in London, staring at his wristwatch. He tapped it with his fingers, put it up to his ear, and tapped it again. It was ticking, the second hand was moving clockwise, but the hour hand was way off. A neon rainbow buzzed on the wall above his bed as he pondered the fact that he was in another world, a place where even his watch didn't work. And there were people just downstairs, waiting for him to talk to them.

After Maharaji had convinced his mother to let him leave her house, getting out of India had been relatively easy. But accepting his departure was not so easy for many of his Indian students. During a large gathering on the day Maharaji was leaving, someone inadvertently spilled the beans that he was on his way to the airport. The audience abandoned the meeting and rushed to the airport in taxis, scooters, and cars, but he was gone by the time they arrived. They headed home despondent, as this was the first time Maharaji had not been on Indian soil.

Months before he touched down at Heathrow Airport, Maharaji's new Western friends, eager to bring his message to their cities, had been searching for suitable houses that might serve as centers, places where people could come to hear the message. They had also begun to talk to people everywhere about Maharaji and Knowledge. For example, David Lovejoy, an Oxford graduate and international-class chess player, left India after meeting Maharaji there and made his way to Australia by hitchhiking and working on ships, talking to people about Maharaji as he went along.

A woman named Venetia Stanley-Smith went to spark interest in Japan, and Sandy Collier found a house in London that would become the first British center.

Carol Hurst, a quintessential hippie in billowy minidresses and clunky high heels, could be seen with a bunch of flowers in one hand and a dipstick in the other, checking the oil levels in her maroon Ford Cortina. In "the old days," she had acted as a mother figure to a coterie of lost boys in a South London hippie commune, taking Glen Whittaker, Peter Lee, and one of their friends, David Thorp, on drug-laced trips in beautiful countryside locations. Now, they were high on their enthusiasm to tell as many people about Maharaji as possible.

When they got the call from India that Maharaji was actually on his way in a few days, Carol and her new husband, Patrick, went on a serious search for appropriate accommodations. They decided the house in Alba Gardens was too small, so they found a tall, elegant town house on prestigious Lincoln Street in Chelsea off King's Road, owned by an affluent and eccentric aristocrat. He agreed that the "boy guru" could stay in his house, and Carol and her husband got the impression that he would charge no rent.

Sue Ratcliffe, who had been laid up in the London Hospital for Tropical Diseases since her return to London from India, helped secure the accommodations. Sue recalls that after discharging herself from the hospital, she and Carol took the town house because "over the bed, there was a rainbow in neon lights." Of course, that was merely a bonus. Their decision was based on their understanding that the house was free for as long as they wanted it.

Now, Maharaji tapped his watch one more time and took it off. No one had mentioned time zones to him. His watch said 8:00 p.m., but lunch supposedly was being prepared. He had never heard of jet lag, and he switched on the television, only to be stunned at the colored images that he had never seen before.

"I could watch the BBC for hours," he says with a laugh. "There was this girl in the color test pattern, and I stared at her, marveling."

With a final glance at the neon rainbow, Maharaji walked downstairs to greet his new friends gathered in the living room. They had prepared a thronelike chair for him, traditionally Indian, but he was keenly aware that this was not India. It was cool, even in summer, and the food, television, and music were different. "What a culture shock," he recalls, "for a thirteen-year-old boy to get on a plane without his parents and land in a foreign country where nobody speaks his language or eats his food."

"How was your flight?" someone asked, breaking the awkward silence.

"How do you think it was?" he answered.

"Must have been fantastic," someone else answered, unaware that Maharaji had not taken advantage of the first-class seats. In addition, he had been a vegetarian at the time and had not found anything he could eat during the entire plane ride. The language barrier was yet another obstacle, since Maharaji's grasp of English was shaky, and his accent was heavy. But soon enough, he took comfort in speaking from his heart to the people in the room about truth and peace. After a couple of hours, exhaustion took its toll, and Maharaji went back upstairs where he rested for a short while.

Sandy was in the kitchen, frantically trying some recipes from a cookbook called *Indian Cookery*. For some reason, they had thought Maharaji might bring his own cook, but Bihari stepped in and showed Sandy how to make hot chili sauce, a favorite of Maharaji's. From then on, Sandy would cook for Maharaji as best she could.

As awkward as he initially felt, though, Maharaji appreciated how hard people were working to make him comfortable. "It wasn't exactly home cooking, was it?" asked Sandy on the third day after lunch, feeling insecure and anxious to please him.

"It *was* home cooking!" he assured her. Sandy got the message that Maharaji felt at home wherever his students were.

After lunch, much to everybody's surprise, Maharaji wanted to take a short tour through London. He went outside and asked for the limo.

"Well," they said haltingly, "it's gone."

"Where did it go?" he asked.

"We could only afford to rent it for a few hours to pick you up," explained Carol, "but I can drive you everywhere in my car."

Off they went in the maroon Cortina with Carol at the wheel. She was tearful, feeling embarrassed about the car situation.

"Where do you usually go when you feel sad?" Maharaji asked.

"Richmond Park," Carol answered.

"Okay," Maharaji said. "Let's go there."

After a beautiful and quiet walk in the park, Maharaji asked, "Are there any other places you go when you are sad?"

They went to Kew Gardens, took another walk, and Carol's sadness evaporated.

On Saturday, June 19, 1971, two days after his arrival, Maharaji spoke at his first Western event at Conway Hall in Red Lion Square, Holborn. Located in Central London, this meeting hall for the Theosophical Institute, a spiritual movement that began in London in the late nineteenth century, was not considered a prestigious location. But it felt right, since the search for an inner experience had motivated its founders, and the simple inscription *To Thine Own Self Be True* was written above the stage. The 400 seats were full, and in the lobby, Glen sold the first edition of the new magazine *Divine Light*.

Maharaji spoke in heavily accented English in a voice that had not yet changed, making it hard for his audience to understand

every word. But his message was clear. He said, "Sir Isaac New-
ton did not invent gravity, but only discovered it. So I will not
invent a god for you, but will show you how to discover that God
is already there within you. If someone comes to me with pure
devotion, I can show them that."

He explained that coming to London to see the sights was not
his intention. He had come thousands of miles, he said, to show
people how they could discover the ultimate within themselves. It
was a fine talk and was well received, a good introduction to himself and his message, the same message that was given to him as a
child and that he would carry with him always as he matured.

As the days progressed, Maharaji's schedule became hectic. He
did a small amount of sightseeing, but he was not interested in
the usual places. Intrigued by the idea of an underground train,
his interest in technology was stimulated as he ran up and down
the escalators in the tube station and whizzed around on the
fast-moving trains to various parts of London. He was fascinated
by the rotating room on top of the Post Office Tower, and once
in a while he walked in the beautiful nearby park, assimilating a
brand-new culture that was nothing like his life in India.

Maharaji gave his second Western talk at the world-renowned
Glastonbury Pop Festival on June 21, 1971. The event was held
on farmland close to a prominent hill called the Glastonbury
Tor, famous for attracting spiritually minded people. British poet
Charles Cameron had invited him to speak between performances
on the pyramid-shaped stage, but due to typical English weather,
the festival was a mud bath, where hardly an attendee was free
from the pounding rain.

At first Maharaji refused Charles's invitation, even though
many of the people around him had gone ahead to Glastonbury
to prepare. He was accustomed to speaking at events that had
been created for him alone, but Charles called him several times
that day, urging him to reconsider. At the last moment, he decided

to go, and they headed off in Carol's car. The drive took about three hours, including a breakdown that Maharaji managed to remedy himself.

There is a photo of him in the passenger seat of the maroon Cortina with Carol leaning over the steering wheel, trying to dodge people who were prostrating themselves in the mud in front of the car. She inched toward the stage where a well-known pop group was in the middle of their set. Someone stepped up onto the stage and clandestinely unplugged the group's amplifier. While the band frantically tried to figure out what had happened to their sound, Carol slipped a chair onto the stage for Maharaji, and he sat down.

The pop group was furious at having been interrupted and raged at the organizers, insisting that Maharaji's talk be as short as possible. That turned out not to be a problem. Maharaji looked out onto a sea of disheveled hippies, quite a few of them naked. He spoke slowly, clearly, and succinctly for about ten minutes, accentuating the fact that everyone wanted happiness. "I'm very sure I can give you what you are really seeking," he said. "God is within you, and I can show you God if you want to see Him. I have that Knowledge, and I can give it to you. My age is so little. My body is so small. I can't serve you as a military officer or a police constable. The only service I can do is to help you by giving you that perfect Knowledge that you are now seeking in materialism.

"All material things are perishable. You, too, will perish one day. So how are you going to find God? You should know such a thing that will never perish and that is inside you. You only need to discover it.... I will tell you who you are and what is the purpose of your coming into this world. If somebody comes to me, I am sure I can give him the Knowledge, and he will be satisfied."

He managed to captivate his colorful audience in that brief period, and to this day, many of them look back at that time with reverence. It was a turning point in terms of the propagation of

Maharaji's message, because years later, people were still showing up at various English centers, saying things like, "I first saw
him at Glastonbury. There was such a glow about him. I knew
right away something was happening." Few people realized what
tremendous courage it must have taken for a thirteen-year-old
boy to walk onto the stage and speak without notes to a crowd of
5,000 wild hippies, none of whom had come to listen to him.

On the long drive back to London that night with Carol at the
wheel, Maharaji began to sing. Later, Charan Anand told Carol
that the songs he was singing were those that Krishna would sing to
his *gopis*, his famous female devotees. Carol, who now lives with
her husband in Wales, says, "Ever since that drive from Glastonbury, I have always felt that there is a connection between us."

When eighteen-year-old Lena Smolkopf received a message from
Sandy saying that Maharaji was coming to Heidelberg, Germany,
where she lived, she was thrilled. She had attended a language
school in London for a month and had received Knowledge from
Charan Anand at that time. When she returned to Germany, she
had written letters to Charan Anand. Unbeknownst to Lena, he
had shared them with Maharaji, who liked them very much. The
idea was that Maharaji would stay in an upscale hotel, and other
travelers would stay in Lena's apartment, where she lived with
her Russian father who was away on business.

But after an hour or so in the luxury hotel, Maharaji sent
someone to Lena's apartment with a message. "Maharaji would like
to stay with you," Charan Anand told her. "He likes to stay where
there is love for him."

"When the doorbell rang," Lena recalls, "I couldn't even go to
the door. I just turned around, and Maharaji was standing in my
living room. I'll never forget that moment when I saw him for

the first time. I was so happy. I felt it coming straight from my heart."

Maharaji looked at her and said, "Hmm. So you're Lena."

"Yes," said Lena, laughing and crying at the same time.

"Do you know what *Lena* means in Hindi?" he asked.

"No," she answered.

"Lena means to get, to receive," said Maharaji. "You're the one who gets and receives. And Maharaji is the one who gives."

"He was thirteen," Lena says, "but I recognized him as my master, which had nothing to do with age."

Maharaji was content to sleep in a small room cordoned off from the living room. A group of people slept just on the other side of a thin curtain, and Lena recalls Maharaji happily whistling from behind the curtain.

After a boat ride on the Neckar River and a visit to Heidelberg Castle, Maharaji got right down to business in this new country. Always focused on telling more people about him, his students rented a small room in Heidelberg University for Maharaji to give a talk. Lena graciously offered money from her savings to rent the hall, put up 5 posters, and distributed 50 leaflets. On the night of the talk, 150 people crowded into a room that was meant for 50.

Lena recalls that a toddler was running back and forth in front of Maharaji. He suddenly said, "You may think this child is disturbing you, so you cannot hear my words. But if we removed him, you would say that the noise outside was disturbing you. These things are not what disturb you, and removing them is not a solution. Your heart wants to listen to my heart, and this child cannot get in the way of that." Six people from the talk came to Lena's home the next day, and Charan Anand gave them Knowledge.

Over the years, Maharaji has reminisced with great joy about the three days he spent in Lena's apartment. Today, at fifty-two, Lena lives in Berlin and works as a management consultant throughout Eastern Europe. "From the time I met him," says Lena, "he helped me discover so much happiness that I live with a constant feeling of gratitude."

Maharaji returned to London, pleased with what he had accomplished in Germany, only to wake up one morning to learn that it was moving day.

"Why?" he asked.

"We don't have any money left to pay the rent," they told him, upset that the man they thought had offered his place for free was suddenly asking for money. But Maharaji was happy to pack up his things and head for the center in Golders Green. In those early days, he clearly preferred staying with his students.

Once in Golders Green, Ron Geaves recalls that Maharaji really let out his playful nature. "He was a child," says Ron, "which was sometimes hard to remember. Now he had a whole bunch of young lunatic devotees with whom he could play. One time, we all had a water fight and flooded the house. He really was having a great time."

At the end of the month, Maharaji spoke at Porchester Hall in London, where he said, "If you want it, come to me, and I will give you Knowledge. But, please, it is not like chocolate or a toffee that I will give you, and you will feel satisfied. It is a technique that you have to follow. If you are sitting here and feeling just a little thirsty, you won't mind whether you are able to get water or not. The more thirst you have, the more you will feel the value of the water. If you have great thirst, then Knowledge will have more value for you. So I want you to take your time."

People take misery and life and mix them together and put them in a suitcase. Every time they open it, they find life and misery together. Life is really not misery. Take the misery away, and what is left is life itself, which is so beautiful.

MARAHAJI,
PROVIDENCE, RHODE ISLAND,
JULY 3, 1976

Assimilation

While Maharaji toured Europe, Joan Apter and Gary Girard called him constantly from Los Angeles. If Joan couldn't reach Maharaji, she would ask whoever answered the phone, "What is he doing? What did he do today? Tell me what he did from morning to night." She didn't have the money to fly to England, so every day, she begged Maharaji to come to Los Angeles.

Mataji and Bal Bhagwan Ji kept calling from India, too, demanding that Maharaji come back home. "What about your school?" Mataji asked.

"Why do you want me to go back to school?" he asked her.

"Because I want you to be educated."

"I also want to be educated," he tried to explain. "I don't want to be a fool in front of anyone. But I am getting more education right now than in school. There, people read about things like time lines in books, but I'm experiencing it for myself. For the nine years I was in school, I have learned much more by traveling six thousand miles. If I stayed in school, I would not be speaking English like I am now. I am having the practical experience of what I was being taught in school, and it's really beautiful."

Mataji reminded him that the yearly Guru Puja Festival was only a few days away. How ironic that only a few years prior, she had been keen to speak at this yearly festival without her son! Now, when it looked like she could finally do that, the tug-of-war was on. With Mataji and the Indian students pulling on one side and Joan and Gary pulling on the other, Maharaji asked Charan

Anand what he thought. Should he go to Los Angeles or return home?

"You know best," said Charan Anand, deferring to him, "but if you go back now, Mataji will send you to school. You told her you didn't want to waste your time because your teachers have nothing to teach you about your subject. I feel this is the right time to convey your message. Let's go to America."

"Good idea," said Maharaji, smiling widely.

When Joan and Gary got the word that Maharaji was on his way, they shifted into high gear. They already had started a center on Alta Loma Terrace in Los Angeles, which had hundreds of steps and was situated among a group of small apartments, just above the Hollywood Bowl amphitheater. Now, in order to obtain a visa for Maharaji to come to America, Joan's father sponsored him, and Maharaji and Ron Geaves spent long hours at the American Embassy in London, trying to arrange his passage. "He took it a lot better than I did," says Ron. "It was difficult to watch them treating him so abominably, but he stayed calm, and we got there in the end."

On July 17, 1971, Maharaji landed at Los Angeles International Airport at about 4:00 p.m. Unlike his dramatic arrival in London, only a handful of people met him. After a brief press conference for TV crews and *Newsweek* magazine, Gary used his father's Lincoln Continental to drive Maharaji to a lawyer's luxurious home in Beverly Hills. This man, who generously offered his home, was nicknamed Mr. Fantastic, since he was so fond of using that word in his conversations.

When a tired and jet-lagged Maharaji arrived at the "fantastic" Beverly Hills address, he wanted to take a nap. But his American friends had made other plans for him, including a reception at the house, followed by an 8:00 p.m. event at The Source, a trendy vegetarian restaurant on Sunset Boulevard. Maharaji complied with the crazy schedule they had set up for him but soon realized that he would have to take control of his own time to avoid burning out. It seemed that as often as he insisted that there was nothing supernatural about him and that he got tired just like any other human being, his students simply refused to acknowledge that he needed sleep.

That night he told people that what he offered was like a very sweet fruit. "If you will take a bite, you will also experience the sweetness," he encouraged.

Within a few days, the apartment at Alta Loma Terrace had become the official headquarters, with dozens of people running in and out of the place, but Maharaji was experiencing yet another culture shock at the home of Mr. Fantastic. In India, there was no sex education, and kissing was cut out of all Western films shown there. And so, one could accurately say that Maharaji was utterly innocent. In order to reach his bedroom, he had to walk through a room where a half-naked girl lay on a bed. He immediately told Joan he wanted to move to the ashram.

She argued that the ashram was inappropriate, that he would not be comfortable since there was only one bathroom and two small bedrooms.

"I don't care," said Maharaji. "I want to move to the ashram." And so he did. He had very little privacy at the ashram, with so many people living there and visiting the crowded little apartment, but he wanted to be with his students above all else.

Staying at the ashram, however, also had its downside. "I remember one girl there," says Maharaji, "who said it was against her religion to take a shower. I know she had profound love for me, but the stench was incredible. I asked the others not to make room for her so close to me, but she always managed to squeeze in." He tolerated the constant street noises and electrical sounds better than anyone else. "Where I grew up," he says, "the house opposite ours belonged to a contractor. At four a.m. they started up their World War II black-nosed Chevy trucks. They had no exhaust pipes, and they shook the windows in our house. I was surprised in the California ashram when one morning, a machine went off somewhere, and all the windows started rattling. It reminded me of home, and I thought it was just great!"

Maharaji held his first large Los Angeles public event on July 18 at the Wilshire Ebell Theater, inviting interested people to Alta Loma Terrace afterward for a question-and-answer session. Jack Whitton, just out of jail for resisting the draft for the Vietnam War, heard Maharaji for the first time there. He says, "I asked him if I could experience what he was talking about now, or if I had to go through a long process first. He said, in his clear, precise way, 'You can experience it directly, and I can show you!'"

The bantering between master and students took on a humorous bent when Maharaji sat around at night, talking to the people gathered there. When asked what he would do if someone had a gun and tried to shoot him, Maharaji answered playfully, "First I'd put my hands up like this. Then, when he wasn't looking, I'd knock the gun out of his hand." He proceeded to kick his leg in the air, and he said, "You should take full advantage of television." The room exploded with laughter.

"What would you do about President Nixon?" someone asked on a more serious note.

Maharaji spoke with a wisdom way beyond his years when he said, "You can't drown a man who is standing on top of a ladder by throwing a bucket of water over his head. But if you wait until the whole room fills with water, when it gets to his chin, he'll do anything you ask of him." Two years later, the Watergate break-in would be the event that filled the room with water for President Nixon, as he resigned from the presidency in shame.

Jack Whitton sums it up by saying, "Maharaji was totally confident. To hear so much of the truth come out of someone so young was impressive. He spoke with power, strength, and authority, and he gave that power, strength, and authority to each of us."

During the next two weeks in 1971, Maharaji spoke at places such as the Macrobiotics House, the Metaphysical Society, the Integral Yoga Institute, the Philosophical Society, and at the center on Alta Loma Terrace. Maharaji called Mataji regularly, keeping her informed about how much he was learning and enjoying his new experiences, but he was getting exhausted.

John Berzner remembers, "We were running him ragged, and he was on a horrific diet of white rice, potatoes, and dhal, because we were so broke. But even in those conditions, the wisdom of the ages would come out of his mouth. And when the talk was over, watch out! He'd grab the water guns and begin squirting everyone." His stay at Alta Loma Terrace was often marked by screaming laughter, like the time he explored the limits of his water bed. He discovered quickly that if he took a needle, poked it into the mattress several times, and jumped up and down, he could control the length of each squirt! Needless to day, the mattress broke and flooded the room. Maharaji's playful nature bubbled to the surface, and when he saw the feast of electronics available in the United States, he was like a kid in a candy store.

"He loved the mega music stores," John recalls, "like Tower Records, with its electronic doors, and his drives to the ocean in my fifty-five Chevy delighted him." Maharaji's English was rapidly improving, as he assimilated the American culture by traveling, talking, and watching television. This was a school to which he could relate—the school of real life!

By the end of July 1971, he made the dreaded call to Mataji to inform her that he would not be returning to India for some time. She had a severe reaction, and some of the people present recall Maharaji yelling in Hindi into the receiver because the phone lines in India were so poor. When he hung up, he looked at Gary and Jack, who had been eavesdropping, and said, "You guys are enjoying this part too much."

During July and August, Maharaji traveled to Boulder, San Francisco, Berkeley, Palo Alto, San Rafael, and Carmel, where he spoke at events and did radio interviews, one on top of the other. On a freezing cold day in San Francisco, Maharaji was rudely awakened at 3:30 a.m. Apparently, someone had scheduled a radio interview for him early in the morning, but no one had let him know.

"You better get up!" he heard someone calling outside his door.

"Who is at my door?" he called out.

"You have to be at the sound stage in forty-five minutes," the voice told him as he hurried out of bed and into the shower.

Maharaji got in the cold car in the dark, shivering all the way to the studio. When he got there, a crew member handed him his first cup of hot coffee. He inhaled the steam, warmed his hands, and took a long sip. It tasted very good and helped him keep warm and awake for the interview. When he got back to the ashram, he had a talk with Joan.

"You're scheduling too many programs," he said. "I'm not going to let you do to me what they did to Shri Maharaji." Several times, he had referred to the way the Indians had clamored after his father and depleted him of energy. "Cancel some of my events, or I'll go back to India."

At this point, Maharaji took control of his own schedule, still going at full speed, but at least he was holding the reins. And he really did take control. In Berkeley, people were booing when he walked onto the stage, thinking that a thirteen-year-old had nothing to tell them. But he nipped it in the bud by saying, "I'm a little kid who has come to talk to you. The least you could do is listen. Stop booing, and don't be a bully." The audience was embarrassed, and they quieted down.

In Carmel, he met Tim Gallwey, a Harvard graduate, Navy officer, and tennis pro, who would go on to write a number of best-selling books on the psychology of sports, including *The Inner Game of Tennis* and *The Inner Game of Golf.* He would also become Maharaji's tennis instructor and close friend. Tim was in Carmel on sabbatical from graduate school when his older sister told him about the boy prodigy who was speaking at the Carmel Cultural Center.

"When I heard he was young," Tim says, "I thought that a thirteen-year-old would never be able to pull the wool over my eyes, which made me interested in meeting him."

Tim enjoyed a metaphor that Maharaji used during that talk. He recalls, "Maharaji explained that God was like a big generator, like Niagara Falls. From the generator, he said, were huge thick wires that fed into the various power plants. From there, they went into power stations across the country, into power lines at peoples' houses, and ultimately into the filament in the lightbulbs. Then he said, 'But I'm getting tired of answering all your questions. Why do you think I know? I'm only thirteen, and everything I say comes from my experience. I'm offering this Knowledge to you, so why not ask me for that and answer your own questions?'"

Tim's final question sealed the deal for him. "By what authority do you say what you say?" he asked Maharaji. "When I was a Navy officer, the captain with four stripes gave directions to steer the ship. I listened to him above anyone who had fewer stripes."

Maharaji laughed. "I don't wear stripes," he said, "but you can listen to what I have to say and what your friends have to say. If you feel in your heart this is what you want, then ask me for it, and I will give it to you. If it fills that longing, you'll know that what I gave you was pure water. If it doesn't, you'll know that either what I gave you was not pure water—or that you were not really thirsty."

Tim realized he was very thirsty. "It was amazing to discover that what I had been looking for was inside of me all the time and always would be," he says. "Here was something that did not exist in the domain of language, but rather in the realm of direct experience. Here was a mirror that reflected what was already inside me. This possibility was so different from anything I had come across, and when I received Knowledge, it was a beautiful experience. I knew it was real, and I started a lifelong exploration of an inner realm that to this day is very beautiful, peaceful, and satisfying."

In Carmel, Maharaji was asked a question that came up time and again along his travels: "Is renunciation the only way to find peace?"

"No," he answered in the tradition of his father, "you can carry on your daily activities, but always remember who you are."

Maharaji spent the week of August 18 to August 27 in a cabin in the old mining camp of Wall Street near Boulder, Colorado, where he sat with his students each morning under a tepee in a field and answered questions. As usual, he reminded them they needn't bother looking for peace on the outside, where it could not be found. "Today people want to find peace in books instead of nature," he said. "But nature is a part of peace, as your soul is, because your soul is also natural. It is not artificial. Your body is also natural. It is not artificial either. So your way of living may be artificial, but your body is not. It is real. It is natural like a tree, and you have to realize the mystery of the nature that is working within your body."

A yoga teacher from Denver named Bob Mishler was at these gatherings in the woods. He had come to meet Maharaji with one of his yoga students, Bill Patterson. Bill had been in India and told Bob about the thirteen-year-old guru. Mishler was impressed. When he met Maharaji, he offered to help in any way he could, and he was so dedicated and efficient that within a year, Bob had become the main organizer in the United States.

Always focused on his purpose, Maharaji spoke at Mackie Auditorium at the University of Colorado in Boulder in front of hundreds, and soon afterward made a "detour" for the benefit of just a few people. The Vietnam War was in the news, and Richard Fredericks, who was doing conscientious-objector service at the University of West Virginia in Morgantown, was not legally permitted to leave his home state. So, he invited Maharaji to come there. Maharaji accepted and stayed at Richard's one-room apartment for several days. At least fifty people came to hear him speak at this university.

Next, Maharaji gave a talk in Washington, D.C., where he stayed in the house of Joan Apter's parents, who were out of town. He also brought his message to New York in September, where hundreds received Knowledge within a few weeks. There, Suzy Witten knew the highly talented designer/artist Peter Max, who created the fabulous graphics for the Beatle movie *The Yellow Submarine*. He designed a poster for Maharaji's talk at Hunter College. At the same time, Milton Glaser, *New York Magazine* art director, offered his town house to Maharaji for a month and also created a poster for him—a four-color rendition of Maharaji's face with a stream of light issuing from his hands. Maharaji asked for the following words to be printed at the top:

> There has never been a time when there has not been darkness.
> There has never been a time when there has not been light.
> In this age of darkness, I have come to reveal the light.

John Berzner and Suzy Witten went on a radio show and talked from midnight to the early morning. Ron Coletta, one of the listeners, says it completely changed his life. "One night, back when I was in high school," he says, "I tuned into my favorite radio station, called WBAI. They had interesting interviews that happened in the wee hours of the morning from midnight to six-thirty a.m., and my favorite disc jockey host, Bob Fass, said, 'Good evening, this is Bob Fass, WBAI. Tonight, I'm sitting here with a group of followers of a thirteen-year-old master, Guru Maharaji, who, I'm paraphrasing now, says he can bring you peace.' Then, seeming to be at a complete loss for words, he said, 'Maybe I better turn it over to these people.'"

Ron recalls, "The mellowness of it, the unusual demeanor of Bob Fass, really drew me in. They spoke about Maharaji in general ways: Thirteen-year-old master. Teaches perfection. Gives you a practical experience. Just came from India, and he's going to be speaking for the first time at Hunter College in Manhattan, New York.

"Then they opened it up for questions. I was really interested to know more about Maharaji and what he did. But all the questions were relating to his age, like, 'Is he really thirteen?' They signed off at six-thirty in the morning, and I remember seeing the sun come up, going out in the backyard, and feeling really elevated. The grass was covered in dew, and I just kind of washed my face and felt part of that whole seminal feeling that they were talking about."

Ron Coletta was really excited after the radio show and called his friends, some of whom he hadn't spoken with in a couple of years. He managed to bring eight people along with him to hear Maharaji speak at Hunter College.

"There he was," Ron says, "this little person way up on the stage. His English was atrocious. I'm really good at understanding English accents, but the majority of people I was with couldn't understand him and were pretty disinterested—except for my brother and my girlfriend's older brother."

The three of them followed up on the event, arriving at Milton Glaser's town house where Maharaji had his living quarters in the basement. Ron remembers, "We were in a big living room, and thirty to forty people were packed in there. Someone asked if we could see Maharaji and ask him questions, and he showed up. So all these people were asking questions, some of which were brilliant and others pretty stupid. I was at a loss, thinking, 'So much of what I've been hearing leaves me with no questions. Everything has been pretty much covered.' And then I decided to ask him the million-dollar question. I raised my hand, and he said, 'Yes?' Back in those days, he would kind of raise his eyebrows. I said, 'May I have this Knowledge?' Humbly and graciously, he slowly closed his eyes and said, 'Yes, you may.' I received it the next day, and I felt that deep within me, this was the real stuff I was being shown. I remember thinking, 'Wow, I could have never figured this out in a million years. It's just too simple.'"

New York was a whirlwind, where Maharaji would meet a steady stream of people each day at the center on 40 W. 11th Street. They would wait, sometimes for hours, for him to show up. Maharaji was clearly on "Indian time," and the audiences were restless and impatient. But no matter how long they waited, when he arrived and began to speak, the people were mesmerized, listening respectfully and visibly connecting with what he was saying.

In a TV interview, host Bill Beebee played a word-association game with Maharaji. "Tell me your first thoughts," he said to Maharaji, "when I say the following words. Let's start with *hate*."

Maharaji said, "Ego. The mind."

"Hell?" asked the host.

"That thing where man loses peace."

"Devil?"

Maharaji said, "Where man is away from God."

"Love?" Mr. Beebee asked.

"Where man is complete."

And finally, "War?"

Maharaji said, "Where man is not satisfied."

Next, Maharaji went to Denver, Colorado, where he stayed at 1560 Race Street, in a house belonging to Bob Mishler. This house also served as a center. From there, he spoke on thirteen occasions in two weeks in Toronto.

When Maharaji returned to New York, the limo that had been ordered did not arrive at the airport for some reason, so one of the students who had gone to meet Maharaji ended up driving him in his Volkswagen Beetle. The next day, a New York newspaper ran the headline, PRINCE OF PEACE ARRIVES IN VOLKSWAGEN. Maharaji stayed at the new ashram on 13th Street and 6th Avenue in a third-floor, walk-up apartment above a bar.

Everywhere he went, Maharaji was making friends. But the truth was that no matter how many people showed up to welcome him and benefit from his message, he was also challenging their familiar frames of reference. It was inevitable that some individuals would develop gripes against him.

In his day, Shri Maharaji had come to accept that his mission included being seen as controversial and having to endure lingering detractors. As a young boy, Maharaji was facing the same kind of narrow-minded opposition. Early on he came to understand that because he was following in his father's footsteps, he, too, would always have to deal with detractors. Of course, he had somewhat contributed to the situation by refusing to compromise or speak with political correctness, especially in the beginning. His boldness brings to mind a famous saying by Krishnamurti, an Indian philosopher: "It is no measure of health to be adjusted to a sick society." But dealing on a day-to-day basis with deliberate disturbances by detractors was an annoying challenge that would never completely disappear.

At a standing-room-only event at Hunter College for a thousand people, Maharaji demonstrated his ability to remain unfazed by disturbances. In the middle of his talk, a man walked down the aisle toward the stage and began yelling at him until someone in the audience with a black belt in karate got up and immediately took the man down with a single blow. The security guards rushed forward to diffuse the situation as the audience took sides, some shouting to throw him out, while others shouted to leave him alone. After about thirty seconds of chaos, Maharaji calmed everyone when he addressed the man lying on the floor with no fear or anger in his voice. "Please let me complete my presentation," he said, "and then I will answer your questions."

The security guards backed away, the man got up and stopped heckling, and the talk continued as if nothing had happened. Those present marveled at the young boy's ability to keep the peace and bring the talk back to his message. Later, when 200 people arrived at the center, Maharaji was grateful that it would take more than a heckler to keep people from listening. In fact, so many people showed up that they moved the entire operation to a martial arts studio nearby that could better accommodate the crowd.

Maharaji's extraordinary popularity in the West in the '70s was indicative of the times. Four years prior, the Beatles had popularized Indian sage Maharishi Mahesh Yogi, George Harrison was playing the sitar, and the common mainstream Western perspective equated the search for inner peace with Eastern philosophy. Harrison's song "My Sweet Lord" had just made it to the top of pop charts, and the lyrics spoke to the longing for inner fulfillment, using many devotional Indian expressions. The idea of finding something inside of oneself beyond the realm of the busy mind had popular appeal, and there was a utopian feeling in the air, as if the world was on the brink of taking a radical turn for the better.

During the time that Maharaji was making his first strides in England and went to speak to the thousands at Glastonbury, John Lennon was in the vicinity recording his song "Imagine":

> Imagine there's no countries
> It isn't hard to do
> Nothing to kill or die for
> And no religion too
> Imagine all the people

Living life in peace...
You may say I'm a dreamer
But I'm not the only one
I hope someday you'll join us
And the world will be as one

What a perfect time for Maharaji to arrive, an innocent-looking teenager who was equally at ease while playing or being serious. Despite his youth, nothing could shake his confidence and warmth. He appeared as a thirteen-year-old pillar of strength and humility, which was appealing to many people of all ages.

"I would have come to the West earlier," he said, "but it didn't make sense. People were too interested in drugs. Today, they are leaving drugs because they can't find what they want there. At this time, the door of the elevator is not too widely opened, and not too narrowly. At this time, the young generation is in search of truth. The world is calling me now, and I am here."

Throughout it all, whether he was watching television, eating the latest American food, or talking to his students, he appeared never to be distracted from his message, an extraordinary feat for a thirteen-year-old. Living day to day, depending on his students for his basic needs, and going without when necessary, he kept spreading his message, not too proud to let people pass the hat when necessary. Ron Coletta, who would become Maharaji's travel companion from 1973 to 1977, says about those early years: "We were living hand to mouth, from one event to the next, from one task to the next, and everything was begged or borrowed. Maharaji was humble and open, and accepted whatever was offered. He was a beggar, in a sense, vulnerable to the graciousness of whoever was open to him in whatever way, right- or wrong-sighted, in whatever place he was."

Ron, now married and an entrepreneur and civic activist living in Miami Beach, Florida, says, "It was a harrowing experience for a thirteen-year-old kid, not only having his difficult role, but also going halfway around the world to a totally different culture that must have been as bizarre for him as India was for us. But the more time I spent with him, I saw that nothing in this world could shake him. No situation or circumstance could divert him from his purpose. It was inspiring to watch him in these situations where so many things were done on a shoestring. Most of us were living hand to mouth, one day at a time. And he was a pillar of steadfastness and humility."

Joan Apter, who knew Maharaji from India, is now a wellness educator and recently introduced an event celebrating Maharaji's fortieth anniversary of bringing his message to people. She recalls, "It was amazing to watch him get acquainted with Western culture. He was like a sponge, assimilating things at such a rapid rate—the electronics, the cartoons on TV. He watched all the cartoons; he watched *The Three Stooges*, getting the input that we all got as children in America. He assimilated all of it so fast and started using colloquial English. And he began enriching his addresses with examples gleaned from his daily observations and life experiences."

Knowledge is like a river. Let a lame man come, it is the same water. Let a rich man come, it is the same water. Let a poor man come, it is the same water. Let an enemy come, it is the same water. Let a friend come, it is the same water. The same water is flowing for everybody. External things do not affect this Knowledge, because it is within.

MAHARAJI
Boulder, Colorado, August 28, 1971

Happiness lies within you, and thus it is your
treasure. You can take it, but you don't have the
key to it. Everybody has lost their keys.
And the true master has the key
for all the safes.

MAHARAJI,
LONDON, ENGLAND,
NOVEMBER 3, 1971

A Jumbo Arrival

In October 1971, Maharaji told his Western students that he was heading back to India for the traditional *Hans Jayanti* festival, celebrating the birthday of Shri Maharaji. They were amazed when he invited them to join him. In an unprecedented move, some of them decided to charter a 747 jumbo jet for the occasion and arranged for the headset audio channels to play his talks. The 300 who flew on the jumbo were joined in India by 200 other Westerners. They gathered in Delhi for the big event and later stayed at Prem Nagar.

Maharaji agreed to an interview with *Nav Bharat Times*. When a reporter asked him if he was a Hindu (a common question), Maharaji said, "If you're talking about my body, I grew up in a Hindu family and the Indian culture. But if you're talking about my soul, soul is just soul. It has no religion."

The newspaper article went on to say that Maharaji had betrayed Hinduism, a familiar accusation. But when a few of his students visited the newspaper offices to protest and hopefully make them retract the statement, rioting ensued. The students said local "hoods" hired by the newspaper attacked them. The newspaper said the students threw stones at their offices. Whichever was true, someone died in a car accident that was caused by the chaos in the streets.

The press had a field day hounding Maharaji and showering him with ridiculous accusations—that he was really forty years old and that he was against Hinduism. The media enjoyed stirring the pot of controversy. To some, he was not religious enough; to

others, he was too absolute in his beliefs. One newspaper stated
that his students' claim that he could show people peace was outlandish hype. The media seemed eager to affirm that Maharaji
had no wisdom to offer and that he should be stopped. Negativity
from the riot hung over him like a dark cloud for weeks.

However, as is often the case, the controversy also brought its
share of interested people, resulting in a fast-growing number
who welcomed Maharaji and honored his teachings. The Hans
Jayanti festival went forward at Ram Lila Grounds, a huge outdoor public gathering place in Delhi, with hundreds of thousands
in attendance.

When the event was over, the Westerners stayed at Prem Nagar, where they celebrated Maharaji's fourteenth birthday with
him on December 10, 1971. A few weeks later, he attended an
event in Patna, where he and his students were harassed once
again, this time by both left- and right-wing militants—including the Arya Samaj and the Bengali Communists. These religious
traditionalists were angry with Maharaji, just as they had been
angry with his father. Now they had grown even more hostile
since his success in the West. How could a group of Westerners
suddenly invade their tradition?

At this event in Patna, someone had hired a group of hooligans
to cut off the electrical installation, turning the area completely
dark as they pelted stones into the audience, causing the attendees
to scatter and flee. Maharaji, sitting onstage, looked at the fires
being set on the ground's perimeter, which cast an eerie shadow
over silhouetted people fighting one another. He continued to speak
while Ron Geaves herded the Westerners into buses headed for
the Prem Bhawan ashram at Mithapur, Patna. Maharaji remained
onstage as long as possible, declaring with unwavering intent, "I
am not as others may have been—a lamb to the slaughter. I have
come to bring peace. Nothing can stop me from doing it."

He was finally forced to return to the ashram, where a huge
crowd had gathered. Gratefully, Rajeshwar Singh, the local judge

who had been with Maharaji five years earlier at his first press conference in the same city, helped put Patna under martial law and a curfew.

As a teenager, Maharaji had philosophically summed up the recurrence of these situations by saying, "It has happened in history that every time a master comes, there are people who don't like him or the message. So it has always been. But there are also people who love to hear the message, and those who are thirsty will listen."

In February of 1972, fourteen-year-old Maharaji returned to London, and with the exception of a short trip back to India, he concentrated his efforts in the West until November. There was very little money to support the work, and few people understood how to book appearances for him and make arrangements for his travels, but he thrived on a feeling of freshness and freedom.

The simple words he said in London on February 28 demonstrated his approach to making the most of challenges in life: "Life is a tide," he said. "Float on it. Go down with it and go up with it. But be detached. Then it is not difficult." Easier said than done, some thought. Clearly the young boy was able to access within himself a place of serenity that allowed him to surf the high waves better than most. He constantly encouraged his students to rely on their meditation for strength and to allow consciousness to inform their judgment. "This meditation is the polish that makes us shine," he said. "If you want to shine, do more of this meditation. If you don't do this meditation, you will become dull, and you will eventually reach the same stage where you were before."

When asked about the role of ashrams at that time, he said he saw them not as a place to lead a "holy life," but rather as a center for furthering the message: "An ashram," he explained, "is a place, a center from which we can air our ideas, a sort of broadcasting station. You can tell people who come there about Knowledge, or you can go out from there and tell them, because everyone must know about it. When we know it, we must bring this opportunity to others, so they might also know it."

‿‿

On March 12, 1972, in Neuchâtel, Switzerland, at an event in a large sports arena, some evangelical Christians held placards and yelled, trying to drown out Maharaji's voice. But they were quickly placated, and thousands of people enjoyed one of the largest Western events to date. Maharaji took the high road and said, "There is only one vibration that dwells amongst everyone, and this vibrates without limit. There will come a time when the world ends, but there will never come a time when that perfect vibration ends. It has to be realized, but not through external means. External means are not perfect, but this Knowledge *is* perfect. When you meditate upon it, there will be no questions. Then you go beyond questions and answers, and you will get peace, and that's the real source."

Maharaji stayed in London through March and April. Then, after a trip back to India to speak at a large festival, he flew to South Africa, where Gary Girard had been doing some advance work since the beginning of January. Gary had been staying with Bhoolabhai Gokal, a distinguished South African gentleman in his sixties who had come to see Maharaji in London before inviting him to South Africa. He and his wife had graciously opened their home, but Gary was overwhelmed by the amount of people who were interested. South Africa had (and still has) a large Indian community, and many people had been Shri Maharaji's students. Gary met with so many interested people each day that he couldn't sleep. "I was in way over my head, and I needed some backup," he recalls.

He wrote Maharaji letter after letter, begging for help, while the number of interested people grew rapidly. They needed

Maharaji to come. One night, Charan Anand called Gary from India. Gary demanded to speak to Maharaji, who could hear the panic in his student's voice. "When are you coming?" he said.

"I don't know," Maharaji said. "What's wrong? You're doing a great job there."

"I'm not taking no for an answer," said Gary. "It's completely out of control here. These people need you, and you have to come right away."

The next day, Gary received a call from Charan Anand, who said, "He's coming." And Gary breathed a sigh of relief.

The month Maharaji spent in South Africa was a landmark experience. His flight stopped over in Nairobi, Kenya, where he stayed at the home of an Indian family. "They had a very large household," recalls Maharaji, "and when I started talking to one of their black servants, the owners got upset."

"You're not supposed to talk to the servants," they chided him.

"He's a human being," said Maharaji, "isn't he? What's wrong with talking to him? I want to know how he lives, how he survives." Maharaji felt strongly about this and later commented that the Indians in Africa were taking revenge for how the British had made them servants during their reign in India. Now they were doing the same to black Africans.

Maharaji spoke throughout South Africa, where interracial gatherings were forbidden. However, as usual, he insisted on doing things his own way. In Johannesburg, he addressed several thousand people at an airport Holiday Inn. He also visited Durban and Cape Town, all the while addressing racially mixed audiences. "In South Africa," he remembers, "I did not have separate gatherings for blacks and whites. All my meetings were mixed, and in a short time, four hundred people had received Knowledge."

Here, at the height of the apartheid system, he told the South Africans that all human beings, regardless of who they were, what they did, or the color of their skin, had hearts that longed for fulfillment. "How wonderful it would be," he told his mixed audience, "to be able to carry on a conversation with your heart, to be able to ask the heart how magnificent it feels to be fulfilled—and for the heart to reply in utter silence. And in that silence, to understand the acknowledgment and to receive internally the most magnificent joy. To have a beautiful smile dance upon your lips because you have carried on that conversation with the ultimate friend you have. Through sad times and happy times, this heart of yours will be your best friend. It will never abandon you."

There in South Africa, Maharaji also took the first step toward realizing a lifelong dream. Cessna had an introductory offer that Maharaji couldn't refuse. For twenty dollars, a person could take a short flight in a small plane to see if he was interested in learning to fly. Maharaji arrived at the airport with Gary and Milky, and the two of them got in the back while Maharaji took the copilot's seat. When the instructor allowed him to take the controls, he did a sort of dive bomb, and everyone in the plane got sick, including Maharaji. But he had already decided that he was destined to be a pilot. Four months later in England, he began formal flying lessons with one of his American students, Bill Bach, who was in the U.S. Air Force and stationed in England. Bill was also a flight instructor, and when Maharaji got a student license soon after, they flew together almost daily.

"When I saw an airplane for the first time in my life," Maharaji later said, "I thought it was going to crash and kill us…. But when I actually flew the plane, it was really easy. Not at all difficult."

From South Africa, Maharaji returned to the United States via a short stopover in London, accompanied by Mataji, Bhole Ji, and Raja Ji. Over the next two months, he spoke at forty-five venues in North America and received honors from city mayors in New York, New Orleans, Los Angeles, and Denver. During the last half of 1971, his touring had been wild and spontaneous, but things were a little more organized now, with more people in many countries and cities backing him up.

At the end of 1971, Maharaji had gone back to India, leaving behind thousands of people who had just received Knowledge. In 1972, as a result of his "World Peace Tour," this number multiplied considerably. Maharaji was still a novelty and was commonly referred to as the "fourteen-year-old guru," and the press was predominantly positive. The news about the young boy now reached more and more people who had been seeking "truth" since the '60s. In the large cities of the Western world, there was hardly a seeker who hadn't heard about the young guru.

Since a major part of the audiences drawn to his message were from this '60s generation, he felt compelled to address the issue of drugs. In New York in June, he said, "Many people in South Africa were into drugs, but now that they have received Knowledge, they are slowly leaving them behind.... If you take a car to get to a house, you don't bring the car with you up the stairs... you leave it at the door. So, if you believe that drugs are the medium that got you to me, now leave them. You have come to me, so you can leave your drugs behind."

Meanwhile, problems were looming on the home front, as family members were competing with Maharaji for public attention. They were trying, not so subtly, to turn his talks into Rawat family events, and the competition was escalating. So, when Mataji had a parade arranged for her in Toronto, Canada, on Mother's Day, John Berzner and friends arranged a parade for Maharaji on Fifth Avenue in New York City on Father's Day, June 18.

"Mataji was getting more and more demanding," John Berzner says. "She was a matriarch who wanted personal recognition and acknowledgment. And then there was Bal Bhagwan Ji, who always needed to have his say." John Berzner recalls being in a car with Maharaji, Bal Bhagwan Ji, and Mataji where Berzner felt Bal Bhagwan Ji was clearly trying to anger Maharaji. The dynamic continued at the first Western Guru Puja Festival in Montrose, Colorado. But Maharaji rose above it as he addressed the thousands of attendees: "What I offer does not come from the

East. The sun also comes from the East, and you don't say, 'I will not let this sun glow on me because this comes from the East.' Sun is not Eastern or Western. Nobody is Eastern, nobody is Western.... This Knowledge is a very old thing, an ancient thing. It existed before the world was created, so realize what is inside of us—vibrating essence, pure energy."

When Maharaji first went to Europe, his message had already been spreading like wildfire in most major countries and cities. Many people had received Knowledge from Indian instructors without ever having seen or heard Maharaji live. A group of Argentineans who settled in the Spanish island of Ibiza after returning from Prem Nagar invited Indian instructor Mohani Bai to visit. She started to spread the message on the island, and then she traveled to Bilbao, located in the heart of the Basque country, the first place in Spain's mainland where there would be a center. People began flocking there.

Three Argentinean students had Danish spouses, so they went to Copenhagen, where someone else who had been to Prem Nagar was spreading the word from a health food store in the center of the city. This attracted best-selling writer Ole Grünbaum. By late July 1972, he became interested in Maharaji and wrote an extensive article in the country's leading newspaper. This article resulted in more than 1,000 people attending a midnight showing of a movie about Maharaji. A month later, Ole went to the Swiss Alps Festival in Saanenmöser, along with about 800 Europeans.

"It was a shock," says Ole, "although a delightful one, to see and hear Maharaji live. A few minutes into his talk, I realized that this was the first time in my entire life I had heard somebody who spoke solely from his own experience and not from what he had read or heard. I had listened to many outstanding people speak and had read a lot of interesting books, but this was profound because it came from experience alone. Later that day, when I stood in front of him and had the chance to invite him to Copenhagen, I had a second shock, or rather a revelation. He was not at all the lofty spiritual master of my imagination. On the contrary, he was the most simple, frank, and friendly person I had ever come across."

Ole, whose father was the finance minister of Denmark, became the Danish and Scandinavian organizer for some years. In the '80s he resumed his writing career, got married, had five children, and for two decades was the country's leading technology writer. In 2002, his book *Tecnofetichism—the Dream about the Friction-Free Society* won the Writer's Guild "Book of the Year" award. He has stayed closely involved with Maharaji to this day.

Ole says, "Maharaji's inspiration gives me a joy that is way beyond what I ever imagined possible, even in the exotic hippie years. The experience of inner peace that he has shown me how to access is deeply fulfilling. Over the decades, even while busy with career and family, I have always wanted to help him reach out to all the people in the world who are hoping that there is more to life than meets the eye."

In Japan, Venetia Stanley-Smith was working relentlessly to generate interest for Maharaji's message. Born into British aristocracy, she had attended lectures by different teachers in London when someone brought her to Charan Anand. She was instantly moved by what she heard. She asked for Knowledge and received it the next day. "I felt so amazed," she says, "that there was inside of me a place where the source of peace, serenity, and fulfillment lay."

Venetia was in the first van that traveled from London to the "Peace Bomb" event in Delhi in the autumn of 1970—the one that made it in time. She was disappointed at first when she met Maharaji. She had only seen a photo of him when he was a small boy of eight. Now he was older, slightly chubbier, and wearing long, black pointed shoes that she did not like. She had a hard time reconciling this image with her idealized picture and did not know what to make of him. After the festival at Prem Nagar, she told him, "I don't know who you are."

He replied, "Don't worry about who I am. Just practice Knowledge." Which she did for hours each day. Today, Venetia says that was one of the best times in her life.

Her great-grandfather, Lord Curzon, had been viceroy of India from 1904 to 1911. The parliament buildings in Kolkata are the same design as the building on his estate in England, and there is a street in Delhi named after him. Lord Curzon donated a considerable amount of money for the restoration of the Taj Mahal and other landmarks in India. Venetia did not generally mention this, but Mataji was impressed when she found out and liked to tell people. Maharaji, on the other hand, never talked about it.

In the spring of 1971, when Westerners were leaving for their countries, Venetia ventured to Japan. After arriving in Kyoto, she supported herself as a dancer in a club but later switched to teaching English. For about a year, she was the only person with Knowledge in Japan, and Maharaji phoned her regularly to ask how she was doing. He arrived there in late September 1972 and spoke at events in Kyoto, Tokyo, and several smaller towns. After he left, about a hundred people in Japan became interested.

Venetia currently lives in a small village outside of Kyoto with her four children and her second husband, who is Japanese. She is writing a book about herself and her life in the Japanese countryside, and she has been the subject of several TV programs.

Maharaji continued to travel wherever his students found an interest and invited him. After Japan, he visited Australia, and then he returned to the Pacific Palisades area of Los Angeles where Jack Whitton had found a house for him close to the ocean. From there, Maharaji conducted interviews for TV, radio, and print journalists until October when he surprised his students by inviting them to come to India.

Some of his students in the United States and Britain organized five chartered jets to take a record number of Western students there in late 1972. By the time they all arrived in India, however, an innocent customs incident involving two people, some cash, and wristwatches soured the press toward Maharaji. They started writing articles that accused him of being involved in smuggling jewels and cash. Not that they needed any more ammunition, since they were already accusing him of lying about his age and of being a CIA agent. Needless to say, these frivolous assertions were never substantiated, but that never stopped detractors from repeating the stories.

"Who is going to give government secrets to a fourteen-year-old kid?" Ron Geaves asked the press. Maharaji laughed about it.

Back in 1949, author George Orwell had written an essay about Gandhi saying, "Saints should be judged guilty until they are proved innocent." Interestingly, this view had been applied to Maharaji since he was a child. Maybe it started *because* he was a child. Whatever the initial reason, the allegations against him and against his work in general were outlandish and eventually would be proven wrong after a lengthy investigation. But at the time, they hampered his efforts.

An article written by Henry Allen and published on September 15, 1971, in *The Washington Post* provides a good example of the media's attitude toward Maharaji. This man, setting a new standard for shallowness in American journalism, wrote, "Maharaji has a fondness for zapping people with a water pistol, for all mankind, and for automobiles. He's the son of a guru from Rishikesh, a region that has spawned holy men the way Appalachia has spawned stock car racers."

When the word got out about the difficulty at customs, a reporter for the British *Daily Mail* announced inaccurately that Maharaji had to face questioning for allegedly smuggling a briefcase containing jewels into the country. Maharaji was called to Delhi repeatedly to attend meetings with lawyers about the incident or to be grilled by the police, questioning his motives. At one meeting, his passport was temporarily taken from him, and he was not sure how long he would have to remain in India. So in the beginning of 1973, the fifteen-year-old was facing yet another challenging time in his life, having to stay in India in order to deal with the false allegations, when all he wanted was to return to his work and his friends in the West.

Maharaji's students explained that the briefcase in question merely held a pool of petty cash for the journey and safeguarded some personal jewelry. Maharaji and the organization would eventually be cleared on all counts.

There are people who think I am doing this work for money. That's not the reason. I do this because I get great happiness from it. I offer this Knowledge to people free of charge, and then they feel great happiness. That makes me happy, too.

MAHARAJI
Johannesburg, South Africa,
April 29, 1972

People really should understand who they are
and what is the purpose of life. And that is
something to feel, not be told. This Knowledge
is an individual experience for everybody.
And everybody can actually feel it
within their heart.

MAHARAJI,
KINGSTON, JAMAICA,
MARCH 17, 1974

The Best and the Worst

Although he was forbidden to leave India for a time during the investigation into the customs incident, fifteen-year-old Maharaji had established himself in the West. He had reached out to tens of thousands, and he was pursuing his dream to learn to fly. And in his personal life, romantic love was just around the corner. In the world at large, the United States and North Vietnam finally had signed the Paris Peace Accords, there was a ceasefire, and U.S. troops were starting to return home. But there were no peace accords within Maharaji's family, and antagonisms were building within the organization that had been set up to finance and manage his tours, now led by Bob Mishler.

Mataji had appointed many new Indian mahatmas, and along with her instructions on how to teach the techniques and where to travel, she also encouraged them to hold on to some traditional Indian beliefs and customs. As a result, Knowledge, an experience of simplicity and inner freedom, was being adorned in Indian clothing. It seemed that while fifteen-year-old Maharaji was becoming more Westernized, many of his new students were undergoing a change in the opposite direction.

More and more, Maharaji was not the only one setting the direction of his work. Many others around him had different ambitions and motivations that were at odds with his. The organization's efforts to finance and support the work were taking on a life of their own, and internal tensions that inevitably occur in organizations started manifesting. In the end, Maharaji's vision was being hindered by other competing visions. What was a student to embrace—Maharaji's pure message of peace or the various additions and interpretations that were now floating around?

He said at that time in London, "I am only a messenger, and what I can do is simply bring two cords together and attach them. That's all I can do. I am a switcher in between. I can just switch on the line," alluding to his offer to show people how to connect with the experience of peace within. In his innocence, he believed that in the end, people would eventually rally around him. Little did he know that things would not be that simple.

This was when he began to mull over the idea of extending a caring hand to people lacking the basic necessities in life. He felt it was time to launch a large-scale humanitarian initiative in which his students could be involved. "Aside from needing peace," he explained, "the whole world needs food. There are still many people who don't have clothing, who don't have food, who don't have shelter.... They need these things. If someone is hungry and we tell him to sit and do meditation, he will say, 'Don't give me peace; give me food first.'"

An organized humanitarian initiative came to life first in India, but it was short-lived, particularly in the West. Perhaps Maharaji imagined that the flow of people rushing to hear him would show the same interest in helping others. But this did not manifest. In fact, it would be twenty-five years before he would once again embark on a wide humanitarian effort. However, this failed initiative shows that at fifteen, Maharaji was already deeply concerned about helping people in need. When his dream for the humanitarian work fell apart, he was very disappointed.

Forced to stay in India until the customs problem was resolved, Maharaji made good use of his time there, attending events and spending time with his Indian students. He even went back to school for a while. However, when Gary Girard joined him in India and brought greetings from the Westerners, the teenage Maharaji missed them so much, he cried. Finally, in June, after seven long months, he was exonerated by the courts. When he got his passport back and returned to England and the United States, his Western students and friends were overjoyed to see him—especially a flight attendant named Marolyn Johnson.

In June 1973, Marolyn, a tall, graceful airline hostess who had heard about Maharaji the prior year, was now living in the Los Angeles ashram. A native of San Diego, California, she had just returned from Chicago and arrived at the house in Pacific Palisades with some sweets for him. She rang the bell and handed her gift to the person who answered the door. She was ready to leave when she heard footsteps coming toward her. It was Maharaji. He smiled at her and said, "You look like an airline stewardess."

"I am," she said, the first words she ever spoke to him. She left with a floating feeling.

A week later, she got a call from Maharaji's cook. "He's going to be traveling to Chicago," the woman told her. "Can you be on that flight? It would be nice if you could help."

Marolyn was not scheduled to work on that particular flight, but she managed to get a seat in the first-class cabin, a few rows in front of Maharaji. "When I turned around," she says, "he was smiling at me. He and his brother Raja Ji were sitting together, and a stewardess working on the flight asked me if I could help. I offered to take Maharaji and Raja Ji to the upstairs VIP lounge where it had been arranged for an Indian meal to be served. Maharaji made me feel very much at ease."

He ate a wonderful meal and engaged her in conversation about a favorite topic—airplanes. "He told me how long he'd been flying and how much he loved it," she says. "When the plane landed, he walked so quickly across the airport, I could barely keep up with him. I stayed for some hours in the O'Hare International crew lounge, where there are beds and showers, but I couldn't rest. I felt like I was out of my body. I used to carry a picture of him with me, and I felt that I truly loved him from a place deep inside. I didn't know him yet as the fun, engaging, enjoyable human being that he was. But I was in heaven after that encounter."

A week after the Chicago flight, Marolyn got a call from Ron Coletta, who was in Denver with Maharaji, acting as his personal assistant. He asked her if she could pick up a piece of sound equipment they had mistakenly left in Los Angeles and fly it to Denver, and someone would pick her up at the airport. She got the small piece of equipment and procured a free pass to fly from L.A. to Denver.

She arrived at the Denver residence to find Maharaji in a playful mood. He was watching an old movie, and he invited Marolyn to stay and watch it with him. "I looked into his eyes," she remembers, "which were so deep, and his smile was so real. I felt content."

When the movie was over, Bill Bach (Maharaji's flight instructor) and Ron Coletta approached Marolyn. "Maharaji was very impressed with you being a stewardess on his flight," Bill told her. "We would love for him to be able to fly an airplane so he can go wherever he wants to bring his message to people. If the position comes up, would you be his flight attendant?"

"That would be my dream come true," said Marolyn. But that same night, in a private conversation, Ron really threw her when he said, "You know, he really wants to get to know you."

Being close to Maharaji had been the furthest thing from her mind. He was her teacher and eight years her junior. This could not be happening. And yet, a part of her thought, "I've always known this, haven't I?"

"I have to think about it," she told Ron. And she did. In fact, she could think of nothing else. "He was not intellectual, but he was intelligent," she recalls, "and very clear and conscious. I was scared because as much as I was drawn to him, I didn't really know him as a person to hang out with, and who could I talk to about it? My parents knew I was a student of his, but they didn't know what to think of it. I had to go really deep inside to accept an offer I wanted but didn't know how to receive."

She considered that he was from India and she had been raised as a Southern California beach girl in San Diego. Cultures, families, and the future loomed heavy on her mind as she pondered the extraordinary possibilities.

When she got another call from Ron, this time inviting her to the house in Pacific Palisades, she accepted the invitation. Marolyn and Maharaji began to spend more and more time together, and it was clear that a relationship was developing. One evening, when they were walking on the beach, Marolyn told Maharaji, "I know that you are feeling these feelings now, but if you ever change your mind, I will understand. I will disappear and will not give you grief."

He looked at her and said, "When it comes to you, I've got my foot on the accelerator, it's floored, and there are no brakes." At that moment, any doubts she may have had vanished. She felt his commitment, his clarity, and it was real. As he slipped his jacket around her shoulders against the cool ocean breeze, she felt his care that would always be with her.

Marolyn's offer to disappear was a loving thing to do but was basically unnecessary, as the relationship was growing stronger with each passing day. And so was the family pressure, as Maharaji tried to hide the courtship from his mother and Bal Bhagwan Ji. On tour, Maharaji and Marolyn traveled separately.

John Hampton, one of the young Americans who heard Maharaji during his first visit in 1971, had become a helper around his house. He says, "I was Marolyn's bodyguard. To avoid attracting attention to the relationship between Maharaji and Marolyn, I grew a beard, she put on a wig, and we would go to events in disguise. We did that through the whole tour, and then Maharaji and Marolyn would get together privately for dinner when the event was over."

No matter where Maharaji was, however, his message of peace would be met with discontent by certain individuals. In August of 1973, he was in a ceremony, receiving the key to the city of Detroit, when someone in the audience threw a whipped-cream pie in his face. The man hit his mark, but in his usual gracious fashion, Maharaji wiped off his face and continued the ceremony. Afterward, a councilwoman gave him an official salute and a key to the city for his peace efforts all over the world. She ended her talk with a profuse apology for the pie incident.

Maharaji immediately accepted the apology by saying, "Love is the major thing between us all. I want to apologize to the person who threw that pie at me, because he might have been hurt by somebody, or maybe they tried to arrest him. I do not want him arrested, and I do not want him hurt, because if somebody doesn't understand something, you cannot blame him for that."

In just a short period of time, the organization had expanded until its international offices filled four stories of an office building in downtown Denver, and national headquarters were cropping up in various countries. Throughout all of this, Maharaji observed how many people got entangled in internal politics instead of focusing on the inspiration and the message, forgetting why they had come to him in the first place. In August he called together a group of students outside of the organization to form a council of people with whom he could discuss his ideas for moving forward, but the first meeting never took place.

Henry Jacobs, a student of Maharaji since he heard him speak at the University of Colorado in Boulder in the summer of 1971, says, "Maharaji was under too much stress. He was feeling strangled by the organization. And he got sick the day the council was supposed to meet. The meeting was cancelled. And he had good reason to feel this way. If anything, I believe he displayed amazing patience."

Bal Bhagwan Ji had insisted that Maharaji go to the hospital, and he had been too weak to argue, as he lay nearly unconscious for several days. Although there was never an official diagnosis of his illness, the press had a field day, proclaiming, "The guru has an ulcer." They were suggesting that he was more like a stressed businessman than the holy person he was projected to be. He *was* stressed, but little did the press or even his own students realize the pressures that the now sixteen-year-old was dealing with.

When Maharaji was discharged from the hospital, he left for Europe immediately. He gave his first talk in Paris, but French anarchists threw tomatoes and eggs at him. Without knowing who Maharaji was or the message he had to share, they were hell-bent on "giving the guru a hard time," and he was forced to leave the stage. In another disturbance soon afterward in Beethovenhalle in Bonn, Germany, Christians holding Bibles stood up in the balcony of the packed hall and shouted, "The Antichrist has come!"

In the house that had been arranged for him in Bonn, he found people sitting outside his room and even on the staircase. He had to walk over them each time he wanted to use the bathroom, so he called the organizer in Copenhagen who had told him about a lovely house there that he could stay in any time. "Is it ready?" he wanted to know. "I'll be there the day after tomorrow."

Maharaji took refuge in Copenhagen for ten days with Ron Coletta and Marolyn. He told only a select few that he was there so he could move around undisturbed. He enjoyed sailing between Denmark and Sweden, walking in the forest, playing chess with Ron, and spending quality time with Marolyn. This rest period was extremely therapeutic, as Marolyn and Maharaji got closer, and his health improved. The oceanfront villa his Danish friends had prepared for him had been refurbished by designer and nationally recognized ceramic artist Bodil Buch, a former member of a vanguard pop band who would later become a life-long friend of Maharaji and Ron Coletta's wife.

The house was extremely modern, with transparent, inflatable sofas and living room armchairs. Maharaji got such a kick out of the furniture that when he left, he deflated an armchair, folded it up, and put it in his suitcase.

By November, he was ready for the extensive media interest in his upcoming Millennium event in Houston, Texas, for 20,000 people. The entire family had jumped on the bandwagon, preparing for this grandiose gathering, where Maharaji would sit on a sixty-foot-tall stage, with a full orchestra creating background ambience.

On the evening of the event, the press was out in hordes. They had a tier reserved especially for them, but they ran into some trouble when they tried to get into the venue. The color of the passes had been changed at the last moment, and they were stopped at the door. It took quite a while to get things sorted out, and by the time the press took their seats, they were hopping mad. Not a good omen.

Here as everywhere, Maharaji spoke from his heart, presented his message, and surprised everyone with unexpected answers to people's questions. When asked if he was expecting future opposition, he said, "Well, if it's going to be strong, and if it is really peace, there had better be opposition. Because if there is no opposition, it means we are not actually establishing peace. There has to be a conflicting reaction. First there is night, and when the sun comes up, it's beautiful. If there was no night and the sun was always up, what would be the beauty of it?"

From early on, Maharaji had been keenly aware of his message's controversial nature and had demonstrated a readiness to face detractors to ensure that the purity of his message was not compromised. He would never waver from this. He trusted that people with a sincere interest in his message would see past any controversy and recognize the diamond that he was offering.

One journalist said that a perfect master could not have gotten an ulcer. Maharaji quickly set them straight by saying, "If an ulcer were the only sign of imperfection, then whoever doesn't have an ulcer must be perfect. Perfect is perfect. It has nothing to do with the body."

The three-day Millennium event received mixed reports in the press. Three thousand locals and about 20,000 of Maharaji's students made up the audience, but it was clear that the attempts to draw new people from all over the United States had failed miserably. Some said that the show lacked soul, while others called it one of Maharaji's great successes. In any case, the organization began to bleed financially when the "Western Peace Bomb" event was over.

On November 28, 1973, a few weeks after the event, Maharaji appeared on *The Merv Griffin Show* on television, where he fielded questions with great confidence. Merv asked him, "Are you rich?"

Maharaji smiled and replied, "I am absolutely rich, the richest man in the world probably. Because you don't have to be rich in money to be rich. You have to be rich in heart."

The year ended with his sixteenth birthday party in New York, the first time he did not go back to India to celebrate. He was in Los Angeles when calls began to come from Ira Woods, one of Maharaji's students from New York. Ira, who would later become one of the first Western instructors, had rented a ballroom in the Commodore Hotel in Manhattan for Maharaji's birthday event, and he had notified everyone. But there was one small detail—he still had to talk Maharaji into showing up. After being flooded with letters, flowers, and telegrams, Maharaji gave in and went to New York to attend the celebration. His family came as well.

Everyone agreed that it was a fabulous party, at which several students dressed up in costumes and did funny skits for the sixteen-year-old. In one skit, Bob Mishler announced he had found a way to double propagation. He put Charan Anand in a magician's box and pretended to saw him in two, and no one laughed harder than Maharaji. In Boston, Massachusetts, someone once asked him why he was so playful when his message was a serious one. "People think that when a guru comes," Maharaji explained, "he is going to be as serious as a stone. But if someone who has found happiness does not smile and laugh, then who will be happy?"

When the party broke up in the early hours of the morning, Maharaji and Raja Ji secretly flew back to Los Angeles on an early morning flight. By the time Bal Bhagwan Ji and Mataji woke up, Maharaji was halfway to L.A., and Mataji was upset, as usual. Her world was coming apart at the seams. Raja Ji was about to marry a Western woman named Claudia, whom he had met while traveling in Germany, and Maharaji was courting Marolyn.

Ron Coletta recalls, "It was clear that Maharaji and Raja Ji were Westernizing, and Mataji was an ultra-orthodox, old-guard Hindu lady with clear ethnic and religious biases. When her sons started to break away, the friction escalated. The fact that Maharaji and Marolyn were getting close was the coup de grâce, since marriage outside of Hindu tradition was blasphemy to Mataji, plain and simple. At the same time, Bal Bhagwan Ji, feeling jealous, believed that as the eldest, he should have been the one to succeed his father and master."

Bal Bhagwan Ji apparently confused transmission of family assets, which in India routinely happens on the basis of primogeniture, with the succession from master to student, which happens on the basis of merit. Maharaji became the successor, not because he was a son of Shri Maharaji, but because he was, in Shri Maharaji's eyes, the most worthy person to become the successor, and he was recognized as such by the students gathered to mourn Shri Maharaji's passing.

The family had successfully coerced Maharaji into complying with their wishes when he was a child, but now, at sixteen, he was standing on his own two feet, brimming with clarity and self-confidence and able to make his own decisions. "Tensions were building," Ron says. "Mataji was devastated at how her family was turning out. Bal Bhagwan Ji, her closest ally, was bitter; Bhole Ji had become a kind of mama's boy; Raja Ji was getting married to a Westerner; and Maharaji was falling in love with Marolyn."

The events of 1974, which could have been a time of celebration for Mataji as two of her sons had fallen in love, would instead mark the final split in the family.

That love that we all talk about, that we all are looking for, can really come. That peace, our dream, can come true. And the truth is that all these things that we have been dreaming of ever since this human race came, we can get it all. Our dreams can really be true. It's very, very possible.

MAHARAJI
Denver, Colorado, May 4, 1974

We are all looking for some kind of satisfaction.
There are different kinds of satisfaction in this
world. But there is one satisfaction that we
all are looking for. And that is peace.
And remember that peace is not outside.
Peace is inside.

MARAJI,
BOSTON, MASSACHUSETTS,
FEBRUARY 27, 1974

I Do

In Denver in April 1974, Maharaji applied to become an emancipated minor, because he and Marolyn were now engaged, and he knew his mother would not condone his marriage at sixteen (or any other age, considering the American wife he had chosen). With his emancipation, he could obtain a legal marriage license without his mother's signature. After spending about forty-five minutes with a judge, he was granted his request.

His talks in the months leading up to his marriage were mainly aimed at his current students, encouraging them to practice the techniques of Knowledge. In early May in Denver, he said, "There are three ways to understand things. If somebody whom you respect tells you something, you'll say, 'Since you are saying it, I'll believe it.' The second way is, 'This is what my concept is, so I believe it.' But the third way is a very independent way called 'seeing is believing.' In this way, you feel and you realize practically, without anybody's concept. And this is what I tell each of you to do."

He was demonstrating the third way as he stood on his own two feet, doing what he felt was right for him. Maharaji, an innovator, flowed with what was happening, while his elder brother and his mother believed staunchly in "the Indian way."

Raja Ji was the first to marry, and the family feud bomb ignited. The family had all been living together in Pacific Palisades, but Mataji became so upset that Maharaji asked her and Bal Bhagwan Ji to move. So both headed back to India in early 1974. Linda Bach, who was cooking for Maharaji at the time, recalls, "He pulled us all in really close at that time, and we were a tight little circle. When he would come to Denver, a handful of us would watch Indian movies with him in the basement of the house each night, and I felt like his sister. He needed us because he was only a teenager and he was losing his blood family."

In a sense, this was a Romeo and Juliet story, as Indian sources say that Mataji had already arranged for her four sons to marry the four daughters of a prominent Indian family of her own Garwhal tribe. Her arrangements were clearly born of an ambition to create a kind of dynasty, and the two elder brothers eventually married two of the chosen daughters. Bal Bhagwan Ji's wife would later become a member of the state government, but Mataji's youngest sons refused to fall in line with Indian tradition and with her ambitions. This was unheard of in a traditional Hindu family.

In the midst of so much turmoil, however, Maharaji stayed focused on moving forward, as he got his driver's license and received permanent U.S. residency. Now he could live and work legally in the United States, even though he was not yet a U.S. citizen.

In early spring, just when it seemed that things around him were calming down, he received a letter from the organization's officers claiming that because he was a minor from India and they were more familiar with Western ways than he was, they would take care of the management, and he needn't come to Denver headquarters at all.

The stunning implications of this letter got more bizarre when, a few weeks later, they sent a follow-up letter acknowledging their mistake. They stated that, although they still felt there were legal things he didn't understand, they needed his inspiration, help, and kindness. Now they were urging him to come and help them.

Maharaji provided some recentering clarity in the midst of their turmoil when he said, "I understand that many of you don't think the organization is running properly," he told them. "But peace is not going to come out of the organization. You have to realize that peace is inside you, not inside the organization. You don't go to a desk at headquarters and say, 'Can I have some peace, please?' Peace is inside of you. Do you understand?"

He met with the officers, as they had requested, and remarks from his public talks during that period demonstrate his ability to rise above criticism and disapproval. He said, "People have confusion, and they want me to help them solve it. But I can give you a thousand answers, and you will never be satisfied. I have given you the answer to everything, and that is Knowledge. If you cannot get your answer from that, forget it. You will always be confused."

⌒

When Marolyn went back home to San Diego to tell her parents about her intention to marry Maharaji, they both saw how happy she looked. But her father, a Navy man, was still somewhat reluctant. He said something like, "Is this another one of those cotton-pickin' gurus?"

But Marolyn felt as if her knight in shining armor had swooped down and asked her to climb on his horse. Not that she was naive. She understood the differences between them and that many people would think she was making a mistake. "But," Marolyn said, "I also knew that he had become a man at eight years old when his father died, and he had already shouldered enormous responsibilities."

When Maharaji heard about Marolyn's father's reticence, he invited her parents to Denver to meet him in person, where he felt he could make them comfortable. He personally picked them up at the airport and drove them to his residence for a backyard garden party. Happily, Marolyn's father and Maharaji hit it off, and the older man told his daughter later that evening, "I have to tell you, he is something else. I know what I said before, and now I have to eat crow. I didn't know what I was talking about. You have found a fine man, and I'm happy for you." This, coming from a strict military man who rarely admitted being wrong, was a welcome surprise.

The date was set, and all were delighted that the marriage would go forward—that is, all except Mataji and Bal Bhagwan Ji, who refused to accept it. When Mataji realized there was nothing she could do to stop the marriage, she gave Maharaji an ultimatum: "If you do this," she said, "if you choose her, I will renounce you as my son."

"Then I don't have a mother anymore," Maharaji said. His commitment was absolute and so was hers.

That March, Marolyn was radiant, with fresh flowers in her hair at her wedding shower at the shared home of Tim and Sally Gallwey and Lynn and Edd Hanzelik. (Edd later would become Maharaji's personal physician). Several weeks before the official wedding in May, Maharaji and Marolyn, accompanied by Ron Coletta, had a private vow ceremony in the Pacific Palisades. "I felt that I was out of my league," she says now, "but no matter what difficulties arose, it always felt divinely arranged, never an accident."

On May 20, 1974, in Gennessee Mountain, Colorado, Marolyn and Maharaji arrived at the Rockland Community Church, a small glass-and-timber chapel in the Denver mountains adjacent to a serene lake. Milky, Ron, Raja Ji and Claudia, Mahabir, newlywed couples Gary and Donna Girard and Bob and Eileen Mishler, and other close friends attended the wedding. Although Milky was given strict instructions not to cry, he wept with joy throughout the entire ceremony, as did many other witnesses.

Maharaji's marriage to Marolyn was one of the most life-changing events for him. At the wedding, in keeping with Indian tradition, he gave his new wife a new name—Durga Ji, an Indian goddess seen as the embodiment of feminine and creative energy.

When they got into their car after the ceremony, the words "JUST MARRIED" were scrawled in soap on the rear window, and tin cans attached to the back bumper clanged together as they drove away. A joyful reception followed at the residence, and the wedding immediately made international news.

When news of the wedding reached Mataji in Dehradun, witnesses report that she rushed downstairs and dramatically took down all of Maharaji's pictures. Raja Ji says, "I think someone with some education could have given our mother a little perspective, because this was not the end of the world. She could have just accepted it, but I think Bal Bhagwan Ji helped turn her against Maharaji to gain the influence he wanted so badly."

Maharaji says, "They said that I could take the West for my work, but the East was no longer my territory, that I was to be just a figurehead, like the emblem on a Mercedes. 'Just shine,' they told me. 'Watch out for the bugs, and don't smile too big.' But the Eastern instructors were my responsibility, and I took charge."

Now the family was divided into two camps—with Raja Ji; Didiji and her husband, Yashwant Negi; and her mother, Older Mataji, siding with Maharaji. "Why did you support him to become the master, when it was my right as the eldest son?" Bal Bhagwan Ji would shout at Didiji when she came to visit in Dehradun.

Raja Ji, who received the first blow from Mataji when he married Claudia, said, "It was quite early on when Maharaji did not want anybody to manage him. He was always perfectly capable of managing himself."

❧

During the first days of July, over 8,000 European students celebrated with Maharaji in the Forum in Copenhagen at an event that marked Marolyn's first public appearance. Maharaji appeared exceptionally happy, especially when he and Marolyn came out on the balcony to listen to a group of Spaniards who sang late-night serenades from the street. Afterward, Marolyn invited the Spanish troubadours into the house by the oceanfront and served tea and cookies.

Meanwhile, friends of Maharaji were actively searching for a bigger home for him and his wife and their future family. One day, Bill Bach and John Hampton passed a beautiful little house in Malibu with a For Sale sign out front. After he toured through the house on the hill, which had a view of the ocean, Maharaji said he would be happy to live there. Now he had truly established himself in the West.

If you go into that beauty from where the source of all beauty is, you can't even imagine how beautiful it is. Within you is the source of that beauty. I can't tell you how blissful it will be, how beautiful it will be. It's completely unimaginable.

MAHARAJI
Kansas City, Missouri,
February 21, 1974

Knowledge doesn't have anything to do with India or America. It doesn't have anything to do with this world, as a matter of fact. But it is for us. It's for everyone.

MARAHAJI,
HAMBURG, GERMANY,
MAY 26, 1976

Clarification

Back in India, Mataji and her oldest son were securing most of the Indian properties that were owned by the organization of which Mataji was the patron. They spread the word that Maharaji's Western lifestyle disqualified him from being the master. Now, Bal Bhagwan Ji could have what he regarded as his rightful inheritance as the eldest son.

To make matters worse, some time after the marriage, Bal Bhagwan Ji was in Los Angeles. While Maharaji and Marolyn were out of town, someone broke into the house in Pacific Palisades and stole Marolyn's passport and a photo of the two newlyweds embracing and kissing, which was on a little bedside table. Shortly after that in India, Bal Bhagwan Ji had the stolen photo printed on the cover of a popular Indian magazine.

Kissing publicly was taboo in India, even between husband and wife. The caption, SHOCKING PICTURE OF BALYOGESHWAR, was like salt on a wound as the family spread rumors that Maharaji was spending time with white women. They never mentioned that he and Durga Ji were married, and someone leaked a rumor to Indian journalists that Maharaji was abandoning his father's mission and opening a Laundromat in Los Angeles.

"It was a sweet photograph," says Marolyn, "that Maharaji's assistant had taken. We were in an embrace, fully clothed in our home, but this marriage was too much for his mother ever to accept."

One can only imagine how that must have affected seventeen-year-old Maharaji, whose family previously had held him in great esteem. Now they were not only deserting him, but also slandering him. He was tempted to go to India to dispel the rumors, but he stayed by his wife's side when they discovered she was pregnant. Marolyn remembers, "We were both very, very pleased when we knew that we were expecting our first child. I was into natural childbirth, and Maharaji was my birthing partner."

Judy Osborne, a student of Maharaji's from England, was their midwife and would be the children's nanny for many years before she became a Knowledge instructor. "He was seventeen," she said, "and he had great maturity and a deep understanding about life. Marolyn and Maharaji were attending birthing classes and were planning for Maharaji to be there for the birth. From what Maharaji said, I became aware that in India it would have been highly unusual, maybe even taboo, for a father to be present during labor. It struck me how difficult it must be for Maharaji to be living in a culture that was so different from the one in which he was born and raised."

During the birth, Judy was impressed with how focused and conscious Maharaji was, how he was there for Marolyn, how seriously he took his role as birthing coach and father, timing the contractions with his stopwatch. "He was there with the midwife during my whole twelve hours of labor," says Marolyn. "He held our newborn baby on his chest, because we knew that skin-to-skin contact is a beautiful way for the father to bond with his newborn baby."

A few weeks later, Maharaji told his friends and students, "On March 9, 1975, Premlata's birth took place. *Premlata* means 'the vine of love.' *Prem* is 'love.' It was such an incredible experience when she took her first breath—such an intense feeling, because something was born; it was just there. And then all of a sudden, the first cry was 'Waaah,' and that was it. To the doctors, waaah was just waaah. They go through it a thousand times. But to me, it was something so beautiful. It just went *mmmpoo* into the body, and it was all there." In time, Premlata became known familiarly as Wadi.

In April, however, a month after his daughter was born, his domestic happiness was interrupted when Marolyn and Wadi accompanied Maharaji to India so he could see his students. They missed him badly, since he had not seen them for two years.

On April 13, 1975, shortly after his arrival, Maharaji gave a press conference in Lucknow, where a reporter asked, "How could a family reconciliation be brought about?"

He answered, "Mataji and Bal Bhagwan Ji are trying to harm me, but why should we blame them? If I keep their deceit in my mind, that will not bring a solution."

When a reporter asked if he intended to see his mother, he answered, "I don't know. I came with the intention to clarify the situation here in India, and my family needs to understand my purpose."

He explained that previously they had supported him, but although he had remained the same, suddenly they were changing their opinions of him and his work. "I am going to stick to my objective no matter what," he said. "One day, the whole world will be able to see beyond the curtains that people are trying to place there today. They will say this person is trying to do something in the world. And they will understand."

Whatever occurred, Maharaji simply rose to the occasion, took the high road, and kept his dignity.

The press conference in Lucknow was to be followed by an event, but Bal Bhagwan Ji's supporters had told the authorities that Maharaji was plotting to instigate riots. As a result, Maharaji had to obtain permission from the Indian military to see his students.

He asked for a short time with his students, just to assure them he was still there for them in every way. In a bizarre turn of events, Maharaji had to show up for his talk in a military Jeep with a police escort, speaking for all of five minutes, just enough time to look into his students' eyes and share a few words from his heart. He promised to come back to do an event, but he never spoke negatively about his family. In the face of such blatant opposition, his ability to maintain his composure and not lash out was amazing.

Shortly afterward, Maharaji and Marolyn had an Indian wedding ceremony. Marolyn says, "Maharaji wanted to share our happiness with his students in India. It was boiling hot in Bihar in the Jhumri Talaiya ashram, so hot you couldn't go outside in the daytime, and I had a one-month-old baby. We were on the run, since we heard that Bal Bhagwan Ji was threatening Maharaji's life, and we often left in the night to get to the next place." Whether in genuine danger or not, they weren't taking any chances. "We had to wait until ten p.m. for our wedding ceremony, but it was very beautiful, and we stayed in the ashram there for some days."

Thousands of people showed up to celebrate the marriage and to partake in the feast. Instead of the traditional elephant ride (Maharaji had no fondness for riding on elephants), they decorated a VW microbus like an elephant, and Maharaji and Marolyn rode in a saddle on top while everyone pushed it around. The Indians were elated and inspired, which was exactly what Maharaji had hoped for.

Since the harassment prevented Maharaji from openly seeing his students, he and his Indian assistants devised a variety of secret ways for his students to see him. Greeting lines were set up at roundabouts in Delhi in the middle of the night, where 500 to 600 people would show up for a private moment with Maharaji, who sat in his Jeep.

Pressure continued to mount until Maharaji was about to leave, and his departure was postponed by a lawsuit instigated by his brother. Maharaji filed a counterclaim against Bal Bhagwan

Ji. But after listening to false accusations for nearly an hour in a private talk with the judge, Maharaji withdrew his counterclaim and asked for the proceedings to be stopped immediately, out of respect for his late father. The judge responded positively. After being shamed by the judge for disrespecting his father's name, Bal Bhagwan Ji withdrew his claim as well, and Maharaji left India, not to return for years to come.

⌀—

By the time Maharaji had his Indian wedding ceremony, his message of peace had spread internationally from its humble Indian beginnings. In the six years since the first five Westerners had met Maharaji in 1969, he and his students had brought his message to fifty-eight countries on six continents. Interest was running high in places where instructors had been spending time but where Maharaji had never visited. The problem was that despite their best intentions, they were Indians and had no prior experience with the cultures they encountered in Europe, Africa, and the Americas.

The reliance on Indian instructors was about to change in July 1975, when Maharaji named four non-Indian students as instructors. For the first time, Knowledge would be taught by people who were not steeped in Indian culture. Over the next five years, Maharaji appointed more than eighty non-Indian instructors from twenty countries on five continents, speaking at least nine languages between them.

⌀—

Political unrest in South America was at its peak when Francisco Arce, a Chilean student of Maharaji's who had been working in Argentina, arrived back in Chile in June 1973, during the time of the democratically elected government of Salvador Allende. He and some others put ads in newspapers with a picture of Maharaji as a child, with a caption that said, GURU BRINGS PEACE.

Nancy Izak, who has been active in spreading Maharaji's message in Chile since then, recalls, "I was fifteen, and I went to the first meeting in my school uniform. The next day, a hundred people received Knowledge, and meetings took place daily in downtown Santiago. My sister Mónica, who had heard about Maharaji in New York, turned her house in Santiago into a center, which eventually was transferred to a church basement where close to a thousand people would come daily."

However, three months later on September 11, 1973, Augusto Pinochet took over the country in a military coup. Nancy recalls, "For two weeks we lived in chaos. Gatherings of more than just a few people were forbidden, so we met clandestinely in private houses up to 1985. People suspected of Communist or leftist sympathies were being arrested, and thousands were suddenly disappearing." In this environment of fear and violence, the swiftly growing group of young people who had discovered Maharaji would meet at people's houses, careful to be back home before curfew.

In February 1974, Francisco Arce was arrested on suspicion of being a Communist. He was then interrogated, tortured, and brought to Tejas Verdes, a concentration camp in northern Chile. The police thought that he was trying to turn the organization supporting Maharaji's work into a holdout for Communist activism. In prison, he shared a cell with a famous Spanish playwright, Fermín Cabal, who would later include Francisco in a book. Finally, the government realized Francisco had Canadian citizenship as well as Chilean, and they had to release him. Never hinting to anyone that he had been tortured, Francisco was an instructor for many years, traveling to Europe and Latin America until he passed away in Canada in 1995.

In Argentina, a junta took power in 1973 that would mark the onset of the same kind of political turmoil. Marta Alemann, a nineteen-year-old woman, was living in a local center when she heard machine-gun fire outside. In the next few days, she and her family moved to the United States, and thirty-three years later, she lives near Los Angeles and still enjoys practicing Knowledge. "What a difference it has made in my life," Marta says. "It has made me so strong that living in a foreign country and raising two boys was not that difficult. Today, there are ups and downs in my external life, but inside, I feel like the luckiest person alive."

In July 1975, Maharaji spoke at a three-day gathering in Caracas, Venezuela, a politically stable country in a region of revolutions, military coups, strikes, and demonstrations. Two thousand South Americans attended the event where Maharaji said, "We come into this world, and the purpose of it has to be recognized. We have to find out why we are here and what is the main thing that really drives us. When we are one with that, that is when the true happiness, the true peace, comes to us."

On February 22, 1976, Maharaji was invited to address members of the U.S. Congress in Washington, D.C., at the Mayflower Hotel to commemorate the United States bicentennial. "As America enters its third century," he said, "many frontiers of land, space, science, and technology have already been crossed. And yet, with endless frontiers of human experience ahead, let us pray that the pioneering spirit that has allowed this nation to excel will not falter. As you go forward, continue to be blessed with the broad vision, temperance, and wisdom to allow America to lead civilization into a New Age, as the befitting sequel to the first nation of the New World."

Strom Thurmond, the late senator from South Carolina, asked that this address be made a permanent part of the Congressional Record. And so it was.

Happiness is not something that you can just simulate. Happiness is happiness. You cannot create an environment, sit in the middle of it, and say, "Yes, I'm extremely happy." But people try to do that. There aren't very many people who have enough courage to stand up and say, "Wait a minute, these things aren't really making me happy. I'm just fooling myself." But if we want satisfaction, it all begins right from that point.

MARAHAJI,
STOCKHOLM, SWEDEN,
MAY 30, 1976

The Umbrella of Knowledge

Maharaji's summer tour in 1976 was colored by his attempt to heal the rift between himself and the organization. At many events, he had given Bob Mishler a place of honor and asked him to speak first. But by July, the organizers' disrespect toward Maharaji had escalated to a new level. A core group of the international organizers were suggesting that Maharaji be nothing more than a figurehead and that his message be spread through the instructors only.

During that period, Maharaji invited Bob Mishler and his wife, Eileen, to his residence in Malibu, where he asked Eileen, "Does he still practice Knowledge?"

"He says he does it constantly," said Eileen.

"But does he actually sit down and practice?" he asked.

"No," was her unequivocal answer.

It was inevitable, then, that organization power plays would escalate. While Maharaji worked relentlessly to spread the word among his students that the practice of Knowledge was the key to realizing what he offered, some of the main organizers had become so caught up in their work that they abandoned this practice in their personal lives. It was a summer of confusion as the organizers were pushing aside the one to whom they had originally come to for guidance.

Marolyn, pregnant for the second time, called Judy Osborne in Denver and asked her to come to Malibu once again as her midwife. Judy says, "I was happy and touched to be asked to go to

Malibu again. After being in the thick of things in Denver, Maharaji and Marolyn's home in Malibu felt like a haven for me."

At the time, Judy was very close to Bob Mishler and Eileen, as they had lived in the same house since 1975. She describes Bob as "a warm and charismatic person" who "cared about people." However, he had his own vision of how Maharaji could best help the world. According to Judy, Bob saw Maharaji as a "humanitarian world leader," a phrase she heard him begin using in 1976. "Maharaji, on the other hand," Judy says, "doesn't describe himself as a world leader. He has a deep recognition of the potential of the human heart and the experience of fulfillment that it brings, and he offers a way for a person to be able to connect with the experience within themselves. The vision he expresses is to help individuals, one person at a time."

In the spring of 1976, Judy saw the difference in these two visions rise to the surface in confrontation. Eileen expressed concern to her on several occasions because Bob had stopped practicing the techniques that Maharaji taught. She felt that if Bob would practice and experience Knowledge for himself, he would better understand and value Maharaji's role. Judy saw Eileen get caught in the middle, loving Bob very much but disagreeing with him on this issue and trying to help resolve the conflict that it created between Maharaji and Bob.

By August of 1976, Bob had severed his ties with Maharaji and had become hostile, at times making bitter statements about him. This was not the case for Eileen. She remained close to Maharaji and his family for over a year and then eventually drifted away. Judy lost touch with her, and the next thing she heard was that Bob and Eileen had died in a tragic helicopter accident in 1979.

In the meantime, in June 1976, Maharaji nearly drowned in a boating accident at Riva del Garda in northern Italy. "I was in a small Zodiac," he says, "a little rubber boat, and I was going really fast. I had insisted on taking the boat out by myself, and when I got to the middle of the lake, the rope was hanging in the water, and I did a stupid thing. I got up to grab the rope and put it back in the boat to make it go faster, when the boat went *boom!* It threw me out. All of a sudden, I was in the water and the boat was circling me like a shark, on its own steam. I was far from land, the boat was going full tilt, and the propeller was in the water, turning. I made a dash for the boat, grabbed it, and started going round and round in circles with it. I was getting sick, and the whole world was turning."

A boat full of friends who had been watching helplessly from the shore finally rode up to help Maharaji as he flailed in the water without a life vest. "I believed I would die that day," Maharaji recalls, "but here I am." He got stitches in his foot where the propeller cut him, but he recovered completely.

With the birth of his second child, Hans, on September 17, 1976, Maharaji began to travel without his family. Long periods of separation marked this era, which began with a conference in Peru and then Swaziland during November. In Mendoza, Argentina, he said, "There have already been so many wars, and people are still ready to fight another. Why? They are human beings, just like you and me. But they are missing that true understanding, that true meaning of life. And not just one person or one leader; it's everybody in this world! If everybody understood the aim of their life, they would go towards that and not towards the crazy things that man is going towards."

In Frankfurt, he said, "In our own heart we have to make the decision. We have all the craziness, but we have the greatest love to experience now in this lifetime. Who makes the decision for us? I would not make that decision for you. I made the decision for myself a long, long time ago when I was very, very little. Now I have it, and believe me, I don't regret my decision. It is beautiful. But it is a decision that I want to experience, I want to know, I want to realize. That's the decision you have to make."

ᗡ

In Atlantic City on December 20, 1976, Maharaji reiterated the importance of focusing on the experience within, and he reminded his students how much his message could help people, if it could only reach them. "I really wish we could all just come together and beat the great drums. I have this dream, not an idea or an idealism, but the aim of my life. I want to beat these drums so hard it might break down the barriers that people have placed between themselves and the possibility of peace in this world."

He explained to everyone that he could provide guidance and inspiration to people and that the organization had to leave him free to do so. He assured them that while organizations could support his effort, they could not do it for him.

Stressing the simplicity of his message, he began training additional Western instructors. As a result, in 1977, many of his students began reconnecting with their original fervor for practicing Knowledge.

Training programs for instructors occurred on seven occasions throughout 1977, and Maharaji spoke over thirty times at multiday events in a dozen cities in the United States and Europe, including events for 4,500 in Denver, 6,500 in Miami, and 10,500 in London. In Marbella, Spain, he said, "When you find the true love, the true harmony that's within all of us, it doesn't matter who you are. It doesn't matter if you are black or white, Muslim or Hindu, Christian or Buddhist, short or tall, skinny or fat. It doesn't matter who you are or where you come from. The love that doesn't vary or go up and down is always there."

In Oregon he stated, "What is the purpose of this life? Why has somebody taken so much time creating us, putting us on this earth, making this earth suitable for us to live in? I am here to show the secret through which you can go inside and be what you are and not be subject to what anyone else tells you that you are. This is what makes the difference between being a king or a beggar inside, an emperor or a prisoner. The purpose of our life is to experience that infinite love, experience that always-smiling smile within. It is possible. It's completely up to us."

The year 1977 climaxed with a five-day international event for 14,500 people that started on November 8 in Rome's Palazzo dello Sport arena. The circular dome, originally built for the Olympics' boxing matches in 1960, elegantly framed the celebration of life at which Maharaji said, "Peace—that's what man is looking for. For whatever man is trying to do, whatever he thinks he is trying to accomplish, he's really only trying to accomplish one thing: peace. That's the only thing that hasn't been accomplished yet. War has been accomplished, total destruction has been accomplished, a lot of corruption has been accomplished, a population explosion has been accomplished. Going to the moon, orbiting Mars has been accomplished. The one thing that really hasn't been accomplished is peace."

On his twentieth birthday, a telephone conference was arranged through which he addressed thousands of his students worldwide. This teleconference marked the beginning of the technological progress that would help promote his message on a much broader scale. "I got up this morning," Maharaji said, "and Marolyn asked me how it felt to be twenty. It doesn't feel like anything to be twenty. What I feel is just a lot more grace than when I was sixteen. It is a lot more incredible."

As a child, Maharaji knew his father often slept on benches in railway stations with barely enough to eat as he traveled to spread his message. From a young age, he had realized that poverty was not conducive to taking a message of peace to the world. He witnessed how difficult it had been for his father to take his message farther than northern India because he lacked the resources to travel and to put on events beyond this limited geographical area. Therefore, as Maharaji's students began building a base of resources and developing a global infrastructure, he was pleased that he would soon be able to bring his message to people and lands he had never reached before.

While the organization developed resources to hold events and publish materials to present the message, Maharaji started working to create financial security for himself and his family. To him, one thing was clear: there had never been a charge for Knowledge, nor would there ever be. He had never charged for his appearances, and he never would. Furthermore, neither he nor his family had ever benefited from the sale of materials: from the very start, he had granted the organizations royalty-free copyright licenses to make materials from his addresses. His personal financial independence would allow him to provide for himself and his family with dignity, while the organizations would cover the costs of creating materials, setting up events, and conducting all activities necessary for furthering his message of peace. But how would he do this?

When he first started out, hundreds of individuals, grateful for what he had shown them, helped him with his personal needs, such as buying him clothes and food, so he could dedicate his time to spreading his message. Also, since he had arrived in the U.S. at the age of thirteen, he was provided support by the organization in the U.S. in keeping with his guest status until he became an emancipated minor capable of pursuing his own interests privately. This support included housing, transportation to and from events, and other relevant expenses.

In 1977, the organization was audited, and the U.S. Internal Revenue Service found these practices to be in full compliance with the regulations governing charities. At the same time, personal gifts of appreciation started coming not just from people but from businesses his students had founded that were doing well. He received stock shares in corporations as gifts, which later generated significant dividends for him. Some of these companies were sold, generating substantial windfalls, and his profits were reinvested smartly. One particular company that developed large-scale software applications for government contractors went public, generating considerable wealth for Maharaji and his family. In this way, he became financially independent and able to provide for his family while also focusing on bringing his message of peace to people around the world.

Maharaji has never had any qualms about enjoying an affluent lifestyle and has made it clear that neither poverty nor wealth bring happiness. Throughout the years, his investments have allowed him and his family to enjoy a privileged lifestyle for which he never has to ask for or accept any compensation from the organizations furthering his message. On several occasions throughout the years, detractors have managed to prompt inquiries into the finances of Maharaji and of the organizations that support his efforts. Each time, Maharaji and the organizations have been found to be in good compliance with the various regulations.

～

Maharaji and Marolyn's third child, Dayalata (Daya), was born on June 26, 1978. Judy Osborne slept in a room close to them so she could help at night if the children woke up. She remembers how very much in love Maharaji and Marolyn were and how much Maharaji loved his family. "The feeling amongst them was amazingly harmonious," she says.

Their peaceful lifestyle was disturbed the following October, however, when a devastating brush fire occurred in Malibu that burned the homes on either side of theirs to the ground. Marolyn remembers that Maharaji kept saying, "Let's go."

She said, "Oh, I think we're okay," but when she saw the fire coming over the hill, she said, "Let's go now."

"I grabbed the diaper bag," Marolyn remembers. "We had to drive on Pacific Coast Highway going north towards Ventura where Bill and Linda Bach were living with their daughter. The fire had already jumped Pacific Coast Highway. It was heading for the ocean, and we saw twelve or fourteen homes on fire along the Encinal Canyon bluffs. I turned around to see a police car behind us, stopping all the traffic after our car had passed.

"We were driving through fire that was burning on both sides of the road. My thought was, 'Oh, my God. This is it. Is this how we will go? Maharaji, me, our three babies, our three children.' I didn't want the children to see it, so I told Wadi and Hansi to get down on the floor, and I held their heads down gently. Daya was only a few months old. It took a few minutes to get through the black and red fire before we cleared it."

Judy Osborne recalls Maharaji asking the staff to leave immediately. "He didn't want any heroics," she comments, "even though this was his home and everything that he had was in there." His concern was for their safety. "The fire came but it blew right over the house," she remembers. "All the trees were burned, and so were the grass, the shrubs, and the hills around there. And then there was the soot. Everything in the house was filthy from soot."

Maharaji and his family stayed with his brother, Raja Ji, for a while, and then within a few months, they relocated to Miami while the Malibu house was being repaired.

⌒

As Maharaji's touring grew, so did his need to have access to a plane. With travel independence, he could reach more people in more locations in less time.

By 1976, the organization was chartering various aircraft, but each had its own set of problems. When the family and event organizers were traveling to Denver from Los Angeles on a chartered Falcon 20 jet, a cabin depressurization incident occurred shortly after takeoff. John Miller, a student traveling with Maharaji at the time, says, "About ten minutes into the flight, the plane suddenly veered to the right and descended rapidly. I thought we were going to crash when the oxygen masks deployed. Premlata was asleep in my lap. I put her mask on first, contrary to what you are told to do, and I passed out for about thirty seconds. When I came to, we had descended below 15,000 feet. A pressure valve had blown in the rear of the plane. When we landed safely, the engineers said they could get it fixed in about three hours, but there was no way we were getting back on that plane."

Airplane trouble continued throughout the year. In March 1977, a Gulfstream II was leased for an extensive tour through Europe. Jeffrey Pease (now a jet captain and one of the people who had lived in the Pacific Palisades house) and John Miller were on board. Both recalled a five-hour delay during a scheduled fuel stop at Shannon Airport, Ireland, because of a cracked wheel. And then, in November of the same year, a BAC 1-11 twin-engine jet, chartered for a trip to Rome, had a malfunction with the autopilot system, causing Maharaji and family to fly commercially instead. When the same charter company flew a replacement BAC 1-11 to Rome to bring Maharaji and his family back to L.A., the aircraft had an engine failure on takeoff due to a failed high-pressure fuel pump.

Perhaps the deciding factor in purchasing a plane for Maharaji's travels was an incident in 1979 aboard a chartered Convair 880 bound for Europe. According to John Miller, during the flight, Maharaji was surprised to see the pilots' lack of concern when they told him that the plane might not be able to reach London with the required minimum fuel reserves, and then flew on to London anyway.

In each of these situations, everyone arrived safely at their destinations, but Maharaji vowed from then on to do what was necessary to maintain and fly an aircraft at much higher standards than was possible with leased and chartered planes.

In the spring of 1979, an old Boeing 707 was acquired that had a long enough range to accommodate his extensive travels and enough space for his family and the people helping with his tours. The aircraft underwent extensive renovations in Miami before becoming operational in 1980. And Maharaji was taking the appropriate steps to secure a license that would allow him to operate such a powerful aircraft.

∽

After Maharaji's dramatic but successful South American tour in the beginning of 1976, political conditions worsened on that continent. He did not go back there for four years, and his students experienced all kinds of persecution. In 1978, the center in La Plata, Argentina, was suspected of subversion against the military rulers. The federal police placed some of their "best" men to watch the nine students who lived there. Meetings were banned, so every night they would go out clandestinely to attend gatherings in private homes while one person stayed back to protect the house.

Laura Salvide, a twenty-four-year-old student who lived in the center, was alone one night when she heard glass shatter. Barefoot and in her short nightgown, she slowly opened the door without turning the light on and felt a cold gun on her forehead. Nine policemen stood armed in front of her. "Hood her!" one of them shouted. "We're taking her with us!"

She knew that rape and torture might be close at hand. They ordered her to lie down on the floor, and she prayed. When she got up with a little bit of calm, she no longer saw these people as monsters, but rather as confused men oblivious to the purpose of life. She felt some compassion toward them and began to speak from her heart about what Maharaji had shown her. Then she offered them some food, which they eagerly accepted.

Laura went to the kitchen. A policeman followed her, showing her his rifle, which was full of nail marks, one for each person he had killed. "When I enter a place, I first commit rape, then I kill, then I figure out if they were guilty or innocent," he said.

At that moment, a very corpulent man who boasted the nom de guerre El Oso came into the kitchen. The policeman asked him, "Isn't it true that we do not deserve to be saved?"

El Oso responded, "You're right. We are going straight to hell, and there is no pardon for us." But in the next moment, he asked for a broom and swept up the glass he had broken. Then he turned to Laura and said, "Convince me."

She started talking to him. When the other students came back, they were all taken to police headquarters. Pictures and written materials were confiscated. The next morning, though, it seemed that El Oso had been touched by what he experienced the day before. He set up a room in the police headquarters and asked the students to come in and talk to his colleagues. "It was amazing to see other policemen coming in and sitting down to listen," recalls Laura. "He even put a picture of Maharaji on his desk."

Time passed, and one day El Oso showed up at the center again. He had taken a leave from the police force because he "could not touch, not even look at a weapon any longer." He started preparing for Knowledge, and in 1979, he traveled to Kissimmee, Florida, to see Maharaji. "I felt so lucky when I met him there," says El Oso. Laura remembers that tears were rolling down his face.

El Oso later went to Uruguay where he cried when he told Mexican instructor Jean-Philippe Lemay that he feared he would never receive Knowledge because he had blood on his hands. He was afraid it was too late for him, but the instructor asked him to show him his hands. "Let me see," said Jean-Philippe, studying El Oso's hands. "I don't see any blood." Thus, the once hardened and brutal policeman received Knowledge.

A multiday outdoor event in Kissimmee, Florida, in 1979 marked the end of the '70s. The 20,000 people who attended heard Maharaji say, "For so many years in our life, we wait. When you're little, you want to be able to do things. And you can't because of your age. You want to grow up so you can do what you feel like doing. Always you're told that you have to grow up first. Life becomes a process of waiting.

"We go to school and we wait till we can go to university. In university we wait till we can graduate. Then we wait till we can get a job, wait till we can become the boss. Then we wait till we can retire. And then we wait till we can die. That's not what this life is for: to just wait endlessly.

"All our lives we want to become happier. It doesn't matter whether you're a janitor or a general. And it doesn't matter whether you have gone to the moon or have never left your village. There is one thing we can all do. We can find that happiness in the place inside that is real. That is the one thing a human being is best at. We were made for that."

These questions have been here almost since there has been a human race on this earth: Why are we here? What are we doing? What is it all about? The answer is in our hearts, all locked up. We want to get at it, and it is like a treasure hunt because we know there is something very precious within us.

MAHARAJI
Royal Albert Hall, London, England,
May 28, 1979

There's an experience that you are not conditioned to believe. It's an experience of yourself when the mask lifts and the real you can come through. And it's shining, and it's unique, because it's you. A creation. A masterpiece.

MAHARAJI,
MONTREAL, CANADA,
JANUARY 9, 1981

From One Human to Another

At twenty-five years old, Maharaji looked back on an amazingly rich, eventful, and successful life. He had traveled the world many times over, inspired millions of people from all walks of life, and had profoundly transformed thousands upon thousands by his message and by what he had shown them. His efforts were bearing fruit on all continents.

His ambition, as he had so boldly described it, was to take his message of the possibility of peace and fulfillment to every person in the whole world. However, he had always been clear that "the world" per se did not exist and, therefore, neither did the concept of "world peace." Only individuals existed, he said, so if peace were to manifest in the world, it would have to start within each human being, one person at a time. And Maharaji would do whatever was necessary to reach and inspire as many individuals as possible, one by one.

It was also clear that the purity of his ancient and timeless message had to be kept intact. But the ways in which he offered it to people *had* to evolve. Times were changing, and he intended to carry his message to more lands and people than ever before, while preserving its impeccable simplicity.

To do this, he needed a more efficient way to travel. During the 1970s, he had been subject to near-fatal breakdowns, unscheduled stopovers, and restrictions regarding airfields that limited his itineraries. Determined to change these circumstances, he worked toward earning the certifications and ratings necessary to operate various types of aircraft on his own. Flying a safe and well-maintained plane over long distances without having to stop and refuel would allow him to reach many more people. He would also be able to make his own schedule and leave on a whim as needed.

In June of 1980, the refurbishing of the Boeing 707 was completed. To be able to fly it as the captain, he acquired various aviation licenses, including his private pilot license, a commercial pilot license, and an air transport pilot license. During 1981, his efforts were rewarded as full access to the 707, a capable aircraft, enabled him to travel to forty different cities and speak on 120 separate occasions. He crisscrossed North America four times that year, touring South America, Europe, India, Nepal, Australia, New Zealand, and Malaysia.

He also needed to free himself from the adulation that had surrounded him since early childhood. He had worked diligently to avoid being called "God" and dozens of other surreal titles that people attached to him. Not only were they untrue, but they also distracted people from the message. "People have always asked me if I was God," he says, "and I always say no. But they decided that I *was* God, because if I were not, I would say that I was. How do you win when someone's concepts are stronger than reality?"

A few years later, he said to an international audience of several thousand of his students, "I've been through it all, more or less. I've sat on thrones that you can't even imagine. I was a very young boy when it all began. And yet, I have my life to live. And I have commitments. I don't have to put myself on a pedestal. I don't have to have a mythical wall around me so that everybody who comes to see me is more or less stunned. I'm me. And what I have to talk about is more human than anything else except for human beings themselves. This love, this expression comes from one human being to another."

During one of his talks, he carried on the following conversation with himself:

"In whose name do you speak?"

"I speak in my own name."

"What is your teaching based on?"

"My experience."

"In which tradition do you stand?"

"I create it."

Maharaji was making it clear that while his father had shown him Knowledge, he had his own style of bringing it to people, and his authority came from his own mastery. He once said, "If we had done it the same way, this would be a religion, wouldn't it?" He also said that, although there was an age-old tradition of masters bringing the message to people and Knowledge was the same as it had always been, his approach to delivering it changed as was appropriate for the times.

He hinted at people's misguided search for a hero outside themselves, saying that the hero they were looking for was already within them, that the heart was the ultimate hero. "Your heart," he said, "is true, good, beautiful, and always there. In your life, you will not find a better hero." But no matter what he said, people continued to project godlike qualities onto him while others criticized him for it.

In 1980, Maharaji returned to India for the first time in five years, where he held instructor-training programs for Indians. After addressing nearly 40,000 students in Delhi, he returned to South America, making his first stop ever in Mexico, where the message was catching fire.

A student named Jaime Mencos, who had met Maharaji in India in 1972, began spreading the message from a small flat in Mexico City in 1973. At first, attendance had been sparse, but in a very short period of time, the place was crowded with people, from wealthy bankers to several elderly people on meager pensions who sold lottery tickets in the streets. The message of the heart appealed to the gentle nature of the Mexican people, and when Maharaji showed up for his first event in Cancún, he spoke to a packed audience.

In another first, Maharaji visited Malaysia on April 27, 1981, where he reconnected with a student named Subramaniam Munusamy, who had first met him at the Millennium event in Houston in 1973. This enthusiastic young man had begun telling people in the Malaysian peninsula about Maharaji, and when instructor Rajeshwar showed up in Kuala Lumpur in 1974, dozens of people received Knowledge, including most of the members of Subramaniam's family.

Now, in 1981, Subramaniam had gathered together about 1,200 students and 700 guests to listen to Maharaji speak in the grand hall of the Malaysian Chinese Association in Kuala Lumpur. Today, Subramaniam says, "Back in 1973, I had not heard much and was actually not well prepared. But in the Eastern culture, if a master gives you something, you take it and practice it. I realized that a seed had been given, and I have practiced every day for thirty-four years. Today it has grown into a mountain. Practicing this Knowledge has given me such an equilibrium, and my life is filled with love and with gratitude."

In 1985, preparations were under way for Maharaji to visit West Africa for the first time. Starting in the early '70s, people in Ghana and Senegal began hearing about Maharaji through friends and families in Europe and Canada. Throughout the early '80s, the message had spread from Côte d'Ivoire to Cameroon, Togo, and Benin. In 1983, a group of people from Benin who were living in Côte d'Ivoire were talking about Maharaji. When two of them returned to Benin, seventy people there received Knowledge within months. One group decided to use cars, motorcycles, and even little boats to take the message to the villages throughout the country.

Eva Roger, a French woman who lived part of the year in Côte d'Ivoire with her fishing-merchant husband, was instrumental in spreading the word in the area. She worked with Joseph Aka, an Ivorian, who had studied in France. Eva and Joseph met in Houston, Texas, in 1973 during the Millennium event. In the midst of the crowds in Houston, Eva noticed an African and introduced herself to him. She was very happy to learn that the young man was also from Côte d'Ivoire, and they made an appointment to meet up when they returned to Africa.

In Abidjan, Côte d'Ivoire's largest city, only Eva and Joseph had Knowledge. Joseph found an apartment where they could have meetings, and Eva helped to finance it. But they were hesitant to contact the European population of Abidjan, and many of Joseph's friends were more interested in magical powers and the supernatural than in an inner experience. Eventually, five young men became interested, and Eva and Joseph repeatedly asked for an instructor to come to Côte d'Ivoire. Their persistence paid off when one finally arrived, and the five young men received Knowledge.

Within months of speaking to their friends about Maharaji, hundreds of people in Abidjan and in several smaller cities became interested. Young people joined those who were interested in the message. Eva held get-togethers on Saturday afternoons in her garden where they had joyful times talking, singing, and generally celebrating. Passersby would often stop to find out what was happening and were invited in to hear about Maharaji.

Eva continued to collaborate with Joseph and other Ivorians who had become her dear friends and from whom she learned a great deal. "I arrived in Africa before there were any modern conveniences," she recalls, "but the absence of comfort did not bother me. I was very happy and enjoyed the experience we all shared. On many occasions, we held meetings in simple homes with dirt floors and had to walk over wooden planks during the rainy season to get into these venues. It was primitive. Sometimes meetings even took place in huts."

So many people were touched by his message and wanted Knowledge that instructors began to arrive there regularly. Eva assumed the spontaneous role of briefing foreign instructors on African customs. One of these instructors was Willow Baker. "Eva's respect, consideration, and feelings of warmth for the Africans was contagious," Willow says. "She helped many instructors understand and appreciate more quickly the local culture that was so different from theirs. She was very encouraging and supportive of the Africans' genuine efforts."

When Argentinean instructor Diego de Alzaga came to West Africa, he visited a small village north of Lomé, Togo. There, Diego gave Knowledge to a king who had seven wives. The king wanted his wives to receive it, too, and he was not pleased when Diego told him that each of his wives would have to experience a thirst for Knowledge themselves. In the end only the king received it.

In September 1985, Maharaji arrived in West Africa. When he went to Accra, Ghana, although travel was challenging for people, hundreds came from neighboring countries to hear him speak. Particularly poignant is a story from his time in Dakar, Senegal. As he was being driven around the city, he told his driver, "Downtown is where the tourist stuff is. I want to see the 'real stuff.'"

When the driver left the city and headed into the suburbs, Maharaji saw people gathered around simple huts, singing, talking, playing games, and laughing with their radios on full blast. "Then I saw this kid," Maharaji says, "wearing a shirt with holes in it. He had no pants on, but he had a toy that he had made himself from a wire coat hanger and a wheel. He was running that wheel on the road, and he didn't care if traffic came and went. He didn't care if Russia or America had nuclear arms. He didn't know if anybody was worried about him. He had that little wire wheel on the side of the road, and he was running. He was happy in his world."

Maharaji was pointing out that for all the comfort, technology, and sophistication that we have become dependent on, the source of joy lies within each person, waiting for anyone who desires to connect with it.

⌒

On New Year's Day 1982 in Miami, Maharaji announced via telephone to thousands of students worldwide that Amar, his fourth child, had been born on December 25. At this point, Marolyn stayed home to care for their four children while Maharaji continued his travels.

At one event, someone asked him why people were so determined to turn his message and Knowledge into a religion. "Because they like it," was his succinct answer. He was adamant that religion had nothing to do with what he offered.

"I don't want to preach another religion," he said in New York. "There are too many religions already. I want this experience to be real. No books. Just real, human being to human being. I am a human being, just like you. I have two arms, two eyes, and two ears. But I am happy inside, and that happiness is not dependent on everything that happens around me on the outside."

He explained that when he was a child and people had projected their grandiose ideals onto him, he had often felt they were making him into a hood ornament. But they were missing out on what he was trying to show them.

Instructor and physician John Horton encountered a Japanese student who was adamant about viewing Maharaji as a mystical being, even when Maharaji told him that he was as human as anyone sitting in the room. "He only says he's human to satisfy those who cannot see his divinity," the student insisted.

"No," John told him, "he is a human being, and he is teaching as a human being."

But the student preferred to maintain his original perception of Maharaji. He told Maharaji in the question-and-answer session, "You were presented to me as a divine being. I know that you will not publicly affirm this, so I want you to tell me that you are special beyond other people."

When the talk was over, Maharaji met with the desperate student face-to-face. "Do you love me?" he asked the Japanese youth, who became immediately embarrassed. No one spoke openly in Japan about loving a teacher—or anyone else—but he managed to say that he was grateful for Knowledge and that he did love Maharaji.

"I love you, too," said Maharaji. "So let's keep it there, okay? All the other stuff is irrelevant."

When he was asked by someone else if there was anything to give up, he responded, "You don't have to give up anything. If you want to renounce something, then renounce your fear and anger." A few years later, when asked the same question again, he added, "All you have to renounce is the emptiness within."

I was on a big pedestal where I didn't belong. That's not me. I'm a human being. I need to be a human being, and I'm proud to be a human being. It's the best thing there is to be. You come down and you realize all you want is to help. All you want is to have that feeling where there is love.

MAHARAJI
New York, New York, June 14, 1985

We have such a hard time understanding that
this life is the biggest, most wonderful trophy
we could ever have. And we already have it.
If there were a race, it has been won. Now is
the time to be, to relax, and to enjoy. Enjoy
this trophy. Admire and appreciate, love and
understand, and be proud to be alive.

MAHARAJI,
CÔTE D'IVOIRE,
SEPTEMBER 25, 1985

Refinement

Back in the '70s, while most Westerners who received the gift of Knowledge simply continued with their normal daily life, some had chosen to move into ashrams. But by 1984, the Western ashrams were all but gone. Maharaji believed that having an experience of inner peace did not depend on embracing any specific lifestyle or culture. And now he was making it clear that the time had come to leave the ashrams behind.

Terry Yingling, an American student who had lived in an ashram for years, recalls, "One day I decided to look for a place to live on my own. The ashram had been an experiment, and culturally it did not fit in the West the way it did in India. But when they came to an end, I never felt that I was being abandoned, the way some people did. The experience that Maharaji had shown me within was my anchor. What was happening felt like the next natural step. Of course, there was an element of uncertainty in going out on my own, starting over in my late twenties, but I had a firm belief that my own clarity and determination—not some ashram—would determine my happiness."

Ron Geaves recalls that his move out of the ashram brought him closer to himself. "I can remember," he says, "when I finally left the ashram and was trying to figure out what I was going to do with myself, where my future was going to be, and what my life would be. In the end, two things came out of it for me. Knowledge worked for me, and Maharaji inspired me. Everything else, no matter how precious I thought it was, got thrown out."

Encouraging his students to hold onto the best things as changes happen in their lives, Maharaji gave this analogy: "There are three kinds of people in this world. One is like a blender. Whatever you put in it, it will just grind it up—nothing escapes. Another is like a tea strainer that retains what you're going to throw in the garbage can. All the good that happens, they'll throw right out the window, and all that's not good, they'll hang on to dearly. Then there is a third kind of person who has the opposite capability. They can get rid of what is not good and extract the beauty from any circumstance they are in. It's not really like there are three different kinds of people. In fact, these three capabilities are in every one of us. It is a matter of which one we exercise."

While Amar was still too young for school, Maharaji and Marolyn homeschooled their other children, making it easier for the family to join Maharaji as he traveled. But when it was time for their youngest child to be educated, they decided to enroll all four children in private school. Maharaji was spending a great deal of time away from his family, and as much as he enjoyed bringing his message to people, he was a family man who missed his wife and children. He constantly flew back home from wherever he was to celebrate every birthday and anniversary with his family until the children became young adults. To this day, each year since he's been married, he has taken time off with his wife to celebrate their wedding anniversary.

He told an Australian audience, "I've got four children and a wife, and I miss them very much. Every day I talk to my wife, and she tells me how the little one is growing up. When I left, he was right in the middle of getting it together to walk, and my other boy is losing his front tooth. I love them so much, when I go back, I'm going to have them sit right next to me all the time."

Whenever he was away, he called home and talked with each of them. On holidays and whenever possible, the family would join Maharaji wherever he was, traveling all over the world. According to one of their teachers, "Stories would come back about visits to the Louvre in Paris, the pyramids in Egypt, the Acropolis in Athens, the Taj Mahal in India, adventures in Japan or Belgium or Mexico. The children developed a practical sense of world geography, and they got to appreciate countless cultures firsthand. For these kids, learning became a natural part of living, enriched by personal encounters and real-life stories."

As family and friends had always mattered greatly to Maharaji, when he got a telegram while in Tokyo in 1985 saying that his beloved friend Sampurnanand had suffered a heart attack, he immediately flew to India. There he met Dr. Edd Hanzelik, who had flown in from Los Angeles. The conditions in the Indian hospital were rugged, and the pathetically inadequate intensive care unit was nothing more than a dark room with four beds.

But when Sampu saw Maharaji standing at his bedside, the life flowed back into his previously fatigued face. Even the doctors observed the change in his life force, and arrangements were made to fly him back to the United States for better care. Sampu ended up in Cedars-Sinai Medical Center in Los Angeles, where he was diagnosed as having had a major heart attack. But with good doctoring and support from Maharaji during his recovery, Sampu lived fifteen more years in relatively good health in a house in Malibu just down the hill from Maharaji's.

In 1986, with several well-trained instructors in place in the United States and Canada, Maharaji spoke at forty-five public events and did follow-up events in twenty-six cities in sixty days. He spoke to approximately 38,000 people on his North American tour alone, a record in the West. On this tour, he said, "Life is perfect by design. It is in itself complete. It doesn't need to be augmented, and nothing needs to be done to it. All I do is carry a little mirror with me, and any time somebody says, 'How should I be? What should my goals be?' I whip out that little mirror and say, 'Look, do you even know what you have?' It would be a shame to be the world's richest person and not know it. You have something more precious than diamonds, more precious than emeralds. In reality, you are very beautiful. I am not talking about looks, but inside of you. You have this life. And you can access the treasure that is within you."

Maharaji turned thirty-two in Brussels in 1989, where he attended a large international event with 10,000 attendees. He said, "Life is so simple. The magic that this Knowledge holds is so simple. Joy is so simple. Happiness is so simple. That feeling of being fulfilled is so simple. It's not riddled with riddles. No big dilemmas. The thirst makes itself apparent. What is our problem? We don't even know what we're looking for.

"Do you realize what a magic it is that you feel a thirst? Do you realize what a magic it is that the heart pounds and cries out, 'I want to be fulfilled'? It is magic when from a deep place within each human being, a voice starts to come that says very simply, 'I need, I want to be fulfilled.' Let it be prevalent in your life. What are you waiting for?

"There is a time to sleep and a time to be awake, and in the awake time is the need for fulfillment, for that thirst to be quenched. That's where it's real. No pictures of the sun will ever light anything. No pictures of a candle will ever light anything. You need that real light that shines. Light does not create. It merely shines. Light allows an object to be illuminated, as does our heart, as does that space from which that thirst and cry comes.

"When do I begin to be thankful? When do I start opening my eyes and see that all around me is that beauty, all around me is that essence? Most importantly, within me is the very joy that I have been looking for."

The teacher doesn't want to stay in the same place. He wants to move, and that's the beauty of the process. The teacher takes the student with him when he moves to higher and higher levels. In that art, teacher and student prosper and teach and shine each other. The teacher shines the student, and undoubtedly, the student shines the teacher. And what a wonderful way to do it. It's magic every single time. Magic!

MAHARAJI
Brussels, Belgium, December 10, 1989

Part Four

1990–2006

Human beings who look for a miracle have
forgotten what miracle has already occurred:
they breathe.

MAHARAJI,
FT. LAUDERDALE, FLORIDA,
SEPTEMBER 13, 1992

Crisis

At the beginning of the '90s, Maharaji had been traveling the world for more than twenty years, and he was in his early thirties. The original hippies who had brought his message back from India had blended into society, but their fascination with his message remained intact. Many still practiced the techniques and kept in touch with Maharaji whenever they could, while hundreds of thousands of new people had embraced his message.

In contrast to the early hippie days, his base of students had now become very broad. It covered the entire spectrum of society, from government and business leaders to the humblest people in small villages around the world. As there was nothing to join and nothing to pay, people were simply enjoying the message of peace and the gift of Knowledge in their own lives.

Although a great deal of technological progress, particularly in communications, had taken place globally, the peaceful society of which the utopians of the late '60s and early '70s had dreamt did not seem any closer to manifesting.

Between 1971 and 1991, some situations had improved and some had gotten worse. The Palestine problem remained unsolved, despite the many peace negotiations and a peace accord. The Berlin Wall had fallen and Communism in Eastern Europe had collapsed, causing an end to the Cold War that had lasted nearly fifty years. In South Africa, Nelson Mandela was released from prison after twenty-seven years, and the much-decried apartheid system was abandoned. These developments suggested growing peace and freedom until the Gulf War in 1991 made it clear that wars would continue, even though Russia and the United States were no longer adversaries.

Since leaving India, Maharaji had traveled almost constantly, bringing hope and inspiration to people. He had a wife and four children who loved one another dearly. He was in his prime and was moving forward tirelessly with a keen sense of his mission. As he said many times over the years, he was determined to offer the possibility of peace to every person on the planet.

Amidst the utopian fervor of the '70s, many of his early students had believed that he would somehow single-handedly bring peace to the world, but by the time the '90s rolled around, they realized that Maharaji's intention was to bring peace to individuals, not to the world. He also understood that peace would manifest one person at a time, and to accomplish that, he would need his students' help. Through the ages, the message of peace had been spread by word of mouth, and that was not about to change.

What mattered most to his students was the gift he had given them—a way to be at peace in their lives. That, in their eyes, made all the difference. So, for them, the '90s marked a return to the fundamentals of the practice of Knowledge and to the inner experience they said it gave them.

In the twenty years since he had started traveling, the makeup of his audiences had greatly evolved. In the '70s and early '80s, he spoke largely to audiences of his own generation that were mostly part of the counterculture. As time passed, he was attracting many people from mainstream society—anyone who was looking for something more in life than what society was offering. He began to present his message in terms that were less reflective of the '70s and more relatable to people from all walks of life in the '90s. His expression had become more elegant and evocative, better articulated, and able to touch people across a myriad of different cultures and lifestyles.

Addressing a distinguished audience of diplomats, government officials, and guests at the United Nations Conference Centre in Bangkok, Thailand, September 12, 2002.

Maharaji and family on his birthday in Miami Beach, Florida, December 10, 1982. From left to right: Premlata, Marolyn, Amar, Hans, Dayalata, and Maharaji.

Maharaji and students delight in the informality of La Tierra del Amor, an outdoor event site near Buenos Aires, Argentina, January 1991.

Veteran TV journalist Burt Wolf conducts a one-on-one interview with Maharaji for the TV documentary *Inner Journey*, Malibu, California, January 2003.

An audience of 130,000 listens to Maharaji at Jawaharlal Nehru Stadium, New Delhi, March 8, 2003. The stadium is filled to capacity for the first time ever.

Delivering the keynote address at the "First Conference on Peace" in the Great Hall of the University of Salamanca in Spain, June 20, 2003.

Seeing Maharaji for the first time after five years, many of the 1,700 attendees welcome him by waving their handkerchiefs at an event in Accra, Ghana, August 2003.

In a helicopter in India, November 2003. The helicopter was used for traveling to villages when distances were too great or road conditions were poor.

An audience of 275,000 people gathered to hear Maharaji at an event in Bhagalpur, Bihar, India, March 21, 2004. Speaker towers and a large outdoor screen made it possible for everyone to see and hear him. A year later, 325,000 attended an event near the city of Gaya, Bihar.

Speaking to more than 3,000 guests at a four-day outdoor event at Ivory's Rock Conference Centre near Brisbane, Australia, April 2004.

President Emilio Colombo, former president of the European Parliament and former prime minister of Italy, greets Maharaji before he addresses senators, deputies, diplomats, and government officials in the Conference Hall of the Italian Chamber of Deputies at Palazzo Marini, Rome, Italy, July 7, 2004.

Maharaji speaks to an audience of 2,000 at an event associated with the Universal Forum of Cultures, Barcelona, Spain, June 14, 2004. The forum, attended by more than five million people and many world leaders, promoted cultural diversity, sustainable development, and conditions for peace.

Addressing faculty, community leaders, guests, and students at Sanders Theatre, Harvard University, Cambridge, Massachusetts, July 22, 2004.

At Roy Thomson Hall, Toronto, Canada, July 24, 2004. The event was broadcast live to 128 cities around the world via satellite.

Maharaji speaks to civic, government, and business leaders at the invitation of Rotary International at the National Centre for Performing Arts in Mumbai, India, February 19, 2005.

Receiving a gift of appreciation from Tengku Rithauddeen, president of the United Nations Association of Malaysia and former minister of foreign affairs. Maharaji addressed a distinguished audience of members of royal families, ambassadors, cabinet ministers, and members of the Asian media. Koffi Anan, the secretary-general of the United Nations, sent his best wishes for the event. Kuala Lumpur, Malaysia, April 20, 2005.

Maharaji at Thammasat University, the leading Thai institution of higher education. He was introduced by Manu Leopairote, permanent secretary of the Thai Ministry of Industry, chairman of the Petroleum Authority of Thailand, and director for Thailand of the Asian Productivity Organization, May 4, 2005.

Following an event in Hong Kong, on May 10, 2005, Maharaji greets some of the attendees. Many are seeing him for the first time.

At the invitation of the United Nations 60th Anniversary Committee, Maharaji addressed diplomats, government and civic leaders, and guests at an event held in celebration of the UN's 60th anniversary at the Herbst Theater in San Francisco, California, where the UN Charter was signed 60 years before. June 24, 2005.

Speaking to a distinguished audience of faculty, students, and guests at Oxford University, Oxford, England, July 19, 2005. The attendees were welcomed by Peggy Morgan, a governor and research fellow at an Oxford research center. Maharaji was introduced by Professor Ron Geaves from the University of Chester.

Composing music, Thousand Oaks, California, 2005.

Giving the keynote address at a special event with the United Nations
Association of Australia at the Australian Parliament in Canberra,
Australia, on the occasion of the United Nations' International
Day of Peace, September 21, 2005.

At the United Nations Headquarters in New York, Maharaji delivers the keynote address at a special event call "Water for Humanity and Peace," April 21, 2006. The event was held in honor of the support provided by The Prem Rawat Foundation to the UNDP Community Water Initiative in Ghana and the National Council of Women of the United States' Water Well Project in Ghana.

Receiving the Distinguished International Humanitarian Achievement Award from Mary Singletary, president of the National Council of Women of the United States, at the special event at the United Nations headquarters in New York, April 21, 2006.

Food for People, a custom-built, well-equipped 10,000-square-foot facility, provides 45,000 free meals each month to people in need in a tribal area of Jharkhand, in northeastern India. Funding is provided by The Prem Rawat Foundation.

Children enjoying a meal at the inauguration of Food for People, March 23, 2006. Free hot meals are served each day, year-round, to 500 children every morning and evening and to 500 adults every afternoon.

In March 2006, TV host Rajiv Mehrotra interviews Maharaji on his weekly, thirty-minute prime-time talk show, *In Conversations*, on Doordarshan TV, the leading Indian TV channel. Rajiv Mehrotra has interviewed more than 1,000 celebrities and world leaders on this show.

Maharaji delivered the keynote address at the Pre-Convention Meeting of Rotaract at the annual convention of Rotary International in Malmö, Sweden, June 9, 2006.

On the occasion of the fortieth anniversary of Maharaji bringing his message of peace, Shri Bhairon Singh Shekhawat, the vice president of India, and 25,000 people under twenty-five welcomed him in the Indira Gandhi Indoor Stadium, New Delhi, July 29, 2006.

After Maharaji gave the keynote address at an event held by the Malaysian Chinese Association at the Tunku Abdul Rahman Chinese University, Kuala Lumpur, August 8, 2006. On Maharaji's right is the minister of health, Dato Dr. Chua Soi Lek. On his left is Tun Dr. Ling Liong Sik, chairman of the university council.

⌒‿

In 1990, a piece of land called La Tierra del Amor (Land of Love) was acquired in Escobar, near Buenos Aires, Argentina. Now, Latin Americans could more easily spend several days at a time with Maharaji. He enjoyed giving informal addresses in a relaxed setting where people in the audience could freely converse with him.

La Tierra consists of ninety acres of *pampa húmeda* (humid flatlands). Cristina Gago, the present-day land manager, says, "Maharaji once compared it to a pancake; it could not be more flat. But it has become a beautiful big garden full of trees. In the beginning there were a piffling two trees on the land. Now there are over 2,500, including majestic oaks and several species of eucalyptus."

A small creek that is deep enough to swim in crosses the land; many species of birds thrive there since they have no natural predators. Resident woodpeckers, hummingbirds, *zorzales* (birds who sing all day), and *horneros* (the "mason birds" that make their nests out of mud) are joined by sparrows that stop there during migrations. Large hares venture out at night to eat birds' eggs.

At night, the air at La Tierra was filled with the tiny twinkling of millions of glowworms. Maharaji would sit under a tree in the center of a large empty field, with his students surrounding him. The openness and informality encouraged them to ask questions, and they could hear the answers in an intimate setting. Whenever such sessions took place, Maharaji provided inspiration and often humorously debunked myths and preconceived ideas.

At one such informal gathering, he said, "More than anything else, we need to begin to feel the real magic—the magic that we can witness, that we can feel. The magic that brings life to so much that is lifeless. There are so many ideas, so many books, so many words and concepts. All those get brushed aside when that realness begins to shine. You become speechless. Words mean so little when you can allow yourself to just feel, to open up, petal by petal, inch by inch, and trust in that opening.

"Then that magic slowly starts to work in our lives. It makes itself so clear. It's totally indescribable. You can try to capture it, and yet it's uncapturable. You can try to slow it down—it doesn't slow down. You can try to analyze it, but it's beyond analysis. You and I, what assets do we have? We think it's our house or our job or this or that. These things are so temporary. Here today. Gone tomorrow. The only thing we have is our hearts. The only asset we have is that feeling that has never looked at us and said no. Everything else has said no at some point or other. Trust it.

"Why? Because ultimately, what do you think is going to happen to us? Maybe you will become a billionaire. Then what do you think is at the end of that? You will become very quiet. Your eyes will close, your mouth will close, and this most subtle thing that causes the breath to go in and out and in and out will be gone. Where will it go? Nobody knows.

"Why fight the fight you cannot fight? Let the bird of your soul, of that heart inside, out of its cage. Let it sit on your shoulder freely. Converse with it while you can. Express to this bird not your desires, not what it can do for you, but what you can do for it. Tell it how thankful you are that it came. Don't try to buy it gifts; it doesn't care for them. Don't buy it cages; it cannot be imprisoned. Just tell it what maybe you have never said before. Turn to this bird, to this existence, and say thank you. Not thank you *for*, but just thank you."

In 1993, Maharaji went back to La Tierra, but there was a huge rainstorm, and many tents were flooded during the night. At this event, a woman asked for Knowledge, and when the instructor asked about her profession, she said honestly, "I'm a prostitute."

The instructor told Maharaji that there was a person who should not receive Knowledge.

"Why?" asked Maharaji.

"She is a prostitute," he said.

Maharaji said, "If she is a prostitute and you disapprove, don't sleep with her. What does that have to do with giving her Knowledge?"

Maharaji told this story several times over the years, stressing that what he offers has nothing to do with lifestyle or beliefs and that he is not in a position to judge how people conduct their lives. In the end, he gave this woman Knowledge in a session with a few others. After spending hours with the participants, showing each one of them the techniques, he commented to the instructor, "I wasn't able to tell which of the women was the prostitute!" Incidentally, within a short time, she left her previous life behind and became a successful artisan, making beautiful jewelry.

As Maharaji continued to travel the world nonstop, his efforts were taking their toll. He told his audience in Florida, "I spend less time at home than I do on tour. It's like 90 percent on tour and 10 percent at home."

Ray Belcher, Maharaji's production assistant during these years, observed his exhaustion. "He had just completed a U.S. and a European tour. We were in Germany and he was sitting backstage, almost weeping with weariness. He looked up at me and said, 'Things have got to change. People have to help me more in this kind of situation.' When he stepped onstage, he was his old self, talking and inspiring everyone, but it was clear that something needed to change."

༄

One day in November 1991, Maharaji was flying from New York to Chicago when a dramatic event occurred. Sampurnanand, after receiving a phone call in the backseat of the plane, made his way to the cockpit. He looked into Maharaji's eyes and said, "I have something to say to you."

Maharaji saw that Sampu was disturbed. "What is it?" he asked.

"Your mother has passed away."

Mataji had not been in Maharaji's life for many years, and, unfortunately, a reunion had never taken place. Joan Apter, who had gotten to know Mataji well during her time at Dehradun, says, "Mataji was a dyed-in-the-wool Hindu. She believed that she had to follow the Indian tradition and be the one to choose her son's wife or she would lose face in her community. When Maharaji chose his own wife, Mataji was devastated, but at one point it appeared that she was going to drop it so she could see her first grandchild.

"One afternoon, she called Maharaji to say that she was coming to his house, and we all raced around cleaning and doing preparations. It appeared that she wanted to meet her first grandchild, and Maharaji was excited, making sure everything was in order. But when her car got to the front gate, it stopped. Apparently she had a change of heart, and she turned around and left. Maharaji must have been terribly disappointed, although he never mentioned it. That was the last time she ever attempted to make contact with her youngest son. After that, she and Bal Bhagwan Ji drifted away in their resentment."

Joan, however, had fond memories of Mataji, who had been so welcoming and helpful when Joan first arrived in Dehradun many years prior. "She tried to fatten me up with rice pudding when I was too thin. She thought something was wrong with my skin because I had freckles, and she insisted I wear a bra. She was a loving woman, a unique personality type, but she held on to her Hindu culture over loyalty to her family." Maharaji traveled to India to attend her funeral, but Bal Bhagwan Ji would not allow him into Prem Nagar ashram where his mother's ashes would be buried.

At that time, Maharaji lost a key associate, who had been with him for nearly fifteen years. Michael Dettmers, a Canadian, had met Maharaji in 1976 and had rapidly replaced Bob Mishler as Maharaji's personal assistant. As Mishler had done before him, Michael attempted to convince Maharaji to focus on becoming a humanitarian leader and to let the instructors deal with the message of peace, but Maharaji was not interested.

In the '80s, while Dettmers was involved with Maharaji, he took Chilean philosopher Fernando Flores's two-year-long Ontological Design course. He became an avid follower of Flores and became more interested in the intellectual and philosophical complexities of Flores's philosophy than in Maharaji's message of peace and the practice of Knowledge.

He increasingly strove to implement the basics of Flores's sophisticated philosophy, which included "interpreting the world as constituted and invented in language," and "seeing that we live in interpretations, not in objective realities," and "seeing that we are biological, historical, and linguistic beings." Needless to say, there was quite a gap between this philosophy and Maharaji's message of the heart.

The gap widened when Dettmers attempted to apply Flores's complex philosophy to managing Maharaji's work. He even tried convincing Maharaji to incorporate the philosophy into his message. In spite of Dettmers's many requests, Maharaji never responded. When Dettmers, in an attempt to transform Maharaji's work into a profit-making business, tried to convince him to charge people for Knowledge, it became apparent that the divide between the two had become too wide to bridge.

In 1991, Dettmers left Maharaji, hoping to succeed as a business consultant. He moved to the Blue Mountains of North Carolina where he lived for a while in an isolated community. No one heard from him for years, until he resurfaced for a brief moment in 2002, making defamatory public statements about Maharaji online, only to disappear again. When he failed to become a successful business consultant, he moved to Florida where he was hired by a small exercise equipment manufacturing firm.

∽

When videotapes of Maharaji's addresses started supplement-
ing print materials in the early '90s, the number of people hearing
about his message swelled a great deal. His message would now
flow from the source directly to the student, from one heart to
another, and students no longer had to grapple with the instructors' personal ideas or biases. For the first time, the dissemination
of the message was not people-dependent. Even in India, video
use was accelerating dramatically with more than 2,500 centers
acquiring videocassette players. There, Maharaji held large sessions where he personally presented the Knowledge techniques to
students via a video camera, a projector, and a large screen. These
sessions, some with as many as 5,000 participants, were held in
tentlike structures with attendees sitting on mats on the floor,
while Maharaji walked through the rows, giving explanations as
needed and answering questions.

When someone once asked him about the purpose of the so-
called *third eye*, he answered humorously, "A third eye doesn't
make sense to me. I don't even want one. Imagine the glasses you'd
have to wear. The third eye is a metaphor. They have it on the
dollar bill but it doesn't help anyone. If you convert the concept
into a metaphor for being able to perceive another realm, then I
agree with that."

Starting on October 14, 1992, a five-day event occurred in
Australia on a piece of land about forty minutes' drive from
Brisbane that had been acquired the year before. The 2,100 acres
of Amaroo (formally known as Ivory's Rock Conference Centre)
had been home to cattle, horses, and pigs for as long as anyone
could remember, as early settlers had cleared the original forest.
Before them, aborigines lived there for centuries.

The aboriginal name for Ivory's Rock is *Muntamben*, derived
from the name of a native plum that grows there. The name *Ivory's*

Rock came from the name of an early settler. An agreement had been reached with aboriginal elders that climbing Ivory's Rock, which towered over the site, would remain off limits out of respect for the rock's significance to aborigines.

In July of 1991, when the land was first bought, the weather was dry and hot, and the land was parched. And yet, there was a certain serenity to the place. Maharaji came to see the property before it was purchased, and he saw that with a lot of hard work, something wonderful could blossom.

"He was in love with the land from the moment he saw it," says Aussie Ray Belcher. "It had an extraordinary feel to it."

Maharaji sat on a tree stump there and watched the sun set. A few days later, a small army of volunteers was hard at work removing brush and manure. They picked up loose timber, chopped down dead trees, bought a used tractor, and built bridges where they were needed. In this way, Amaroo was born, where people from all over the world could come to spend days at a time with him in a peaceful environment.

By October 1992, excitement bristled in the air as 3,500 people arrived from all over the world for the first Amaroo event. Sanitation efforts were in full swing, kitchens were constructed, and tents were put up. About 450 people were accommodated on-site at the first event. Maharaji sat on a rattan chair on a small podium on the grass at the foot of a gentle hill. People sat on the grass around him and listened over several days during this magical time—the beginning of many more events there.

Today, the 2,100-acre site is home to more than 650 species of eucalyptus trees, plants, and shrubs, some rare and almost extinct, such as the hoop pine. Wild dingoes live in the rocky outcrops, and four species of wallabies roam in the tall grasses—including the rare rock wallaby—along with a wide variety of wildlife. More than 100 species of birds can be sighted, including the rare peregrine falcons and wedge-tailed eagles.

With new bridges and roads, cleared land, modern camping facilities, and a state-of-the-art outdoor amphitheater that seated 4,500 people, Amaroo had been transformed from a run-down cattle property into a well-equipped event site. Maharaji enjoyed the rustic quality of life in Amaroo, cooking his own food on an outdoor barbecue pit and sitting with his family around the fire under the stars at night. "Beautiful kangaroos, wallabies, and opossums roamed the land," Maharaji said, "and we watched their babies being fed."

But the expansion of his work around the world produced a growing drain on finances. "We do not have a money tree," he said in Florida in 1994. "People make contributions and that's how it happens. I charge nothing for this Knowledge. It's priceless. There isn't enough money in the whole universe to pay for it, because an act of kindness can never be paid for. We have no billboards or TV or newspaper advertisements. Somehow the thirsty seem to find me, always."

The dissemination of Maharaji's message has always been paid for by voluntary contributions to the organizations by those who appreciate his message and want to bring it to more people around the world. Knowledge has always been free of charge, and so have many of the materials. Those that were not free were usually sold at cost. These materials never generated profits, since the priority was to make them available to as many people as possible, at a price that people could afford, even in the most disadvantaged countries. And there were always enough volunteer contributions to continue bringing the message to more people in more places.

At this time, in 1993, a significant event occurred when Older Mataji, Maharaji's stepmother, died. When he heard she was ill, Maharaji came to see her in India. When he visited her in the hospital, this once-vibrant woman was close to death, fighting for each breath. "Let's bring her home," he said. "She may as well go in comfort, not in some impersonal hospital room." They made her as comfortable as possible at the ashram in Delhi until she passed away, and Maharaji made the cremation arrangements, helping prepare the body and build the funeral pyre. He obviously had deep feelings for his stepmother, who had shown him nothing but kindness, affection, and respect throughout her life.

⌒

Maharaji now circumnavigated the globe often more than once a year. The 707 had served him well for a few years, but it had to be sold in 1984 because it did not meet the new noise regulations of the American Federal Aviation Administration. Maharaji was now back to using a succession of aircraft, either leased or purchased. These included, between 1984 and 2006: two Learjets, a Challenger, a Hawker-Siddeley, a Citation, and two Gulfstreams. He spent a great deal of time away from home, arranging for his family to join him whenever it was possible. But on August 14, 1995, he was in Buenos Aires, Argentina, when he got a phone call that would bring him back home for a while.

Marolyn had suffered a headache so severe that she blacked out and ended up in the hospital. A CAT scan of her brain and a spinal tap revealed blood in her spinal fluid, indicating a brain aneurysm. When Maharaji was told that the aneurysm was life-threatening, he immediately canceled the rest of his tour and flew straight home.

Dr. Edd Hanzelik says that Maharaji was calm and practical. "He immediately accepted what was happening," says Dr. Hanzelik, "and he was so concerned. He called at least ten times on that flight home to see how she was doing and to participate in decisions about her care."

From the airport, Maharaji went straight to the hospital, and he was in the waiting room during Marolyn's surgery. The neurosurgeon came out of the operating room looking pale and shaken. He said that when he opened the skull, the aneurysm ruptured and blood hemorrhaged into the brain tissue. He had to react very quickly. He told Maharaji that he did not know whether Marolyn would ever speak again or even wake up—that she could remain comatose for the rest of her life.

Edd Hanzelik recalls, "Maharaji immediately started thinking in terms of what to do next. He considered what would happen if she could or couldn't talk, how they would care for her at home, no matter the outcome. I was amazed how he never got unhappy or expressed despair. He was clearly shaken, but very practical and hopeful, focusing on how to make the best of the situation, whatever it was."

However, it turned out much better than they had expected. The doctor told Maharaji, "She's bucking and kicking, and she'll be okay." Maharaji got permission to park a motor home in the hospital parking lot where he slept each night and personally cared for her during the three weeks she spent in intensive care.

"He brought me cooked meals three times a day," Marolyn recalls, "and he got so good at reading the monitors, the nurses started calling him 'doctor.' He would show them when my numbers were falling, and some thought he was my special doctor."

In fact, according to Edd Hanzelik, Maharaji apparently saved his wife's life one day when he noticed that after being administered a particular medication, she exhibited signs of a stroke, as her arm and leg weakened on one side of her body, her facial muscles drooped, and her speech became garbled. At first the doctors resisted the possibility that the medication could be causing the problem, because it was a key aspect of the treatment, but when the medication was finally stopped, the symptoms disappeared, and the doctors were grateful that Maharaji had noticed something they had not. After several weeks, he was finally able to bring her back home, where he converted the bedroom into an in-home nursing facility so she could regain her strength and make a full recovery, which she did within a few months.

Maharaji spoke of this trying time in Florida several months later, describing it as a "real disaster." He said, "This is one of those classic stories where this mind does not allow you to rest for a single moment. Reality as you thought no longer exists, and something is trying to say, 'What is the reason?' There is no reason, but something inside is crying, 'Why is this happening to you? What have you done wrong?' You look for an explanation—it's like a storm. You try to find out why the storm is here by reading the weather books, or you find a safe haven where you can tie your boat. That is when you need real reality."

Today, eleven years later, Marolyn has no neurological damage whatsoever, and Edd Hanzelik recalls Maharaji's behavior during that time with great respect. "He remained amazingly grounded the whole time and never allowed his emotions to distract him. To help her feel at home in the hospital, he brought the silk sheets from their bed at home and personally served her meals to her. I could see the effort he was making to make her feel cared for and to uplift her spirit as she went through such a difficult recovery. I was touched deeply to see this caring side of him shine under such trying circumstances. It said a lot for his character."

What is the ultimate wish? There is only one wish for all human beings on the face of the earth. Just one. And that ultimate wish is to be content. To be satisfied. To be in harmony. To be in that place where this life is adorned with the jewels of joy. That is the ultimate wish.

MAHARAJI
Cotonou, Benin, August 5, 1995

Ask yourself for a moment what is really important to you—not by anyone else's definition, but your own. Peel away the roles you act out every day, and you will find a being. A being that cannot be put into a box. A being that isn't good or bad—just a being. A being that wants to exist, that wants to learn, that wants to appreciate. A being that just wants to be.

MAHARAJI,
SEATTLE, WASHINGTON,
FEBRUARY 1, 1994

Language of the Heart

In 1996, the number of Maharaji's students was climbing into the hundreds of thousands. While his message, his mission, and his ambition had not changed in the twenty-five years since he had started traveling the world, the way he expressed the message had evolved considerably.

Not only had his Indian accent become less noticeable and his grammar and syntax more correct, but he had also become a master of speaking to people heart-to-heart. His message was resonating better than ever, wherever people lived or whatever their backgrounds. He had developed a unique ability to inspire people to seek peace within. And while his approach was not one of intellect and reason, as Danish writer Ole Grünbaum puts it, "he came to master the language of touching the heart of those who were open to being touched."

He had always excelled at speaking in the simplest terms. With insight, humor, original stories, and metaphors, Maharaji kept traveling the world, touching the hearts of people from villages in India and Africa to the halls of the United Nations and prestigious universities.

In 1997 in Barcelona, Spain, he told the audience, "I have traveled the world. I have gone from one country to another country where they don't speak the same language, the driving is different, the way they conduct business is different, the way people look is different. And amongst all those differences, I have seen a beautiful, simple similarity—that we all yearn for that beautiful thing within."

A few months later, in Leicester, England, he said, "You are a human being. Your nature is that when you have pain, you wish for it to stop, but when you experience joy, you do not. So, understand this nature of yours: That when you're experiencing joy, there's no limit. But when you're experiencing pain, you want it to stop. You need that joy, not for one day or two days, but every day, all the time. That is your nature."

Maharaji brought his own meaning to words such as *understanding* and *knowing*. For most people, *understanding* usually denotes a recognition that is rational in nature, while *knowing* implies some measurable proof. But in Maharaji's vocabulary, true understanding and knowing originate in the heart, not in the mind. He has said on several occasions that knowledge of the self was the only nonscientific knowledge, and while all other forms of knowledge could be known through the intellect, this one could only be felt in the heart.

At an event in Rome, he said, "The rules of the game are incredibly simple. With every breath, remember what is important to you. To know. Not to pretend to know, but to know. You must feel and understand. Nobody can understand for you. You have to understand it yourself. It is your journey. That's why this Knowledge is different."

In 1998, addressing about 86,000 people via a live interactive global satellite broadcast from Pasadena, California, he said, "One lifetime, this is all I have. Do I comprehend that? Because unless I know that's it, how can I shape my future? What can I learn from my past? What can I apply to what is coming? If I want to be fulfilled, is there an urgency to it? Every moment that comes brings with it the possibility of me being fulfilled, and this is no small matter—me, being fulfilled. Me being able to understand, to comprehend my life, my existence. And what is 'understanding'? Understanding is this narrow glue, this thin layer between information and this Knowledge. There is no shortage of information in this world, but what good is it? What you need in your life is the know-how to go inside.

"The world is full of information, but how much real knowledge is there? Very little indeed. It's rare to be able to go within and experience life. There is no shortage of information on how you could possibly enjoy this life, but there is a distinct shortage of people actually being able to enjoy it. Why? Because we have overloaded ourselves with information. What are we looking for? What do we need? What does it mean to be alive right now? That is what we all have been given. It is time to accept the love of this existence. It is time to accept the joy of this heart."

By 1998, Maharaji's speeches were relayed on a regular basis by direct-to-home satellite. As more people around the world were able to afford satellite dishes and receivers cheaply, his discourse could be heard in the most isolated places. People in Nepal who lived in villages without electricity started using generators to power donated satellite dishes and video projectors. They would gather in the village center at night and watch the message of peace beamed down from the skies. The same thing was happening in villages in India, in the Andes in South America, in the Australian bush, and in remote areas of central Africa.

During that year, Maharaji's oldest daughter, Premlata, asked him for Knowledge—and he gave it to her. "She makes an effort to practice every day," said the proud father, "and seeing the reactions of her siblings was amazing. The night before, when they found out that their oldest sister was going to receive Knowledge, their jaws dropped. All of a sudden, this thing was no longer 'someday.' It was real."

When Maharaji talked about giving his daughter Knowledge, he humorously admitted there was a conflict between being

the father and being the teacher. The father was worried about
whether his daughter would practice, while the teacher simply
trusted the student.

In 1999, Maharaji launched a personal Web site, www.maharaji
.net, that contained poetry and other writings. At first he was
reticent about having his own site. He felt that the Internet was a
cold medium and did not provide the closeness that he liked to
have with people. But eventually he accepted the fact that even
with all its imperfections, the Net would make it possible to reach
people in a manner that other channels could not afford. In a
touching and intimate welcome page to his Web site, he wrote:

> "Know thyself" has echoed through the ages. This
> simple statement has been revised and updated but
> has never lost its charm or intrigue.
>
> We all, in our own ways, want to better ourselves,
> be it in our career, our family, our friends, our skills—
> whatever our chosen endeavor may be. So we should,
> and to this end many avenues are available to us.
>
> However, one cannot forget one's self. Knowledge
> of the self is also important—to some, indeed, para-
> mount. Knowledge of the self begins with the self.
> Your universe resides within you, waiting to be dis-
> covered.
>
> What does it take? It takes a sincere desire, an
> earnest thirst. Understanding is a wonderful surprise.
> That which didn't make sense all of a sudden does.
>
> My efforts have always been to help people under-
> stand and feel the feeling within. People through the
> years have tried to place me in a mold, and from the
> very early years, I have not been able to oblige them.
>
> When I was very young, people were looking for
> the "old, silver-haired guru with flowing white robes."

I was only eight. When people were flocking to India for their search, I was in the West.

When people were looking for sophisticated discourses, I spoke of simple things. When people wanted nirvana, I said, "You need peace." When people said, "Tell us of the scriptures," I said, "Look within you." When people asked, "What is your qualification?" I said, "Judge me by what I offer."

To this day, people want to see me the way they want to. After all, I guess it is rather inconvenient to see things how they really are. I have evolved, but my message stays the same. Externally, I have changed, but within me, something stays the same.

And the Web page concluded with, "This Web site is not here to make you want Knowledge or to show you what it is. That is a journey that needs to be undertaken with one's own thirst."

Since he first came in contact with the media as a young child, Maharaji had learned over and over that he could not rely on it to spread his message or even to report about it fairly. He had also noticed that most journalists, when writing about him, had no qualms about overlooking the message of peace. Instead, they had a keen interest in writing about trivia and in fueling controversy, regardless of how old and irrelevant the stories may be. For this reason, he had decided in the late '70s to keep a low media profile and to rely instead on people who appreciated his message to reach more and more people by word of mouth.

Throughout the '80s and '90s, he largely flew under the radar, and the media seemed to have forgotten about him. He no longer met their stereotype of the child guru freshly arrived from India.

Unsure what to make of him, their interest had faded, and they had moved on to other faces in the news.

But with the explosive rise in the Internet in the late '90s, the media landscape underwent a radical change all around the globe. Suddenly, anyone could be a publisher. While this may have been a boon for freedom of speech, it gave a voice to those whose pursuit was to spread misinformation or, worse, animosity.

Many leading voices for peace, including the Dalai Lama, Nelson Mandela, and Mother Teresa, found themselves at the receiving end of hostile, unfounded opposition. Maharaji was no exception. When his audiences grew to millions, there were bound to be a few among them who, for reasons of their own, would make him a target of their antagonism.

And so, in 1997, a handful of disgruntled former students, disappointed not to have received the preferential treatment they had hoped for, joined up on the Internet with a few radical extremists. Together they launched a Web site from which they started defaming Maharaji on a daily basis. Since the Internet was not regulated, and since most of them were posting anonymously, they could write whatever they wanted without fear of legal consequences. Misinformation, slander, and outright fabrications were all permissible, and they had no hesitation engaging in these practices.

Maharaji, from the outset, made it clear that he was not interested in suing for defamation. First and foremost, forgiveness was, in his view, the most effective approach to dealing with animosity. Also, he didn't want to be distracted from his efforts to bring his message of peace around the world. Additionally, he must have been aware that these detractors were actually hoping that he would sue them. Even though they knew they would lose, they thought that by having him appear in court, they would be able to generate a media frenzy that they could use against him.

Much of the original impetus for the detractors' Web site had come from a lawyer from Vancouver, Canada, who made his living defending arsonists and murderers. He once boasted on the Internet that he had embezzled money from the organization supporting Maharaji's efforts. A few weeks later, when confronted, he recanted.

Soon he had amassed a few acolytes with checkered pasts, such as a drug dealer and the owner of a porn business, who now peddled hard-core videos over the Internet. The group soon recruited a garbage collector from Australia, who later did prison time for illegal weapons and drug sales, and a notorious cyberhacker investigated for domestic violence. And then there was an unemployed surfer found liable by the Supreme Court of Queensland, Australia, for theft of private credit and financial data, and a San Francisco lawyer who bragged online about being arrested three times and who now works for the public defender's office. This motley group of misfits was determined to put an end to Maharaji's work, as they started flooding the search engines with thousands of messages defaming him. Over time, their slandering developed into an all-consuming obsession.

If they had dedicated themselves to helping humanity as intensely as they did going after Maharaji, they might have generated some benefit from their actions. But for whatever reason, this core group spent hundreds of hours on the Internet, desperately seeking to create a media circus around Maharaji. To project the appearance of being more numerous than they were and to increase their ranking on search engines, each of the handful of detractors started posting many messages each day under multiple aliases.

For a while, the anonymity of the Internet allowed them to fool the search engines with impunity. However, Google soon realized that it had been a victim of vicious spamming by these detractors, who had used unethical means to gain undue prominence in search engine rankings. Google then stopped caching their messages and scaled down the number of indexed pages from 13,600 to 900. To this day, however, a handful of detractors, using anonymity, multiple aliases, shady spamming tactics, and a webmaster based in Latvia, continue to have a prominence in search engine rankings that is totally out of proportion to the small size of the group.

When Maharaji showed no interest in responding to these detractors, their previous libel, slander, and defamation turned to harassment and then to intimidation and threats. A core group of four or five obsessed message-posters, engaging in an anonymous smear campaign, harassed managers of event halls, trying to make them cancel Maharaji's events. Editors of newspapers and magazines who published fair articles about Maharaji received daily barrages of anonymous, intimidating calls and e-mails.

When Dr. Eduardo Padrón, president of Miami Dade College, invited Maharaji to speak at a benefit to support the United Nations World Food Programme, hate group members sent the governor of Florida, the Board of Education, and the entire faculty e-mails requesting that the doctor be fired immediately. When their harassment proved ineffective, their anger escalated. One person even tried to incite people to kidnap Maharaji and members of his family. Shortly thereafter, they started feeding misinformation to gullible journalists in the mainstream media. They sometimes even posted as official spokespersons of the organizations, misleading journalists and feeding them bogus incriminating information.

In London on July 14, 1999, spurred on by the hate group and promised a juicy story, columnist Francis Wheen wrote an article in the *Guardian* entitled, THE MAILMAN, THE MAHARAJI AND THE EXPLODING LOVE BOMB. The article falsely stated that Maharaji owned ninety-nine Rolls-Royces (they were confusing him with an Eastern sage named Rajneesh who had done time in prison) and owed the government $4 million in back taxes when his tax record was impeccable. The article went on to say that

Maharaji called himself the "Exploding Love Bomb"—here also confusing him with another Eastern teacher—and they posted a photo, this time of the Krishna Consciousness movement's leader, with a caption under it saying THIS IS MAHARAJI. The *Guardian* made no effort to fact-check the information the hate group fed to it. A few days later, the paper printed a retraction, acknowledging that these statements were incorrect and that the photo was of the wrong person.

As Maharaji's message spread by satellite, many of his students still lived in places where he couldn't visit. In 1999, when NATO airplanes bombed Serbia in an attempt to stop "ethnic cleansing" in Kosovo, a dozen or so of his Serbian students met secretly twice a week to watch videos. At times, bombs fell so close to their meeting place that the whole room shook. Yet, through it all, they still found some peace and tranquility.

One of these students, Nenad Novkovic, recalls, "Twice a week, about ten of us attended meetings and events, literally in the midst of exploding bombs and screaming sirens. We had a small hall and a TV set where we spent magical moments watching videos of Maharaji's addresses while the thunder of exploding bombs shook the earth. In a normal situation, I'd have been afraid, but listening to him transported us to a completely different place where we felt secure inside. We all enjoyed and shared that beautiful feeling and ended up forgetting that the army headquarters, targeted by the bombers, were only 500 meters away. When the bombs fell, we just looked at each other and went on listening. There was no fear. How amazing it was to feel an ocean of peace and joy inside, in the middle of a war zone."

Nenad remembers walking out into the street one night after watching a video to find that the nearby army headquarters had been turned to rubble. "The local mail services were not reliable during the war," Nenad says, "so we sent a letter via Bosnia to Maharaji describing our activities and appreciation. You cannot imagine how happy we were to hear that later on, he mentioned us in his speeches as an example of how possible it is to enjoy Knowledge—even when a war is exploding around you."

Some people trust in leaders, but people don't trust in themselves. Why? When we, the citizens of this earth, start to trust in ourselves and the changes we want to bring, when we start to trust that truly, truly we want world peace, then it won't even take one day to establish.

MAHARAJI
New Delhi, India, November 4, 2005

Don't forget the commitment to this heart. Grab the moment. There are many things important to you, and their priorities will change. But your heart, your feeling, your fulfillment. This priority will never change.

MAHARAJI,
MALIBU, CALIFORNIA,
JANUARY 3, 2000

The Millennium

At the turn of the century, the number of people interested in learning the techniques of Knowledge had grown to such an extent that it was no longer feasible for Maharaji to conduct these sessions himself. Some sessions had several thousand participants, and it was just too many. Also, in some locations, people had to wait for months or even years for Maharaji to come.

In response to this, he developed a multimedia presentation that could be shown around the world to people with a sincere interest. He made a video of himself instructing people in the techniques, which was released to a small number of trained helpers. They traveled the world holding sessions where people could learn the techniques from Maharaji himself, albeit not in person.

On April 25 in Santa Monica, California, Maharaji used this video presentation for the first time, and from then on, he was no longer required to attend each Knowledge session. No matter where a person lived, they could receive the same instruction straight from him. The presentation was translated, and today, people receive the instruction in more than fifty-five languages.

In contrast to the '70s when people often received Knowledge within days of hearing about it, they were now required to spend some time watching videos and growing in their understanding of what was being offered.

Maharaji had not assumed his children would become his students, but if they wanted the gift, they would have to go through the same process of preparing and meet the same conditions of sincere interest as everybody else. A few years after Premlata, both his eldest son, Hans, and his second daughter, Daya, asked him for Knowledge. Daya became a gifted singer and songwriter, performing at many of his events.

The year 2001 marked the thirtieth anniversary of Maharaji's message arriving in the West. He said, "After thirty years, I'm still carving the same rock, and it is evolving and evolving. I don't care it if takes another thirty years or forty or seventy. Whatever it takes, that is what I am going to do because I know that anything and everything is possible. Thirty years ago, I stepped off that airplane, and I didn't know what was going to happen or how I was going to be received. I didn't know what people expected of me. Events began and we started traveling all over the place. Now, after those thirty years, my determination is still that strong."

In the fall of 2001, the United States experienced one of its most horrific incidents with the terrorist attacks on the World Trade Center and the Pentagon. Maharaji posted an original prayer on his Web site that has since been included in the permanent collection on the United States Library of Congress Web site:

> In this hour of need, dear God
> Grant us your grace,
> Guide us from darkness to light
> From confusion to clarity
> From pain to joy
> From hate to love.
> Give us the strength to endure.
> Give us the courage to go on.
> Bless us with your kindness.

In November 2001, Maharaji established The Prem Rawat Foundation (TPRF), an idea he conceived during a conversation with Linda Pascotto, an active philanthropist and one of his long-time students. Maharaji was attracted to the idea of having his own foundation through which to further his message of peace and to provide humanitarian aid to people the world over. No one was more surprised than Linda when, a few months later, he made her president.

Linda, a gracious woman who exudes warmth and kindness, recalls, "I didn't feel that my role was particularly important other than to help him in his work. I don't even think he was excited about the Foundation in the beginning, but he became more so. I think he was waiting to see what direction it would take, since he had had some bad experiences with organizations in the past. All I did at the start was set it up, and Maharaji made it clear that there would be no activity without his consent."

After the launch of the Foundation's Web site, www.tprf.org, in April of 2002, Maharaji, who had not given press interviews for decades, started talking with journalists who had a sincere interest in his message. He gave an interview to *LEADERS* magazine, a business publication. David W. Schner, the magazine's president and executive editor, wrote, "Maharaji has a unique ability to speak simply of the most profound. With sparkling humor and unexpected insights, he has a rare gift for inspiring people to see life with a fresh perspective and to find within themselves a sense of personal freedom, regardless of circumstances."

Maharaji was quoted as saying, "Of all the things that we could be, of all the things that we could achieve, of all the mountains we could climb, of all the oceans we could swim, there is a yearning for contentment, which is neither a mountain, nor an ocean, nor an infinite sky. There is a want to get to that, to achieve that. And that cause is the noblest cause on the face of this earth."

Schner asked Maharaji, "How do you define *success?*"

Maharaji answered, "The way I see it, if you don't feel successful within yourself, then it doesn't matter how successful you are on the outside. There is always going to be a distinction between the two. Even if you are the CEO of a big corporation, you have to come home, and what happens then? You may have a big office, a lot of power, and a range of awards, but when you come home, you're just yourself. You need to be a success there, too. Ultimately, you can be exceedingly wealthy and still be happy and satisfied, or not have a penny to your name and be equally fulfilled. Once you draw the distinction between you and everything else, it's very easy to see that outward success is not what really matters."

Schner went on to ask him, "Is it difficult to convince people that inner success is as important as success on the outside?"

Maharaji answered, "It's not really a question of convincing them. Once you accept that success begins with you, everything else becomes secondary. People have to experience this fundamental shift for themselves."

⌒

Maharaji continued to circumnavigate the world eleven months of each year, and in July 2002, he spoke at the Barbican Centre in London. He said, "Your nature is to want peace. In this moment called *now*, there is that peace. There is that tranquility. There is that joy, and it is now. That will be as forever as the forever will ever get. Home is here. Understanding is here. The joy is here. The place without doubt is here. The ocean of answers is here. The ocean of peace is here. I know you have always thought, 'I am looking for peace.' What if I told you that peace has been looking for you? How many times have you crossed paths with peace? Many.

"Within you comes this incredible gift of life with every breath. It touches you, and you go on for another moment, and another, and another. Don't forget that it is but a drop, and a drop, and a drop that accounts for the mighty river. Your life comes one moment at a time. Be ready. Be ready to welcome it. Be ready to say, 'Come.' And when you can be in that place, perhaps someday, you'll be able to say, 'Thank you for coming. Thank you for this existence. Thank you for this moment.'"

After that event, Elisa Davies, a mortgage broker from London, commented, "What Maharaji said felt like it was addressed to me individually. After all my searching, only now do I understand that what he is talking about is exactly what I have been missing."

Another attendee, fashion stylist Adam Camden, remarked, "Maharaji speaks in a way that is both concise and profound. He gives the best description of an underlying feeling in words that I have ever heard. I find him both inspiring and empowering."

Heather Alverston, an interior designer, said, "Listening to Maharaji makes me feel happy, especially when he touches on the subject of falling in love with life, of enjoying every moment, knowing myself. It was as if I was seeing myself for the first time."

That year, Maharaji was interviewed by Carmen Posadas, one of the most famous writers in Spain and the recipient of the Premio Planeta literary prize. She is known for her semifictional books, which describe characters from the Spanish jet-set society, and for her children's books. Maharaji also gave an interview to John Krukowski, the editor of *U.S. Business Review,* a national monthly business magazine.

Following is an excerpt from this interview:

USBR: *Please tell us a little about your work.*
MAHARAJI: My work is to reach out to people and introduce them to a possibility of peace that lies within each one of them. I hope that reaching within and finding that peace in themselves provides them with a more complete, more balanced life. And I

hope they can find the inner joy that so many people look for on the outside. So many people don't find it, and their vision narrows to, "I'll try this, maybe *this* will bring me what I'm really looking for." And so, that's what I do.

USBR: *How exactly are you defining* peace? *Just being comfortable with one's self or self-confidence?*

MAHARAJI: You can have many definitions for peace. Peace is one of those things that we definitely have a word for, but it is a feeling. A feeling where a person feels content in him or herself, a person feels a simplicity that exists within. People are looking for joy, simplicity, happiness, and peace in so many things on the outside when all those things really lie on the inside.

USBR: *You mention joy, simplicity, peace. Those are precious things in this busy society that we have now. You know, there isn't a lot of time; we are quite driven by money and concerns about material things. How does one balance these things?*

MAHARAJI: Well, that's exactly what I try to reach people with, and that's what the main core of my message is—that in your business, you should find the pride that you have accomplished something. But when you're just looking for that simple joy, that simple peace, it lies inside.

USBR: *So people are more apt to take action on external things, like their business rather than internal.*

MAHARAJI: Yes. Our whole society and our outlook is very much, "Can somebody please make a button that I can push and that will make everything good and make all my problems go away?" But a button like that does not exist, and secondly, what we are looking for is really within us.

We make objectives and we make plans for our business, but sometimes we don't make very clear plans for what we want in our lives. We think, "If I succeed in business, I will have all of that." That is a major assumption. And if you look at the track record, that is an assumption that does not come true. It stays an assumption.

And I am trying to get people to look at themselves and say, "Here I am. I am alive, and that *means* something, and I have this potential that I can do something. Well, what can I do? How can I make it all very right for me, or very joyful for me, or very simple for me, so every day that I am alive I can truly say, "Thank you"? Thank you for this life; thank you for what I have.

Maybe this is too idealistic for a lot of people, but to me, this would be a great game plan to have and to work toward succeeding in that because life is all too precious.... You know you cannot go to a bank and withdraw a little more life. Just can't do it. What you have is what you have, and you've got to make the most of it. I mean, so many of the business things that we do, if we could just apply some of that to ourselves, I think it would be wonderful.

USBR: *Almost like a strategic plan for our own well-being?*
MAHARAJI: Yes. A plan that says, "Look. This is my goal. This is my vision for myself. I see myself happy" rather than just, "I see myself prosperous"—a plan that says, "I see myself prosperous *and* happy." And when people are looking towards that happiness, I think I can help.

On September 12, 2002, Maharaji delivered the keynote address at a special event held at the United Nations Conference Centre in Bangkok, Thailand. The event, emceed by a well-known Thai television anchorwoman, was attended by several cabinet ministers, diplomats, and high-level United Nations representatives. Maharaji began his address by stating provocatively, "Institutions can't bring peace." It was his first appearance in such a setting, and his address naturally dealt with the theme at the core of the United Nations' mandate—peace. He used this occasion to share his view about the nature of true peace and about individual peace versus world peace.

"The absence of war," Maharaji said, "is not peace. It is people—it is us who start the wars. When differences become so great, and intolerance reaches epic proportions, wars will happen. When I fail to see another being as I see myself, wars will happen. When the causes and reasons become greater than the sanctity of peace, wars will happen. When I fail to realize the value of being alive, wars will happen. And whenever war begins outside, it will have begun on the inside first. And the war on the inside is far more dangerous because it is a fire that may never be quenched. It can rage on, and on, and on, and on. In the battle outside, at least you will hear a noise, but in the battle inside, you may not hear a peep. The battle outside may have strategies; the battle inside may be just going on with nobody even negotiating. This is your time on the face of this earth. This is your opportunity to be alive.

"When peace begins within me and has taken hold of me, when I have allowed it to blossom, then peace is also possible for me on the outside. Then peace is possible for me because I have felt it.

"Peace isn't about words. It is about feeling. For a thirsty person, saying, 'Water, water, water, water' will not quench their thirst. They need water. And not only do they need water, they actually need to feel that their thirst has been quenched before they can say, 'Ah. That feels good. Thank you.' We have forgotten that simplicity.

"The search for peace is not a quest of this millennium, or the next, or the next. For as long as there have been people on the face of this earth, the one thing they have all admired is peace. They have gone to great lengths to have peace in their lives. And peace comes when you can begin to look within. Peace comes when you can begin to appreciate this existence."

Here, we remember that Maharaji never cared about being politically correct. Perhaps he found delight in challenging prejudices, but more likely he simply refused to compromise what he knew to be true. He clearly felt compelled to bring his message to people directly and in its entirety, no matter how boldly it flew in the face of established dogmas and beliefs. He had accepted that, by the very nature of his message, many would find him controversial. He was speaking from his heart to people's hearts, independent of social or cultural norms, and he was more interested in authenticity than in convention. To him, the inevitable controversy he would attract was a small price to pay for keeping his integrity.

A few years later, in Brighton, England, he gave his audience an analogy using the tale of the Chinese emperor who so loved the nightingale's song that he had a mechanical nightingale made and put it in a beautiful cage. Everyone came to see it and raved about it. But while the mechanical bird looked good, the king's longing to hear the song of the bird was not fulfilled.

Maharaji used this tale to highlight how people often settle for formulas that appear to bring satisfaction but really don't. "It is the song you are after," he said. "Do you hear the song in your life? Do you feel the song? I am the one person out in the crowd who says, 'Where is the real bird?' Remember why you got the cage? It was for the bird. I say, 'The cage is useless. Where is the bird?' Many people don't like that. That's why I'm considered controversial. I don't go along with the flow."

Both he and his father had been constantly criticized. For Maharaji, it started when he was eight years old, and the Indian tabloids accused him of being a member of the CIA. Now a real reason behind the controversy became apparent: his message revealed some beautiful yet challenging truths about human nature that some found too confronting.

In 2003, his students in India filled the largest stadium in the capital. No one in India had ever done this before, not even the most popular politicians or music groups. During the first two months of 2003, his students had held many small events in Delhi, telling people about Maharaji's message and about his event at the stadium.

Then on March 8, on a glorious sunny day, people started pouring into the huge Jawaharlal Nehru stadium. Everyone wondered if it would be filled to capacity. The plan was to keep 10,000 seats empty behind the stage, and if all other seats were taken, the stadium would be considered full. But not a single seat—in front of or behind the stage—ended up empty, and thousands of people had to stand. The wall behind the stage had to be quickly torn down to allow people seated there to see Maharaji. More than 130,000 people were in attendance.

Maharaji talked more about the nature of human beings: "The moments in our lives that have passed will never come back. What will happen after we die, I do not know. What is important is to understand that supreme joy is inside each one of us and that the thirst for that joy is within as well. This is not our doing. The joy and the thirst for it are inside of every human being. It is our nature, just as it is the nature of a dog to bark. People try to change it, but they can't. When we feel joy, we smile. If you feel a thirst for that joy, I can help."

The next day, 60,000 people showed up for a follow-up event. Maharaji commented, "It is really wild—we are breaking new ground in India. It is a new horizon."

In April 2003, Maharaji embarked on a tour of U.S. universities, which brought him to Nova Southeastern University in Fort Lauderdale, Florida, and then to the University of Colorado at Boulder, where he had spoken when he was thirteen. At the Nova campus in Florida (where he had been invited by the head of peace studies programs), there was a packed audience of students, faculty, and guests. He addressed the obsession with external achievements and its failure to help people acquire personal happiness and fulfillment.

"We do so much to fulfill ourselves on the outside," he said. "We create massive institutions as we seek to expand our outer horizons, yet we overlook our inner horizons. It's perfectly fine to learn about the world, but we must also learn about the heart because true peace is not found outside. Within the heart of every human being lies the possibility of being fulfilled and discovering what is real in life."

To those who have asked if being fulfilled is selfish, Maharaji has often replied as he did a few months later in Barcelona where he said that seeking peace is no more selfish than breathing. "The most noble of ventures a human being can undertake," he said, "is to be fulfilled. People ask if that is selfish. Is sleeping selfish? Once you feel the need, it isn't selfish. Is it selfish for the bee to go to the flowers or for a bird to fly in the sky? No. And is it selfish for a human being to want to be fulfilled? It is the most noble of all actions that can be."

While his message of peace was attracting greater attention, his remaining detractors persisted. A few days before an event in the largest auditorium at the University of California at Berkeley on April 30, 2003, a troubled former student of Maharaji, a paralegal from San Francisco, managed to dupe rookie journalist Martin Ricard from the *Daily Californian* into writing an article based on fabricated testimonials, all supplied by detractors. The paper's editor later acknowledged the error, but the slams and slander continued.

In June of that year, British journalist Charlie Morton from the *Bristol Evening Post* wrote an article allegedly exposing some dark secrets about Maharaji's organizational finances that proved to be unfounded. A so-called whistle-blower calling himself Andrew Carpenter dramatically appeared on the cover in dark silhouette, as if fearing for his life. In his exclusive interview with Morton, Carpenter said that after three months of research, he had filed a complaint with the UK Charity Commission—implying that Maharaji should be put in jail. But the truth was revealed as "Carpenter" (later revealed to be a fictitious name used by a detractor from South Bristol, England) was identified as a member of the hate group that had been harassing Maharaji and his students. The Charity Commission conducted an inquiry and promptly dismissed the complaint.

At the same time, John MacGregor, a Sydney-based freelance investigative journalist and ex-student of Maharaji, published an article in the *Sydney Morning Herald*. Previously a loyal follower, he had been influenced by some angry detractors. With no factual support, MacGregor accused Maharaji in print of keeping a secret tax haven in the Channel Islands. MacGregor insisted that Maharaji's indiscretions included flying money out of Australia and into Swiss bank accounts.

Some of the group's covert activities were uncovered when MacGregor and another person were caught in a bizarre scheme to steal information from two computers belonging to organizations that supported Maharaji's work. The Court ruled against MacGregor in a summary judgment that stated that Maharaji and the local organization had done nothing wrong and ordered MacGregor liable for the costs of the action, which topped $100,000.

Although MacGregor had been a respected journalist, the Queensland Supreme Court found that he had violated civil law in the unlawful acquisition of confidential computer data. He was found in contempt of court in the conduct of his defense, and it was later discovered that he had perjured himself. When an arrest warrant was issued, he fled the country and went to hide in the mountains of northern Thailand, where he soon developed a psychological condition.

After placing himself under psychological care for six months, MacGregor felt remorse. And on the road to emotional recovery, he accepted responsibility for what he had done. On April 27, 2005, he testified under oath in an affidavit and gave chilling details about the hate group of which he once had been a member. He wrote, "I began to communicate with former students of Prem Rawat who maintain a series of Web pages, one goal of which is to create an atmosphere of ill will and malice towards Rawat and his students.

"I was one of the worst offenders, and the goals of this group are often obsessive, malicious, and destructive in nature. Through the use of the Internet, they interfere with the rights of people to experience their own spiritual discovery. The group's actions have included false and derogatory stories about Rawat designed to cast him in a false light, the publication of entirely false stories of a defamatory nature on the Internet, and encouraging media to report these fabrications as fact.

"In retrospect, I am of the opinion that many of these persons are irrational, obsessed, and motivated by ill-directed anger. During my involvement with this group, I filed several complaints to tax and regulatory bodies hoping to initiate expensive and burdensome investigations of Rawat and related volunteer entities. I had no factual basis upon which to make such allegations. The complaints I filed were supported by unauthenticated, incomplete, or out-of-context documents designed to paint a sinister picture. I owe Prem Rawat and all of Rawat's students an apology for my actions and for allowing myself to be used by the group."

These conciliatory statements and public apology marked the abrupt end of the career of this brilliant journalist, once the darling of the Australian media. And along with that came the demise of the credibility of this bitter group. When MacGregor was facing legal and emotional trouble, they abandoned him and began to quarrel among themselves. With the sworn statement of John MacGregor and his apology, the hate group's leaders, methods, actions, and wrongdoings were suddenly exposed by someone with credibility in the media. Eventually, the group weakened through infighting, as members started inflicting upon one another the hate they could no longer channel toward Maharaji.

Maharaji has always spoken with a spirit of equanimity about people who have turned away. In 1971 in London, he had said, "If this gives you peace, well and good, go ahead. If not, don't follow it anymore." Later, in 1999 in New Delhi, he explained, "There's one thing with Knowledge—if you want to leave it, you can leave it very easily. Just stop practicing. The door is open for people to come in, but because it's open, the ones who want to leave, can leave. That's the way of a door. There are many people who leave Knowledge because they don't want to make the effort." Maharaji always welcomed back without judgment those who had left and wished to rekindle their interest in his message.

In 2001, when Maharaji was asked about the hate group, he said, "They may garner hatred toward me, but I do not garner hatred toward them. I have no reason to. If they extended a hand of friendship, if it was real, I would accept it. Not because I am looking for friendship, but from where I sit, I'm comfortable enough to do that. I'm secure. I don't have to bad-mouth anyone. It's as simple as that."

Later, during an event in Australia, he added, "It would be, indeed, difficult to find a master that was not criticized," he said. "A reason, perhaps, is that if you find a candle, you will also find some matchsticks next to it that didn't quite light. People came, and the generosity of the master was at fault. They should never have received Knowledge, because that's not what they came for. They came for something else. But the master was still generous, and he gave them the benefit of the doubt and gave them Knowledge."

In November 2005, the members of this hate group were exposed as engaging in *phishing*, an Internet scam in which innocent people are asked to reveal their personal information to thieves posing as financial institutions. Since this was uncovered, the group has greatly shrunk and now manifests itself only in spurts. In a last, desperate episode, a member of the hate group, a public employee of the State of California Public Defender's Office, filed a libel suit in a California state court seeking permission to depose Rawat's students and ultimately, she hoped, Prem Rawat. The court expressly denied her request after lawyers argued that she intended to use discovery as a means of harassment. Finally, most likely sensing that she could not prevail on the merits, she withdrew the complaint. The group's subsequent efforts to gain public and media attention failed after these episodes stripped away their last shred of credibility.

This latest development marked a significant downturn for this angry group. While there will probably always be a handful of individuals around the world trying to flood the search engines with defamatory messages in an attempt to undermine Maharaji's message and humanitarian efforts, the road is now open for him to advance with more impetus than ever before.

In November 2003, invitations were pouring in from all around India, including many places that had no paved roads. Cars or buses could not travel more than twenty miles an hour over pothole-riddled roads, and some of the villages were hundreds of miles apart. There were no airports where a jet plane could land. Maharaji decided to use a helicopter, which he piloted himself across great distances, going from village to village, speaking at eight public events in eight cities, addressing more than 800,000 people.

In order to support this tour, Bill Storey, an Australian student of Maharaji's, went ahead of Maharaji through India, setting up stopover points for the helicopter. He recalls, "The helicopter typically would land in the midst of scrub where Maharaji might stay in a small cabin with goats and the tinkle of cowbells in the distance. The take-up of his message in those areas was absolutely amazing. It was literally exploding, and with his helicopter, he could get to places in forty minutes that took me eight hours by car. The closer we got to an event venue, the more we would see bullock carts, rickshaws, taxis, and trucks teeming with people. It looked like photos of World War II with columns of refugees in exodus, except that even the poorest of the poor wore bright colors and expressions of joy on their faces.

"Many of them never had seen a helicopter, and it was a bit precarious as youngsters rushed to meet Maharaji when he landed. But it was okay. The most amazing thing was that Maharaji, talking to 350,000 people in the heart of India, said the same thing he said when he spoke at the United Nations, and people clicked with him in the same manner."

On December 7, 2003, over 650,000 people gathered in more than 2,500 centers throughout India to hear Maharaji speak via live satellite broadcast. "There were 2,000 different centers in India with linkup capabilities," Maharaji later said of the event, "and we set up a studio environment in a tent. People would ask questions in their local cities, and the questions were sent to Delhi on the airwaves. Someone got the question in Delhi, typed it out, and sent it over to me. When I stepped onstage the first time we did this, there were only ten questions. But by the time I left the stage, twelve hundred questions had come through."

During this broadcast, someone asked, "What does it mean to you when you talk about *feeling* what it means to be alive?"

Maharaji answered, "For a lot of people, it's just words, but I offer people an experience of that—of really feeling what it means to be alive—not from the good and bad perspective. Not from the judgment perspective. But really feeling every moment of your existence. This is the possibility that exists for everybody. There is something inside of me that inspires me to actually enjoy. I see a real possibility that I am not just a busy bee, but I can be in that beautiful place where I am content, where I am enjoying peace."

At this time in 2003, the war in Iraq was full-blown. Maharaji spoke about how to live in peace in a world at war. "There is a lot of chaos in this world," he said, "but there is also a lot of beauty. There is a lot of ugliness and cruelty in this world, and there is a lot of kindness, and both are coming out. It's just that people latch on to cruelty because they think it's more intriguing than kindness.

"Where does your attention go? That's what's important. You've got to keep your sanity. You, by the way, are responsible for that. Nobody else is responsible for your sanity, so don't go off the deep end looking at the bad in this world, because that will drive you insane. If you see the bad, also see the good. And hopefully, someday, you will become the lover of the good and you will reject the bad. On that day, you will live in a different world."

Let today be the day when you take a step towards you in the truest, most earnest fashion of looking for peace. Because the day you start looking for peace, peace will start looking for you. The day you start recognizing your potential, your potential will start recognizing you.

MAHARAJI
Universal Forum of Cultures,
Barcelona, Spain, June 14, 2004

Whatever happens around you, there is a place in you that is unchangeable. It is not subject to age. It is not subject to all the turmoil of this world. How beautiful it can be if I know where that place is. So I can actually be busy feeling real contentment in my life because my life is very real.

MAHARAJI,
DELHI, INDIA,
DECEMBER 7, 2004

Outreach

By 2003, The Prem Rawat Foundation was putting into action a key element of its primary mission—to provide the essentials of life for people in need. Maharaji was talking about clean water, nutritious food, and eye care. A rapid succession of natural disasters across the world compelled him to help people in need: batteryless flashlights to Hurricane Ivan victims in Grenada, rice to war refugees in Côte d'Ivoire, and free medical clinics in India.

Linda Pascotto, TPRF president, explains, "Maharaji was really concerned that the money actually got to the people for whom it was intended. He had read in the media about other charities where donations were being sifted through so people did not get the benefits meant for them, and he wanted to make sure that the contributions made to TPRF would reach the people." To help ensure that, the Foundation started working in partnership with reputable organizations such as the United Nations World Food Programme, the United Nations Development Programme, the Red Cross, and Oxfam. When such partnerships were not possible, the Foundation found trustworthy monitors on the ground to ensure that the contributions reached the intended recipients, with the lowest possible overhead.

As the Foundation's humanitarian outreach expanded, Maharaji continued reminding people that finding peace and contentment was much more than a passing want. It was an absolute, innate need. "Every day that you wake up," he said, "something within you yearns to be fulfilled, to be happy, to be in joy. If the thirst for peace is within you, then the peace is within you. And finding that peace is what drives us, like an engine that runs the world."

In the spring of 2004, Maharaji toured India, attending gatherings in Allahabad, Ranchi, and Bhagalpur, that drew 175,000, 160,000, and 275,000 people, respectively. "Of all the events I have done in my life," he says, "I have actually never felt like, 'Oh, my God, this is too much.' Never—until I got to Bhagalpur. Coming in the helicopter, you could see something different about the place, but you couldn't recognize it as a mass of people. That's how many there were. The event was happening right at the airport, which is only used once in a while. None of these people had ever seen a helicopter, but they were there for a different reason: They wanted to listen. They wanted to hear a message that was unique."

Maharaji told the 275,000 people, "The world has told you many things, that you need this, you need that. I don't say that you need this or that. What you need is within you. If that thing is in your life, whether you are poor or rich, educated or uneducated, you can make your life successful. You came empty-handed, but you do not need to go empty-handed. You cannot take food with you, but you can take that joy with you. Every human being should have peace in his or her life. This is important because our heart says that it is important. Without peace, we will keep roaming. However much money we make, we will remain poor until our heart is fulfilled."

People from the villages expressed their appreciation. Ahmad Ansari, a farmer from Naugachia, said, "I felt very close to Maharaji. A common man like me can understand what he is saying. I feel I need the Knowledge he talked about. I hope for the opportunity to hear him again and again." Jichha Vishwakarma, a weaver from Bhagalpur, said, "When I listened to Maharaji, I felt a unique kind of joy. I wondered why I had been deprived of this for so long. I am standing at the threshold of the well, and I am thirsty."

Maharaji followed up these large events with a live satellite broadcast event where people could ask questions. More than 600,000 attendees watched the broadcast in more than 2,500 centers. Thousands of questions were received, forty-four of which Maharaji answered over two days.

ᢙ

A few weeks later, on a sunny afternoon in Cambridge, Massachusetts, Tim Gallwey (Maharaji's tennis coach, a Harvard graduate and former member of the Harvard varsity tennis team) introduced Maharaji at Sanders Theatre, Harvard University. Many venerable academic, political, and literary figures of the nineteenth and twentieth centuries have taken the podium in this ancient, wood-paneled theater, including Winston Churchill, Theodore Roosevelt, and Martin Luther King, Jr.

In his introduction, Tim recalled his years at Harvard, listening to philosophical lectures and leaving with a feeling that something important was missing. He described Maharaji's message as "simple, from the heart, and directed towards our own profound capacity to understand and to recognize truth in a way that intellect alone could never hope to." He mentioned that he was struck by the fact that Maharaji's message was not just theory, that it was verifiable, not by logic, but by personal experience. "I credit Harvard," he said, "for opening many doors in my mind. And I credit Maharaji for opening the door to my heart, for allowing me to access feelings of peace, of joy, of fulfillment in a practical way, without external dependence. This," he said, "has made all the difference."

Maharaji said on that day, "The heart can capture a picture that will last the rest of your life. When you become good at looking at the moment, and in that moment you capture the peace, capture the joy, you're going to have quite a collection for the rest of your life. And you can. You have the camera of this heart to capture it for the rest of your life."

Soon afterward in Toronto, Maharaji was introduced by Richard Patten, a member of the Ontario Provincial Parliament. Patten credited Maharaji for bringing a "remarkable message of hope" to this event, which was broadcast via satellite to 106 locations in 28 countries.

Then, on August 8, Maharaji spoke at a global, live interactive satellite event in a TV studio in California, where people in more than 150 locations in 29 countries throughout the world were able to ask questions and interact with him.

A woman from Mar del Plata, Argentina, asked him, "How can I overcome having lost someone I love very much?"

Maharaji answered, "There is not a question of being able to replace that person or overcome your sadness, but know that in your memories that person still lives on. Extract the beautiful from the situation. The love you have for that person never has to end. That love never has to die.

"And that person, although they may not be alive physically, will live in your love, in your feeling, and can live there for the rest of your life. Love is what is important. Love is what brings us together. Love is not about lamenting. Love is not about looking at the past and wondering how it could have been and how it wasn't. Love is not about the things that are not. Love is about what is, what is felt in the heart in this moment.

"Fortunately for all of us, even though there's a loss, there is something that we will always have. Something that nobody can take away from us, not even death. And that is the love."

❧

As Maharaji's audiences grew, so did the number of people asking for the techniques of Knowledge. Historically, Maharaji had insisted that people go through a phase of preparation before being taught the techniques. This preparation consisted mostly of watching videos to develop a better understanding of his message and how to make the most of Knowledge.

The preparation process, however, had taken various forms in different countries across the world, and Maharaji felt the need for a more personal kind of preparation. He wanted people to feel that he was preparing them directly, rather than just showing them videos of his events.

So Maharaji spent a few weeks in Malibu in the late summer of 2004 to focus his attention on this project. Almost every day for eight weeks, he worked relentlessly on the production of custom videos that people could watch at their own pace to prepare for Knowledge. The concept of "The Keys," the name he gave to these videos, had occurred to him many years earlier. He had nursed this vision, allowing it to change form over time. Now he spent every waking hour for two months bringing it into reality.

There are six Keys. People who are interested watch the first five Keys at home at their own pace. Each Key includes one custom-made video by Maharaji and a dozen hours of his addresses, grouped by topics. When people finish watching the first five Keys and feel ready, they may ask to be taught the techniques. No questions are asked from the applicants. Then they are invited to a special meeting where they watch the sixth Key, the multimedia presentation of Maharaji demonstrating the techniques. Maharaji has often said that Knowledge has a built-in protection mechanism: those who are not sincere will not reap its benefits.

The Keys have been translated into many languages and are available free of charge through mail-order lending libraries around the world. The Keys can be accessed on the Internet at www.thekeys.maharaji.net and by telephone for those who do not have access to the Internet. By 2005, for the first time, people could go through the whole process of preparation without having to interact with anyone.

ᴄ᚜

In late 2004, despite its economic difficulties, Argentina was the first South American country to start broadcasting Maharaji's message on cable and satellite television, with many South American countries to follow. Infinito cable TV, launched in nineteen Latin American countries, allowed Maharaji's message to be heard by millions overnight. Very rapidly, over 70 percent of aspiring Latin American students were being introduced to Maharaji's message via television. One of these viewers, Alejandro Santiago wrote, "I have listened to many of Maharaji's talks on the Infinito Channel. They fill me with hope and help me to be strong during the difficult times that come."

Another viewer, Patricia Ortega, said, "I have been listening to Maharaji on cable TV for over a year now. He speaks to the deepest part of my heart, and I already feel that a big change is taking place in my life. Maharaji's message is wonderful food for my spirit."

Words of Peace, a weekly TV series featuring Maharaji's message, received the award for best television programming from the Brazilian Association of Community Television Channels the following year (November 2005). Fernando Mauro Trezza, the president of the association, said, "While many programs are special, some are essential. *Words of Peace*, which presents Prem Rawat's message, is one of these unique programs. This program is receiving this distinction because of its important contribution toward building a culture of peace in Brazil. The feeling of peace that Prem Rawat introduces people to is very important for everyone. It is essential to spread this feeling to everyone in Brazil. This program is a great contribution toward the triumph of inner peace. Prem Rawat's message has the potential to unite all Brazilians in inner contentment. I know that peace is really possible in Brazil."

Dr. Arnaldo Jardim, a member of the Brazilian Federal Congress and a guest of honor at this award ceremony, added: "I find

Prem Rawat's message interesting, simple, from the heart, and relevant for all human beings. This award means that we would like to see more of his message on television, and for many more years to come."

∽

At this time, TPRF was honing its approach to humanitarian work. Linda Pascotto, president, says, "The humanitarian side of the Foundation took on greater importance as opportunities to provide assistance developed and as contributions started to come in from all around the world." It all began with an eye clinic in India in 2003, where, as Linda puts it, "millions of people are unable to function at work and at home because they are too poor to purchase properly prescribed eyeglasses." The first clinic provided free consultations to 800 people; thousands more followed.

The Foundation's humanitarian efforts picked up speed after the tsunami hit Asian shores in late December 2004. Maharaji called Linda and said, "I'd like the Foundation to send some money. How much can it afford?" TPRF didn't have much money at the time, so Maharaji donated several works of art he had created. They were auctioned, and the money raised enabled the Foundation to give enough money to the United Nations World Food Programme (WFP) to feed 9,000 tsunami victims for a month, as well as to fund future endeavors. The contribution was handed to a representative of WFP at a ceremony at the Senate in Rome, Italy, hosted by Emilio Colombo, former president of the European Parliament.

"The purpose of TPRF is to help people," says Maharaji. "I believe that the greatest gift you can give someone is Knowledge, but people need other things, and we can help. A lot of food that is sent to these places ends up as cow fodder, and we can help make sure this does not happen." He was referring to the poverty-stricken tribal area near Ranchi in northeastern India, where well-meaning philanthropists had sent soy bars for protein. But the tribal people had never seen soy bars and they had fed them to their cattle.

Linda Pascotto says, "The main humanitarian focus of the Foundation is to provide nutritious food and clean water for people who don't have access to them. And not just ready-to-eat canned rations. Maharaji wants these people to have good-tasting foods and to give them the dignity of a decent meal. He's talked to me about when he was a child, how hungry people would come to his house, knock on the kitchen door, and any time of day or night, they would get something good to eat. And he's often expressed how gratifying it is to see the face of a person who was hungry and has had a satisfying meal."

Maharaji says, "Just because these people are poor does not mean they are miserable. They all have beautiful smiles on their faces, but they need food, and this project will deliver real food to them. Babies and small children will get three meals a day. Children of school age will get two meals a day, and for adults, it will be one. I don't want to change their culture; I only want to feed them."

On March 23, 2006, Maharaji was happy to be present for the laying of the cornerstone of Food for People, a permanent facility in the tribal village of Bantoli, India, that would soon provide 45,000 free hot meals a month to people in need.

While the Bantoli project was getting off the ground, TPRF was bringing relief to victims of natural disasters around the world:

In the African nation of Côte d'Ivoire, where political rivalries had escalated into widespread violence and tens of thousands of people had fled to neighboring countries, the Foundation provided meals for 4,500 refugees for a month.

In Sri Lanka, after the tsunami, more than 1,500 meals were distributed to children in refugee camps each day for a month.

In Pakistan, when entire villages disappeared when an earthquake shook the region, the Foundation provided food for 6,000 people for a month.

In Niger, in response to a widespread famine, the Foundation provided food for 2,000 people for a month.

When a hurricane destroyed thousands of homes in Guatemala, the Foundation provided food for 4,500 schoolchildren for a month.

When Hurricane Katrina landed along the Gulf Coast of the United States, the Foundation's donation made it possible to provide three meals a day to 8,500 hurricane victims for three months.

And when Hurricane Wilma hit Mexico, the Foundation donated construction materials to Mayan villagers to rebuild the roofs of 600 houses, providing shelter for 3,500 people.

After attending the inauguration of Food for People, Linda Pascotto said, "Each day, year-round, 1,500 hot meals are now being prepared and served at this thousand-square-meter, custom-built facility in the midst of this forgotten tribal area. Part of the food served is grown on the six-acre property, and workers have been trained to operate the facility at high nutritional and hygienic standards unseen in this part of the world. This facility marks the launch of an innovative TPRF model of giving, with food-aid programs developed and operated in concert with local village elders. The Foundation is actively working to replicate this innovative model around the world."

After inaugurating the facility, Maharaji said, "These were the poorest kids you can possibly imagine, but I could see in their eyes a thankfulness that is unique. They didn't have to do anything to deserve this, but somebody came to their neighborhood and gave them an opportunity to have some food that they obviously thought was tasty because the first day, they were back in line with empty plates, saying, 'More.'"

Village elders were supportive of the facility, as were the villagers, and the Foundation helped make it possible. To Maharaji, what happened in Bantoli was a good example of the social dimension of his message in action.

◦◦◦

Going back to 2005, in April the United Nations Association of Malaysia, in collaboration with the United Nations Development Programme, invited Maharaji to Kuala Lumpur. There he was asked to address a distinguished audience, including members of royal families, ambassadors, cabinet ministers, and members of the Asian media.

The landmark event came about as a result of two members of the Malaysian elite who were touched by Maharaji's words. In the '90s, Tan Sri Mahadevan, a Malaysian psychiatrist who headed the country's national health services and lectured at Harvard, had heard about Maharaji and became interested in his message. At age seventy-five, Tan Sri, a colorful character much beloved in Malaysia, still travels the world to play polo.

Tan Sri dreamed of introducing Malaysian high society to Maharaji and giving him a chance to present his message to them in a setting that was befitting of him. He called upon his friend Tengku Rithauddeen, president of the United Nations Association of Malaysia. Tengku, a member of the royal family and a barrister educated in England, had been both foreign minister and defense minister. He was now chairman of the Ethics Committee of the United Malays National Organization, Malaysia's ruling party. As a widely respected elder statesman, his illustrious career and distinguished achievements gave him considerable clout in Malaysian society. Tengku and Tan Sri decided to work together to invite Maharaji to present his message to their networks of friends. Dr. Richard Leete, UN representative of the UN Development Programme for Malaysia, Singapore, and Brunei, joined them in their efforts.

Members of the royal families of Malaysia and Cambodia, as well as ambassadors and cabinet ministers attended the highly successful event. Much of the Malaysian aristocracy was also in attendance, including leaders of the Muslim, Indian, and Chinese communities.

Tengku began introducing Maharaji by reading a special message sent by United Nations Secretary-General Kofi A. Annan. Maharaji then addressed the audience, speaking about the fundamental necessity for peace. "We detest war, and we wonder why people have to fight, why there has to be bloodshed. And we come up with incredible explanations about societies and nations, but we don't talk about the individual people. War is representative of what takes place in the vacuum of the fundamental fulfillment that each individual needs to feel. Peace is not a luxury. Peace is as important as breathing air, eating food, or having shelter, because it is the fundamental necessity of every heart on the face of this earth."

In May 2005, Maharaji was in Bangkok once again, invited this time by leaders of Thammasat University, the leading Thai institution of higher learning. He had been asked to address civic, academic, and government leaders. "Peace begins with you," he said. "Peace is possible with you. Will governments bring peace? I don't know. Can governments bring war? Yes. Look at their track record. Can people feel peace? Yes. Again, look at their track record.

"This life is yours. It is a gift that you have been given. Understand the beauty that is dancing in front of your very eyes. You are the stage where the peace dances. This is your time. Grab the request for peace in your heart; find the contentment in your life. That is the only way to enjoy. Peace is beautiful. Peace is real. Peace is that passion for existence. When I'm not caught up in all the 'goods and bads,' but a feeling, an understanding of what life means —what every day means, what every hour means, what every breath means. Then I can begin to savor what peace is all about."

While Maharaji was traveling in the North Pacific, somebody sent him a bowl through the mail as a gift. He thought, "How nice, something for flowers," but then he read the accompanying note. A Sri Lankan man had decided to shine an old copper bowl that had been in the family for a long time. A couple of hours later, the tsunami hit Sri Lanka. When he was able to rifle through the devastation some days later, he saw something shining in the sun. The bowl that he had cleaned had been returned to him from the ocean. It was a perfect metaphor, as it reminded him that having Maharaji's Knowledge had allowed him to go through many hardships in life while still shining on the inside. He sent the bowl to Maharaji with a little note, and Maharaji referred to this story from time to time.

"I see the contrast so beautifully," he said at one event, "that in the middle of the devastation, in the middle of all the destruction, a bowl is shining. It's shining because somebody took the time to polish it, to clean it. That bowl is us. If you keep looking outside for what is inside of you, your bowl will never be clean.

"Let me admire what I have been given. Let me take that polish and clean my bowl so that it'll shine. And it will. Even the tsunami could not take away the shine of that bowl. The sun came out and there it was, sparkling."

Maharaji has always been careful to remain unassociated with political partisanship, and during humanitarian crises, he has spoken of the inability of all governments, regardless of their orientations, to help people in need find what they require most: peace within. "Prosperity is where governments can help. But governments cannot help you with peace."

He described a conversation from years before that had stuck in his mind. "I was coming from Canada to the U.S.," he said, "and a customs officer asked me where I had been and what I was doing. I told him I was in Canada, talking about peace.

"'Peace is not possible,' the agent told me, 'because as long as there is so much greed and power struggles, there will be no peace in this world.' I thought about it and realized he was right if he was talking about the concept of peace that everyone has. I'm not talking about that. I'm talking about personal peace, which is very possible because it has nothing to do with the struggles on the outside. It is time to rethink what it means to be alive, what it means to exist."

In June 2005, in San Francisco, at the invitation of the UN 60th Anniversary Committee, Maharaji addressed diplomats and government and civic leaders at a special commemorative event at the historical Herbst Theater, where the UN charter had been signed sixty years earlier. On this occasion, he said, "Every human being on the face of this earth wants freedom to pursue their religion, to pursue their convictions, to pursue their opportunities, and most importantly, freedom of the heart to pursue its opportunities, its demands of peace and of a real life of admiration and understanding. A life of beauty. We want to admire and to be fulfilled. Anything else is a compromise."

He added, "What are people like? They speak different languages, but what do they want? The amazing thing is that regardless of all these differences, the want of every single person on the face of this earth is the same. We look at the differences. This is what we have trained ourselves to see—the differences. Some people even say, 'Difference is good,' and I agree. But, in the middle of all the differences, see the similarity. See that for every human being, the demand, the desire for peace is there."

After the event, Patricia Tenbrook, an urban planner who had just heard Maharaji for the first time, said, "I love the original way he expressed himself. Every idea, every phrase was expressed in a way I have really never heard before. And then another new expression! And then another one. Listening to him gives me hope that real peace is possible."

John Sutter, a physical therapist from nearby Marin County, said, "Seeing Maharaji for the first time, I was very touched. What is most important to me is that he wasn't trying to teach me something new, but rather was reminding me of what I already have and to look within and explore."

Dance teacher Irma Rosenfeld said, "Everything Maharaji said was so clear and simple. I felt touched in the deepest possible way. I have never experienced anything like it. I feel as if I am taking a big gift home."

A month later, in July of 2005, Maharaji was invited to speak at Oxford University, where Ron Geaves, one of the first Westerners to visit Maharaji in India in 1969, was an alumnus. Ron faced his professors, colleagues, and friends and introduced Maharaji. He said, "Over the years, I have come to admire Prem Rawat's passion for existence, and I remain enthused by the content of his message in my own personal growth as a human being. It has had a significant impact—sometimes a source of strength when required, sometimes a force for stability when everything else shifted. And I must confess that even in my career, it has helped me develop a worldview that underpins my thinking and writing."

In this ancient hall where so many illustrious speakers had spoken before him, Maharaji said, "I have been given the power to feel, and we know that human sorrow can be mighty. Human pain can be mighty. What have I done today to secure my joy, to secure that happiness for myself? Have I begun to listen to those fundamental needs that I have, needs that say, 'Be content'? Of all the things I can do, if I did that one thing to acknowledge my thirst in my life, then I did something to secure that joy in my life."

~

On October 10, 2005, an event was held to celebrate the centennial of University of Malaya, the most highly respected university in Malaysia. Maharaji was invited to present his message there in front of the minister of higher education, Datuk Doctor Shafie Mohammad Salleh. Maharaji was introduced by Vice-Chancellor Captain Dato Professor Dr. Hashim Yaacob, who said, "Prem Rawat's message is intriguing in that he looks at peace primarily as an individual experience of inner fulfillment that can and needs to be discovered by each person for themselves. He maintains that if each person responds to their innate calling for peace, peace for them and for this world is possible. Peace, he says, is already in the heart of each person and needs to be discovered. 'When people in the world are at peace,' Maharaji says, 'the world will be at peace.' His message of peace is original in nature and singular in the possibilities it introduces."

During his address, Maharaji said, "We need to understand and recognize our fundamental need for peace. We say it is incumbent upon governments to make peace. A lot of people are surprised when I say that peace is a personal responsibility. It is incumbent upon every single person to find that place within their own self, where peace lies."

In an emotional moment after Maharaji left the stage, the vice-chancellor came back unannounced, took the microphone, and said in a choked voice, "As I sat and listened to you, for a moment, I thought you were a Malay person because your name is Rawat. *Rawat* in our language means *to heal.* That is what you are and do. Thank you very much."

Around this time, The Prem Rawat Foundation used a worldwide satellite broadcast to release the documentary *Inner Journey,* a conversation between Maharaji and popular journalist/filmmaker Burt Wolf. Wolf, a veteran TV producer, had created hundreds of hours of programming on culture and civilizations for network television. A connoisseur of fine food, he had also authored several books on gastronomy.

When Burt and Maharaji were introduced through common friends one cold winter night in upstate New York in 2003, it was instant chemistry for both. Maharaji seemed to enjoy Burt's "sympatico" personality and debonair approach to life. Burt, a lifelong traveler, seemed fascinated by Maharaji's insights into what Burt called "the inner journey."

Burt suggested to Maharaji that he do a one-hour television special in the form of a candid conversation about life. Burt, with his warm and engaging personality, was at ease in his role as an interviewer and was genuinely interested in what Maharaji had to say. For him, the taping was a chance to ask Maharaji—someone he believed had a unique perspective—any question he wanted about inner life. Maharaji clearly enjoyed spending time with a consummate professional who asked him rich, intelligent questions in front of a camera. The ensuing one-hour television documentary is reminiscent of the interviews between Joseph Campbell and TV host Bill Moyers. This instant hit has been broadcast on television in various countries around the world, and the DVD has sold many thousands of copies, with a half-hour version also available.

In November 2005, for the first time in many years, Maharaji was back in the foothills of the Himalayas. Enthusiasm for his message had grown in Haridwar, his birthplace, and he was invited to hold an event there. Tens of thousands of people were expected. But Maharaji was unaware that his eldest brother, Bal Bhagwan Ji, still bitter and hoping to have the event shut down, had told the local authorities that the event could potentially cause great unrest. Bal Bhagwan Ji and his wife, both local politicians who had some influence, pressured local police to shut it down. The local police gave in at first, but they were overruled when the regional police chief recalled that they had never had problems with Maharaji's events. The forecasts of unrest indeed proved false, as over 45,000 people assembled peacefully at Awas Vikas Ground to hear Maharaji speak.

In December 2005, Maharaji was invited to speak to inmates of Tihar Prison in New Delhi. Comprised of eight separate prisons and with a population of 13,000 inmates, it is one of the largest prison complexes in the world. Maharaji's students had obtained permission to allow inmates in Jail #2 to watch tapes of his addresses. When prisoners requested additional tapes via the suggestion boxes in each prison unit, the prison superintendent wrote to Maharaji, inviting him to speak at the jail. He said, "A good number of people have benefited through sessions conducted under your expert and wise guidance. Considering the tremendous impact it can have on the mind-set of prisoners to lead them to the path of reform, we solicit your kind services in holding an event for inmates here."

The prisoners did most of the work setting up the event, which a thousand inmates attended. Maharaji said, "Everybody hears about good and bad, but there is a truth that is beyond worldly good and worldly bad. That truth resides in everybody's heart. It resides in all of your hearts. It resides in my heart.

"There is something special in every human being. It is up to us to somehow bring forth that something special. That something special is about real beauty. And that real beauty is about real humanity. Real humanity, which resides in everybody's heart, is not in countries but is in every human being. It doesn't matter who he is or where he is from. It resides inside of everybody. That specialty, that love, our Creator has given to everybody. So if you really want to see a miracle, you are the miracle and there is a miracle inside of you. Bring it out. Let the lamp of hope be lit in your life and let there be light in your life. It is possible."

After his talk, one prisoner, Shyam Sunder Mehto, said, "I feel elated and blessed after listening to his address. I never thought he would come to this jail and be amongst us, but he did. Even though I am behind bars, I feel a freedom that is eternal."

"I was happy that could happen for them," Maharaji says about the prisoners, "because they are human beings. They have done this or that wrong, and they have already been judged, and they are in prison. The one thing the world could take away from them was their freedom, their liberty, and it did. But as long as they have a heart, the world cannot take joy away from them. The world cannot take peace away from them. That is the peace I am talking about."

Maybe on the outside, there is a difference in the color of our skin. The difference is this extremely thin layer of epidermis. While we perceive our differences, we are in fact very similar. Peel away the skin of this world and you will find that everybody is looking for peace. Everybody is looking for fulfillment, for joy, for the ultimate satisfaction in this life.

MAHARAJI
Mumbai, India, February 19, 2001

I believe the worst evils of the twenty-first century are the same as they have always been—not being able to understand one's self, not being able to understand what we are all about. Those become the worst evils because they cause us to distance ourselves from our true nature. Our nature is not war. It is peace.

MARAJI,
Business & Class MAGAZINE,
JUNE 27, 2006

A New Beginning

S ince 1966, when he was eight years old, Maharaji has been traveling widely with his message. Today, the same age-old message travels before him, carried by enthusiastic people from all over the world who have been touched through magazines, TV, videos, and DVDs. In 2006, one such place was Cuba. Ever since one person received Knowledge there in 2002, nearly a thousand have received the gift and several thousand are preparing themselves through the Keys.

Toward the end of the '90s, a Cuban woman living in Miami sent Maharaji's videos to Havana, where a group of fifty professionals started meeting to watch them once a week. Among the physicians, scientists, and government workers gathered was Ana Isis Otero, who had retired from her work for the Cuban delegation at various UN institutions around the world. In 2002, she traveled to Australia to see Maharaji live for the first time at Amaroo.

Now, at seventy-one, she has witnessed the phenomenal spread of Maharaji's message in Cuba. There is a distinct possibility that Maharaji will be able to visit Cuba in the near future. His message is already known there among health and education professionals, who began incorporating his videos into wellness programs for young and old people alike. Cuba, with its socialist government, has been isolated by Washington for many years, but it seems that Maharaji's message about inner peace has transcended these political divisions.

Maharaji is also being called to Cárcel Pública Municipal de Cancún, the largest prison in Mexico. Screenings of his speeches there in 2005 created such an impact that the prison warden, Maestro Jesús Rodríguez Almeda, sent him an invitation. "Your talks have brought about a harmonious atmosphere and an improvement in the inmates' self-esteem," he wrote. "Your presence and your words are encouraging and have a clear impact on the lives of our inmates. Let me inform you that we have currently some 1,000 inmates who are very enthusiastic about making progress towards living a dignified life. For these reasons, it would be an honor to have your message of peace incorporated and welcomed for the first time in the prison."

Today, dozens of the prisoners have signed up for the Keys, which are screened in the prison library with equipment donated by Maharaji's students. "I don't talk to these people about how incomplete they are," Maharaji says. "I'm not there to tell them, 'You can *improve* yourself.' I want them to know they were made by the most incredible Creator. They can do justice to that Creator by looking not at the flaws, but at the beauty that has been placed in every human being."

Oliver García, who has been a prisoner for four years and who viewed a DVD of Maharaji entitled *Introducing Peace*, comments, "It helps me to grow spiritually and internally. It has changed my life inside the jail because I enjoy the time more, and I don't want to fight or argue like before."

Another prisoner, thirty-two-year-old Rafael Castillo, says after five years of incarceration, "It's very interesting, above all, to learn about finding the inner peace that all human beings need. Hearing this message has totally changed how I am, how I act and think."

In late March and into April 2006, Maharaji was back in India, using a helicopter to reach many small villages where he could never go before. He traveled in the states of Bihar, Uttar Pradesh, Madhya Pradesh, and Haryana, focusing on remote areas where people were too poor to travel. He addressed more than 1.7 million people in less than two months, many of whom had walked for days with their families to come and hear him. For decades he had dreamt of having this kind of access to the most simple people, and with the new technologies, this was now possible. Maharaji believed that in the remote villages, where people lived quieter lives and had less distractions and simpler ambitions, his message could take root more easily than in the big cities.

But the obstacles were daunting, such as how to make sure hundreds of thousands of people at a time could see him and hear him properly, when no appropriate technology was available locally. How could they make him visible to more than 200,000 people? And how could a small traveling crew take down the set in hours, instead of days, to go to the next village? This was when he came up with the idea of a traveling stage and a traveling multimedia truck, including a self-contained sound system and an audio/video recording facility.

Maharaji designed trailers that would provide a self-contained stage and all the equipment necessary to accommodate any event up to 350,000 people. Two sets of custom trailers were soon built in New Delhi and arrived at each event ahead of him. One trailer opened into a small stage with high-quality audiovisual equipment, including a state-of-the-art, 300-square-foot daylight projection screen imported from Europe. This would allow as many as 300,000 people to see him clearly from a distance at any time of the day or night.

A small group of successful international businesspeople made a substantial financial investment to build these trailers. The investment immediately justified its worth when people in the last row in an audience of 200,000 could clearly see and hear Maharaji. They could see every expression on his face, as a profound silence replaced the usual rumbling and shuffling that occurred at the largest events.

There were also six towering speakers that rose hydraulically more than forty-five feet from within the trailers. This was quite a spectacle for the villagers, many of whom had no electricity or indoor plumbing and had never seen a television.

But where would Maharaji stay along the way? There were no hotels even near these villages, not even a bed and breakfast. In some places, people lived in huts that had no doors or windows, and malaria and dengue fever were rampant.

Maharaji and the traveling crew stayed in tents in the wheat fields or in trailers near the event grounds. But these hardships did not bother Maharaji in the slightest. Deepak Raj Bhandari, who heads the efforts to bring Maharaji's message throughout the Indian subcontinent, says, "The response was nothing short of phenomenal. Wherever he spoke, people from many villages would come on foot, on bicycles, or an entire village would come in trailers pulled by farm tractors. In one state, 8,000 people who knew about his message brought 200,000 guests."

Deepak added, "Maharaji emphasized that he could help people find peace in a practical way. But at the same time, he encouraged them to make sure before they come forward that what he offers is what they really want, and if not, to look elsewhere and come to him only if they do not find the peace they are looking for.

"Each time, he told them that what he offers is not just words, but an experience within to be had, a practical way to feel peace within themselves. He also said that while we all have our plans for how our lives should unfold and for how we would like peace to come to us from the outside, we need to find peace within in order to be truly successful. I heard some of these people say they always had known somewhere deep inside that what he said was true, but that they never heard it expressed clearly by anyone. I can see how hearing Maharaji unleashes a lot of hope in people. There is something in them that knows that peace is possible, and finally they see it can become a reality, even though they may be poor and disadvantaged."

Stephen Sordoni, a longtime student, volunteer, and financial supporter of Maharaji's work, traveled with him by helicopter to some of these villages. He recalls, "The helicopter landed a short distance from the stage. The event site was in an empty field of twenty acres or so, outside a large village. By the time we landed, the field was filled with tens of thousands of people from many surrounding villages. It was amazing that as we flew over the surrounding villages, there was no sight of people or human activity whatsoever. The homes and streets were deserted, while the venues shone with color from the women in their turquoise, orange, and bright yellow saris and the men in colorful turbans."

At one event, more than 100,000 people from two dozen villages in a fifty-mile radius arrived all through the night, on foot and on bicycles. Twenty people piled up in Jeeps and large dumpsterlike carts drawn by tractors. The crew slept in tents in the field, hearing the villagers singing songs that wafted through the star-studded night. At daybreak, a huge cloud of dust was seen, and a low rumbling vibrated the earth as the first 20,000 villagers rushed, en masse, to the cordoned-off field to find places to sit close to the stage. The atmosphere was electric, and everyone wanted to be as close as possible. When the event began, a beautiful tranquility filled the air as people sang songs and watched videos, waiting for Maharaji to arrive. Finally, he came onstage and spoke for almost an hour.

In the village of Waidhan in Madhya Pradesh, Maharaji compared a human being's life to a drop in the ocean: "A drop falls in the ocean. We don't give much importance to a drop, but so many rivers are there, and all of them started with a drop. When it rains and there is a flood, even the rain comes drop by drop. And when all the drops come together, they become rivers. A drop cannot harm anyone, but when a drop joins with others, it can destroy cities and countries.

"In our life, we are like a drop. We want to unite with the

ocean of joy in our heart, but we don't know how to do it. We can be united with such an ocean; the heart is there in all of us. As long as you are alive, you can experience that joy. Life is about experience, not just words. We have a mind, and we think a lot, but we never think that there is something that is beyond this mind and thought. How can we catch that with this mind? That is why we need to have an experience from the heart.

"Being a human being, you can fulfill your life. As long as you have breath, you can fulfill your life. Fulfill your life now. What will happen later on, no one knows. If someone wants help, I can help. You only need to understand your thirst."

*

On April 21, 2006, Maharaji was honored at the United Nations in New York for support provided by The Prem Rawat Foundation to the United Nations Development Programme's Community Water Initiative. This initiative aims to eliminate the shortage of water in parts of Africa where access to clean water is almost nonexistent. The Foundation supports this program's initiative by providing clean drinking water and sanitation for thousands of men, women, and children in villages in Ghana. The event, called "Water for Humanity and Peace," was attended by many distinguished UN representatives and guests.

The senior water policy adviser of the UN Development Programme (UNDP) opened the event by saying, "Thanks to the generous support of The Prem Rawat Foundation, the UNDP's Community Water Initiative will bring water supply and sanitation services to thousands of poor children and families in Ghana.... This contribution will provide them with dignity through sanitation and water for good health to aid them in achieving their dreams."

Maharaji presented Terence Jones, director of the UNDP Capacity Development Group, with a substantial check from TPRF for the water governance program in Ghana. He also gave a check to Mary Singletary, president of the National Council of Women of the United States, to install electric wells with faucets in the same region. This would enable villagers to obtain clean underground water rather than having to walk miles only to get contaminated water.

Mary Singletary presented Maharaji with the Distinguished International Humanitarian Achievement Award, saying, "He who brings water brings life. With the gift that you and your contributors have made today... you are saving the lives of families who would otherwise die from drinking contaminated water, and sparing the lives of babies who would otherwise perish because their mothers were too dehydrated to nurse them. This gift will go on bringing life, saving life, and improving life in these villages, every day for many years to come. We honor you today because your work around the globe exemplifies humanitarian action. Instead of staying at home and having a comfortable life, Prem Rawat has chosen to travel the world continually for the last forty years, sharing his simple message of hope with everyone who comes to hear it."

Addressing the distinguished audience, Maharaji said, "Of all the accomplishments that you can accomplish, there is one more, and that one has something to do with you, not the world. Generations down the road will look at us, and they will scrutinize us.

"They're going to look at our wars, they're going to look at our failures, and they're going to look at our successes. And they're going to say, 'They were so excited when they got to the moon. That's so sweet!' But then will they say, 'One most important thing that they pursued in their lives was peace'?

"The face of peace has not changed. It has nothing to do with technology. It was talked about by the Greeks. It was talked about by the Romans. It was talked about by the Indians. The idea of people being in a state where they feel real joy. The time has come for personal peace. It is incumbent upon our generation and generations to follow to pick up this banner and to bring peace to this world."

⌒

It's been thirty-five years since the first travelers discovered Maharaji in India. This wave of youth has matured and is now silver-haired. A new wave of youth has emerged, reminiscent of those who first came to discover Maharaji, not necessarily in how they dress, think, or their lifestyles but rather in the intensity with which they are captivated by his message.

An example of this new wave of interest occurred in mid-2006, when Maharaji received an invitation from Carl-Wilhelm Stenhammer, president of Rotary International Worldwide, to deliver a keynote address at the Rotary International Convention in Malmö, Sweden. Stenhammer asked Maharaji to address delegates from Rotaract, Rotary International's division of young men and women, who number 182,000 in more than 120 countries.

June Webber, chairwoman of Rotaract Committee 2006–2007, introduced Maharaji by saying, "It is fitting today that he would address our audience. We live in a frenetic society. There is little time for silence. We are on communication overload. We need to go within. We need to find the peace that is there within ourselves."

Maharaji told the young delegates from more than forty countries, "I commend you for your noble gesture to accomplish what you have set out to accomplish. By the same token, I also invite you to take a peek inside to know what this existence is all about. Be who you are. Be fulfilled every day so you can fulfill others. Be fulfilled every day so you can fulfill the responsibilities that are ahead of you. It all begins with you, so understand that if you don't feel peace, you may not be able to give it to anyone. If you want to quench the thirst of another, the least you need is water. Without water, you cannot quench somebody else's thirst. The water of peace flows within you. I'm not talking about creating something, but about discovering what already exists inside of you.

"Just be who you are. Carry out your noble causes. Be the knights, but wear the armor well so you can succeed in your noble cause to be all that you really, really want to be. No limits. Success has nothing to do with age. Success has nothing to do with accomplishments. Success is to feel alive every moment in your life. Not just to carry a backpack of responsibility, but also to savor the freedom, the peace, and the understanding of this life every single day."

In June 2006, Maharaji visited Cotonou, Benin. He had been there in the mid-1990s, and now busloads of people traveled to hear him from all around West Africa, many of them seeing him for the first time. Antoine Omontecho, who received Knowledge in 1998 in Cotonou, is currently an animal breeder. In July of 1999, he brought an audiocassette of Maharaji that had been translated into the local language, Fon, to his native village of Attata. He also translated the talks into the dialect Tchabe for both audio and videocassettes. Now, seven years later, over 400 people have received Knowledge in the Tchabe area of Benin.

Micheline Douyeme, an executive secretary in Cotonou, received Knowledge in March 2005. She says, "I feel joy that I could have never hoped for. I am no longer driven by doubt, but I'm motivated by an unwavering self-assurance. Problems are still there, but they come and go like waves. After practicing Knowledge, I feel energy like I could uproot a big tree. I cannot explain it. When I heard Maharaji was coming, I was delighted, and spontaneously, my mother, friends, and colleagues were interested in coming. I was happy they attended and enjoyed the event. Nothing can make me pull back, now that my ideal has been achieved. Now my objective is to help all the people I know to taste this joy. Maharaji brings a peace that all humanity should know."

The hall in Cotonou was packed with people from the West African region who had traveled over rough roads in sometimes hazardous conditions. Arriving from Kêmon, Anatole Tai-o, a primary-school teacher, said, "Now that I practice this Knowledge, I feel free. I am no longer weighed down by the constraints of social tradition. More than ever before, I feel responsible for my finding my own happiness, and I am comfortable with that. True happiness is really this peace inside." Anatole's wife, who also has Knowledge; his three brothers and their wives; and several teenage children came with Anatole to Cotonou to hear Maharaji in person.

Maharaji said, "My message is not about the world politics. It is not about the world economy. My message is about you. Just you, because in this world of economics and politics and wars, you have been forgotten. Nobody remembers you, and you have forgotten yourself. I go around the world to remind people of themselves. You. You, who were given the opportunity to be alive. Where is freedom? Freedom is within you. Where is joy? Joy is within you. These are your companions, but you don't know it."

On July 13, 2006, Maharaji visited Copenhagen, Denmark, the city where he had spent time with Marolyn both before and just after they were married. This was his first visit since 1997, and he was introduced to the audience of more than 1,500 by twenty-eight-year-old poet and writer Marie Smitt Nielsen. She said, "I watched a satellite transmission of one of Maharaji's speeches, and his words immediately sank into my heart and warmed it... because for as long as I can remember, I have had a longing to hear something of this kind, something that I felt was relevant to *me* and *my* life. I thought, at last something useful! A kind of human intelligence I can use. Funnily enough, I felt that I knew every single word beforehand. Maharaji's words were like an echo of an inner truth in my heart and that longing for peace."

She continued, "All through school and university, I was waiting to discover some useful information that could make sense to me in my life about this existence... about why I am here and what it means. In school I learned a lot about Danish, English, history, society, and mathematics and later at the university about storytelling, Shakespeare, Karl Marx, theories about text and languages, but I never felt, 'Yes, now it all makes sense!' That feeling came the night I heard Maharaji for the first time. It feels like I have embarked on a new education, the real education about life and my experience with this existence. And I am very much looking forward to enriching my life further with the experience that he speaks of and offers."

Maharaji was direct and encouraging in his address. "Who tells you about your strength?" he asked. "That strength that every human being has, that is unwavering? Who tells you that you have the strength to plow through the roughest oceans, to shine bright in the darkest night? That is your strength and your reality. That is your heart and your goodness. And that is your wisdom, the truest wisdom. Of all the knowledge you can accumulate, the greatest knowledge would be the knowledge of your own self."

A few weeks later, on July 29, 2006, the fortieth anniversary of his bringing his message of peace to the world, Maharaji was in New Delhi. At a special event at the Indira Gandhi Indoor Stadium, the largest of its kind in the country, he was welcomed by Shri Bhairon Singh Shekhawat, the vice president of India, and by 25,000 young people under the age of twenty-five who had come to hear him.

The vice president said, "I am amazed at the magnitude of this event and at how many people are deeply moved by Maharaji's call to peace. I'm convinced that the people of India and our brothers from other countries need to embrace in their hearts his call to peace. For the last forty years, as a messenger of peace, Maharaji has been making a constant effort to teach a lesson of peace to people. I would like to express my heartfelt feeling towards him, as a most trusted and respected person who takes a message of joy to society and society puts it into practice. Doing so is the greatest success there can be in life. I want his message to reach the people around the world."

⌒

At the publication of this book, a new generation is discovering Maharaji's message, and his words of peace are reaching ninety-seven countries in over seventy languages. Some people hear it in big cities, such as in Australia where the program *Words of Peace* is on television on Channel 31 twice a week in most large cities, often getting top ratings, or daily in the UK on the Sky Channel 173. At the same time, in Indian villages where there is no electricity and few know how to read, some may hear about it from someone reading one of Maharaji's addresses to a group gathered under a tree near the village center. He has refined his message and developed an infrastructure so that anyone, anywhere can enjoy the message and if they so wish, prepare to learn the techniques of Knowledge.

Remarkably, in spite of past disappointments, he has developed a new confidence in dealing with the press, as he regularly spends time talking candidly to journalists who have a sincere interest in what he has to say.

What comes next for Maharaji is anyone's guess. Over the years, he always has managed to surprise those closest to him with ever-new ways of breathing life into how he presents his timeless message of peace and the gift of Knowledge.

One can only assume, however, from his past track record, that no matter where Maharaji goes or how he gets there, no matter the state of the world, the intriguing glow of his age-old message will remain intact. It is almost certain that he will continue to tell people about their thirst for peace and how to quench it. Whether the people are eighteen or eighty, if they ask with a sincere interest, Maharaji will show them how to find a practical experience of lasting peace, joy, and contentment within themselves, an experience that will remain with them for the rest of their lives.

These very things that he has reminded people of since the day he could talk he is certain to say wherever he is and to whomever is there to listen. When he is satisfied that he has reached those who are ripe for the message, it is safe to assume that he will leave the stage of the moment, get into his plane or helicopter, and soar through the heavens to deliver his timeless message to a multitude of thirsty human beings waiting at his next destination—and the one after that.

I've been talking about peace since I was very young. I go around the world and try very simply to put my message in front of people, and I say, "Peace is possible." Begin by accepting that possibility in your life. You are the source. From each one of you, it begins. It will be the effort of everyone that will make peace possible. Each one of us. If there ever was a gift, this is the gift. If there ever was a time, this is the time. If ever there was an opportunity, this is the opportunity.

MAHARAJI
Barcelona, Spain, June 14, 2004

Personal peace is very possible because it has nothing to do with struggles on the outside. It is time to rethink what it means to be alive. It is time to think about the gift we have been given. All the citizens of this earth need hope. Future generations need hope. Peace has become a hollow word that people say but don't mean because nobody knows how to go about it. The clue lies in knowing yourself, knowing who you are. Wherever you go, you carry the well of peace with you. You have to know how to turn within. There is a beautiful possibility. This is what my message is.

MAHARAJI
Kuala Lumpur, Malaysia,
October 12, 2005

Part Five

Address by Prem Rawat in Kuala Lumpur, Malaysia

August 2006

At the invitation of the Malaysian Chinese Association's School of Political Studies and University Tunku Abdul Rahman, Prem Rawat delivered the keynote address at a special event called "Peace Is Possible," held for members of the Malaysian Chinese community on August 8, 2006. After being introduced by Datuk Dr. Chua Soi Lek, minister of health, he delivered the following address:

Distinguished guests, ladies and gentlemen. You have all come here to hear about a topic that is both fascinating and, in my opinion, very elusive.

We look at the world and see its problems. There is good and there is bad. Of course, being who we are, we want to get rid of the bad and retain the good. There are certain values that we want society to have.

We want people to be kind to each other. We want people to have a little consideration for each other. There are times when this is automatic for us. When we feel content, when we feel good inside, we become kind. Nobody has to tell us.

I know that if I am standing in line at a cinema waiting for tickets and somebody wants to cut in, if I am feeling good inside, I don't have a problem. I'll say, "Go ahead." If I am feeling frustrated or at odds with myself, I'll say, "No! No!" The same thing happens on a highway or in a parking lot. When I am feeling good and somebody wants to cut in front of me, I let them. When I feel frustrated, I honk and move even closer to the car ahead of me.

There are certain traits that are innate to every human being, that are our truest nature. Some people may say that a human being's nature is to fight because we do it so much. I disagree. No soldier wants to go to war. For every soldier who is out there, there is a wife waiting at home, praying every day that he returns. There is a child waiting for a father, a family waiting for a son, a brother, an uncle. And this family at home cannot stop the war. Maybe the only thing it can do is pray for the safe return of the soldier.

In times of trouble, we do not hesitate to lend a hand to help someone when we feel contentment within. The issue is not how the world should behave, but knowing the fundamental thing that, when it is there, naturally causes people to be the way they truly are.

What is our nature? Peace does not belong to any religion. Peace does not belong to any country or society. The address for peace has been given again and again throughout history. Peace resides within the heart of human beings, within you and me.

A long time ago, the bar was set for mankind that peace is important. A formula was given: peace, then prosperity. We have forgotten about peace and remembered prosperity. The formula is not going to work without peace. We've gone to the moon, but we have been unsuccessful in establishing peace on this earth. We have developed weapons of mass destruction. Creating them has become an art form, with billions of dollars spent on research. But when it comes to peace, we just wave our hands and say, "Peace. Peace. Peace." We need to try to understand what peace is and where it can be found.

Is peace when the neighbors stop fighting? Then build a house where there are no neighbors. If the family is not fighting with each other, is that peace? Then surely all the bachelors must be in peace. Is peace in a monastery? On top of a mountain? At the bottom of the ocean? No. Peace is within every human being.

Human beings are like unlit lamps that need to be lit. If you want world peace, it does not begin with the world. It begins with every individual. It is people who need peace. Not the crows, not the monkeys, not the giraffes. We are the ones who hunger for peace. We are the ones who need peace in our lives.

But peace remains elusive. Why can't we get it by doing what we do in this world? If you try to start a car and it won't start, how long are you going to keep trying? A day? Two days? Five days? The battery is dead. This car is not going to start. The engine may not even be there, so are you going to keep sitting there trying to start it?

This is what people are doing—they're working on formulas that haven't worked for thousands of years. We keep thinking, "This will fix it. No, this will fix it." But none of these things are going to fix it. The only thing that is going to fix it is the clue Socrates gave so long ago: Know thyself. Look within you for the answers you want. Look within you for what you think is missing. If peace is missing in your life, look no further than yourself for that peace. Do not be alienated from yourself.

Here is a little story to think about. One day, as a shepherd was coming out of the jungle, he saw a baby lion cub that had lost its mother. So he took it home, nursed it, and then put it in the barn with his sheep.

Every day, the sheep would go out to graze, and the cub would go out with them. The cub was raised with the sheep. One day, a big lion came out of the jungle and roared at the sheep. All the sheep went to hide and so did the little lion.

When the big lion saw the little lion trying to hide, he walked over to him and said, "What are you doing?"

"I'm hiding."

"Why are you hiding?"

"I am hiding because I don't want you to eat me."

The lion said, "I'm not going to eat you. Don't you know who you are?"

"No, but whatever you do, don't eat me."

So the lion said, "I'm not going to eat you. You have forgotten who you are. Come with me. Let me show you."

He took him to a pond and said, "Now, look at your reflection."

And when the little lion looked at his reflection, he said, "I'm not a sheep. I'm like you! I'm a lion."

We need to look in the mirror of our hearts to see who we truly are. Having been raised with sheep, we think we are sheep, too. But we are lions. We think peace will come from someplace out there. We think it will come on a certain date. We never look in our own hearts where peace is dancing every single day.

This is who we are. This is our true nature. Of all the things that we do in our lives, how much time do we actually spend with ourselves? Do you know what is considered the worst form of punishment? It is solitary confinement, where the only person you are allowed to be with is you. This is how far we have come.

Young people say, "This is not the time for me to be looking for peace—I am young." But the time to look for peace is not a matter of being young or old. As long as you are alive, search for peace. Have peace in your life because that is what is most important.

You might ask, "If peace is within me, how do I get to it?" First, truly understand that it is within you. Accept the possibility of peace being inside of you. If we keep believing that peace is somewhere else, we will never find it.

We become distracted. So many issues come up. Yet, the peace I am talking about is so innate that it even can be felt in the middle of war. It is the freedom that can be felt by a prisoner inside of a jail. Nobody can take it away from you. It is dependent only on you, not on outside circumstances. You carry that peace within you wherever you go, whatever those circumstances may be. That's the peace I'm talking about, the fundamental peace. That is the peace that you must feel every day.

Peace is not something to feel once and then say, "Okay, that's it." Peace needs to be felt every single day, every single moment if possible. And you have to be the judge of whether you feel it. Nobody else can tell you, "Now you are peaceful; it's okay."

People think you must be happy because you earn a good living, have a wonderful family, a good job, great prospects. But the innate happiness within every human being does not see caste or color or riches. A poor person can be happy and a rich person can be happy.

When I travel, people come to me wanting to find happiness in their lives. Once a farmer asked me, "I am uneducated and I am old. Do you think I can be happy?" A few days later, a wealthy industrialist asked me the same thing. "Do you think I can be happy?" He was young, very well educated, and wealthy. But he asked me the same question.

There is the happiness of having a good family and the happiness of having a good job. But there is another kind of happiness. And that's the happiness I am talking about. So my answer to both of them was, "Yes, you can be happy, because the happiness, the peace you are looking for, is inside of you."

This is not a concept. It is reality. You are alive. You exist, and your existence is the miracle of all miracles. Three major things happen in your life: One, you are born. Two, you are alive. And you know what that third one is. One has happened, one is happening, one will happen—not might, *will*.

It's not about what has happened—it's happened. And it's not about what will happen because it will happen. It is about what is happening. What is happening is that you are alive. And the potential that being alive brings is always there. Tap into it.

Some people want to become a "better" person. And I say to them, "Forget about being a better person. You are the best."

Learn who you are. Understand that peace is possible and that peace is within you. Celebrate that you exist. Don't wait for your birthday. Celebrate every breath that comes into you, every day you are given. Find peace in your life.

Search for it. Wherever you find it, good. If you don't find it, I can help. I have a way to go inside. People say, "Why don't you tell us what it is?" This is what I do, but first you have to connect the dots—one, that peace exists inside of you, and two, that it is possible. Without knowing those two things, you will search and search, but you will not find it. When you know that those two factors exist in your life, you can begin to look. Then you can be serious about what peace is.

Wherever you go, however lonely you become or however many friends you are with, peace is always inside of you. That is where it resides. Whenever you feel like not being a sheep and want to see your true face, look in the heart's mirror and you will see who you truly are. Until you know your truest nature, you will be an alien to your very existence.

What is really important is that you are alive. A gift is being poured into you every day. Understand what it means before it is too late. Understand the preciousness of each breath. Then you will begin to see what you have never seen before, to understand what you have never understood before—about you. You will not find faults. There is a lamp in your heart. Light the lamp and remove the darkness.

Ignorance is mankind's biggest failure. We love to plead ignorance. The saying is, "Ignorance is bliss." It's not bliss. Be enlightened in this lifetime. Whatever it takes. This is your potential and you should fulfill it. You are blessed beyond what you know. It is time to discover every blessing you have been given so you can be thankful. So you can be fulfilled.

Thank you very much and have a very pleasant evening.

(This address has been edited for brevity)

Interview with
Business & Class *Magazine*

April 2006

Eva M. Peña, a Spanish journalist, interviewed Prem Rawat for Spain's *Business & Class* magazine on April 27, 2006.

Q: *You live to spread the message that peace can be found, but what is peace?*

A: There are many interpretations of peace. Some people think peace is the absence of war; some think peace is the absence of sound. But there is another kind of peace, which is inherently within every human being. People have known about this peace for a very, very long time, but in today's world, it is even more important to be in touch with the peace that is inside every human being.

Q: *If peace is within each person, why are human beings constantly struggling?*

A: We are so geared to look for solutions outside us, that when it comes to peace, we look for it on the outside as well. It's a bit like somebody who has a gold mine under their house but doesn't know it. Maybe they beg all day long and they suffer, but the solution is so close to them and so simple. If they could find a way to access the gold mine under their house, they would never have to beg again. People struggle because they cannot find the peace within them. That is my message: Peace is within you. And not only that, I offer a way to be able to get in touch with that peace.

Q: *Do you think that man is often his own worst enemy?*

A: It is true that the wars that rage on within a human being can be terrible. But if man is his own worst enemy, then he is also his own best friend. When you know yourself, you become your best friend. When you don't know yourself, you become your worst enemy.

Q: *Why, in your view, are so many politicians ready to go to war with those who don't see things as they do?*

A: Because mankind does not see peace as a solution. People look at all the problems of the world and think that war is the solution. Peace has been talked about but never applied. It has become one of the things we like to discuss over dinner. Yet, when it comes to the practicality of it, it remains a theory, an abstract concept, because people have not found it. But peace is not abstract. It's very, very real. And it's within every single human being. That is why I am able to take my message of peace to people who are in prison and to people who are in the middle of a battlefield. Even in those incredible circumstances, people can find that beautiful feeling inside of them.

  People tend to do whatever they think is the easiest. Wars are easy to begin. Peace takes a truly cohesive effort. But make no mistake about it, peace has been an ideal of mankind from time immemorial.

Q: *You have stated that a person doesn't necessarily have to be going through hard times to have hope, but then why do many people stop pursuing hope when things are apparently going their way?*

A: There is a very beautiful saying in India that when everything is going well, we take the credit. But when things go wrong, we like to blame others. We forget that good times come and bad times come. It is in the time of plenty that you need to think about the drought. It is too late to think about it when it has already come. In the same way, when things are going our way, we think it's never going to change.

Good times and bad times are like seasons. Summer comes; fall comes; winter comes. A wise person will take note that good times and bad times both come. We think we only need hope in bad times; we don't see the value of it in good times. But the person who understands about garnering the good all the time is the one who will be able to truly enjoy life. We need to understand the value of peace, the value of hope, in good times and bad.

Trying to think about peace only in bad times would be like trying to think about food during the drought. You can think about it, but you can't do anything about it. It's only in the time of plenty that you can do something about it.

Q: *What do you consider to be the worst "evils" of the twenty-first century?*

A: I believe the worst evils of the twenty-first century are the same as they have always been—not being able to understand one's self, not being able to understand what we are all about. Those become the worst evils because they cause us to distance ourselves from our true nature. Our nature is not war. It is peace. When we are in turmoil, we naturally want to get out of it.

Sometimes you see pictures of places where disasters have occurred, and people are leaving. They want to get away. We don't like turmoil. We like it when it's nice, when it's peaceful. So many people are involved in doing things that hurt others. There are people who go hungry, who go without shelter. They suffer and struggle. All I can say is that if we understood our truest nature, we would understand that compassion is part of it.

Peace is in our nature. If we understood that, we would make things happen that would actually help each other. We would work towards eradicating these problems. We think that external technology is more important. So we don't develop the technology for peace. We don't develop the technology to help people not go hungry. We develop the technology to kill each other because we do not understand who we truly are.

Q: *You were a "child prodigy," so to speak. Do you believe that today's youth has a dream?*

A: There are many diversions for today's youth. It is easy to become distracted. If we can get away from the distractions and be attracted to the call from within, there will be hope for everybody. I see that it is not just a question of *this* day and age.

If you look back in history, you see that people lost their way. Things that were not important became important. And that brought suffering and destruction. It is actually not so much a matter of all the distractions. But what are we attracted to? If we can be attracted to peace, to the innate call of who we are, then I think the youth of today will have incredible hope. And they should.

Every generation has the possibility of making things better on this earth. Mankind has always had the desire to be in peace. Maybe this new generation once again needs to hear that call to bring peace and serenity to this world instead of war and turmoil.

Q: *Do you believe that mankind might be afraid of freedom?*

A: If we were afraid of freedom, all hope would start to dwindle away. Freedom is a call from inside. And *that* we cannot be afraid of. Maybe there are concepts of what freedom is. Somebody might say, "If I can do this or that, I am free." But even if they can do these things, do they really feel free from the inside? You cannot deny what you feel. If you are hurt, saying that you are not does not take away your pain. Freedom is not just a concept. You really have to feel free. We can definitely be afraid of conceptual freedom, but we cannot be afraid of the real freedom that we want to feel.

Q: *Precisely how does your method for finding peace help people? What makes it different and better than other methods?*

A: A lot of people talk about conceptual peace. There are people who say that if you go and live in the mountains, you will find peace. Or if you sit down and be quiet, you will find peace. If you read a book or chant these words, you will find peace. But there is a peace within you, and for that you have to be able to take your focus from the outside and put it on the inside to truly feel peace.

It's just like when you are thirsty. You can imagine drinking water. You can imagine the glass, the coolness, the clarity, and the sweetness of the water. But all this imagining is not going to take away your thirst. You need to drink the water. Once you have found the water, you don't have to imagine drinking it. What I offer is a practical means to be able to feel that peace within.

There are a lot of people offering a lot of things, and I'm sure that people are helped by them. And people are also helped by what I am offering. I tell people: Search. And if you don't find what you are looking for, I am available to help you. So I'm not saying I am the only one—only that if you don't find it, I am here.

My message is different because it is not about ideas. It is about feeling. Concepts and ideas have their place. It is okay for a family to discuss what they're going to have for dinner. It just cannot stay at the discussion stage. Somebody has to cook, and those who are hungry have to eat because the discussion is not going to take away the hunger. What I offer is something to take away the hunger.

Q: *How is it possible for people who have suffered the effects of
violence to make a fresh start? Do you believe forgiveness is
possible? If so, how?*

A: I think that when the ideals of people are greater than the
sum of all the bad that has happened to them, they rise above
their anger, above their fear, to a place that can bring them
true peace and tranquility. When people have a vision of
hope—not of struggle, or violence, or suffering, but of hope
for a better life—they can rise above anything because that is
also our nature. We fear what we do not know. We love that
which comes from deep within us, something that comes from
our heart. Forgiveness has to come from the heart. And peace
has to come from the heart. So many people have been hurt,
and so much violence has happened. It is going to take incredible ideals. It's going to take a clear vision of peace for people
to rise above their anger. And yes, I think forgiveness is possible.

It is incumbent upon all of us to move toward that vision
of peace. If we leave it to one person, it's not going to happen.
We must all play our part in rising to the occasion and fulfilling the dreams we have.

Q: *You were born in India, and the Foundation that carries your
name develops many humanitarian initiatives there. How do
you view the future of your country?*

A: I think the future of India is very bright. When people really
come together, amazing things can happen. India is a very
old country with some very simple values. And one of those
values is to move forward, to take the next step. Even though
there is poverty and there is hunger, people help each other.
People in India believe in each other. When people have that,
no matter what they have gone through, they will have a
bright future.

Q: *Do you think happiness can be attained?*

A: Each person is born with an infinite mine of happiness. Inside of us, we have incredible sadness and incredible happiness. It depends on what the catalyst is. Light a candle, and it will bring light. If you light gasoline, it will make big flames and possibly bring danger. The catalyst for true happiness is inside us. And the catalyst for incredible confusion and sadness is also within us. Ignorance will bring sadness; knowledge will bring joy and happiness. That's what we need to understand. We look for these catalysts on the outside, while we need to look for them within.

Q: *Thank you very much. It's been a great pleasure to talk with you.*

A: Thank you.

(This interview has been edited for brevity)

Index

Books & Collaborations by Andrea Cagan

Andrea Cagan has written, edited, and collaborated on a variety
of biographies. Her work focuses on topics that raise public
awareness and social consciousness. She has brought seven
books to the best-seller lists, including three *New York Times* #1
best sellers and one *Los Angeles Times* #1 best seller.

Diana Ross, *Diana Ross Memoirs: Secrets of a Sparrow*

Somebody to Love?: A Rock-and-Roll Memoir, with Grace Slick

Make Up Your Life, with Victoria Jackson

A Bend in the Road Is Not the End of the Road, with Joan Lunden

Lynda Obst, *Hello, He Lied*,
Los Angeles Times #1 Best Seller

Up and Running: The Jami Goldman Story, with Jami Goldman

Marianne Williamson, *A Return to Love*,
New York Times #1 Best Seller

Marianne Williamson, *A Woman's Worth*,
New York Times #1 Best Seller

Marianne Williamson, *Illuminata*,
New York Times, #1 Best Seller

Romancing the Bicycle, with Johnny G.

Held Hostage, with Michelle Renee

Dr. Joyce Kovelman, *Once Upon Asoul*

Andrea Cagan, *Awakening the Healer Within*